Lilith Dark

and the Beastie tree

D1373217

Created, Written and Illustrated by CDowd

LilithDark.com • CDowd.com

Interior Cover Illustration by Joel Poirier

google.com/+JoelPoirier

For Allison and CJ

LILITH DARK AND THE BEASTIE TREE
VOLUME 1
2014 FIRST PRINTING
Published by Alterna Comics, Inc. Office of Publication: 23 Trumpet Lane, Levittown, NY 11756. Alterna Comics and its logos are ™ and ©
2007-2014 Alterna Comics, Inc. All Rights Reserved. LILITH DARK and all related characters are ™ and © 2014 CDOWD. All Rights Reserved.
The story presented in this publication is fictional. Any similarities to events or persons living or dead is purely coincidental.
With the exception of artwork used for review purposes, no portion of this publication may be reproduced by any means without
the expressed written consent of the copyright holder.
PRINTED IN CHINA.

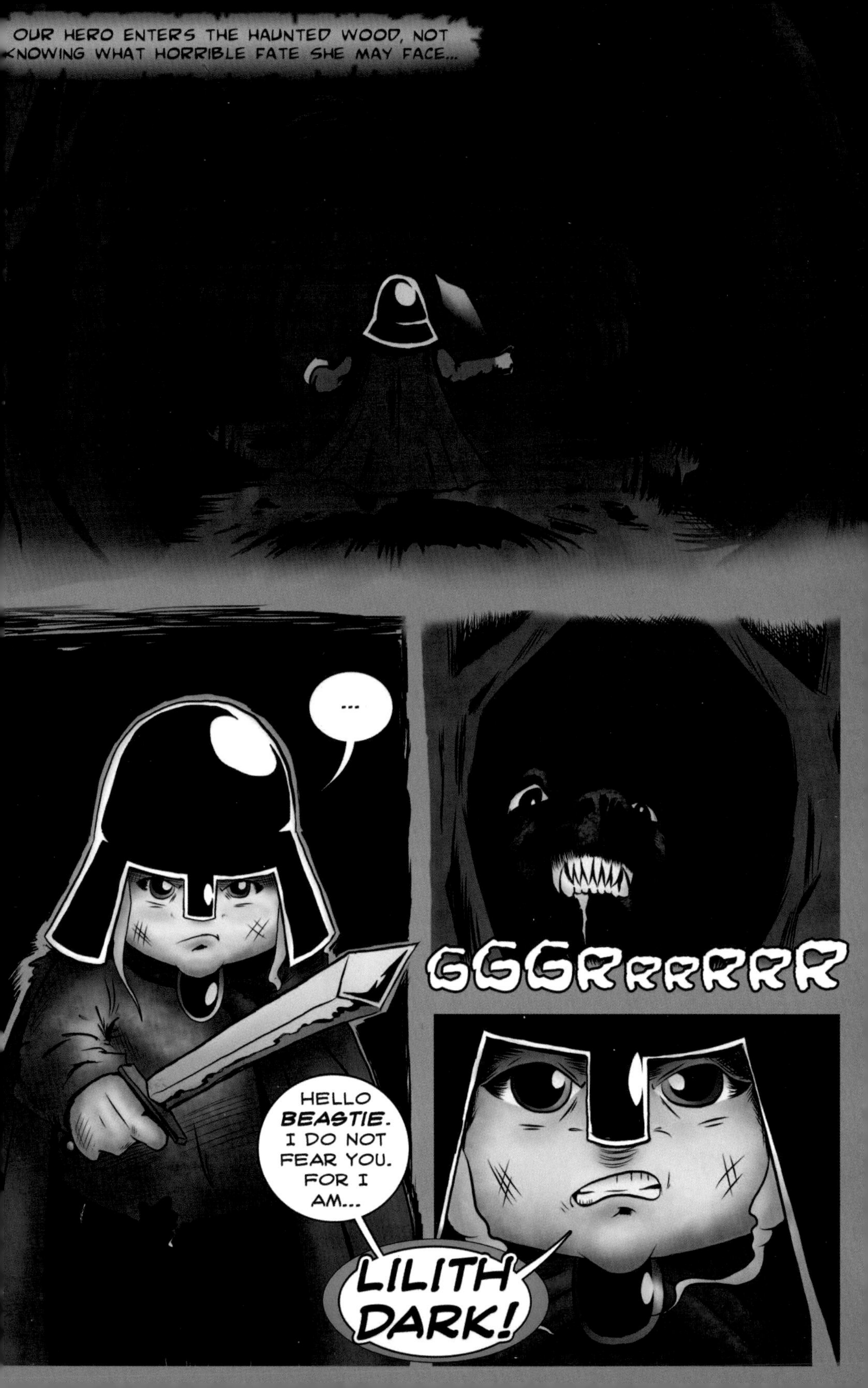
OUR HERO ENTERS THE HAUNTED WOOD, NOT KNOWING WHAT HORRIBLE FATE SHE MAY FACE...
...
GGGRrrrrRR
HELLO BEASTIE. I DO NOT FEAR YOU. FOR I AM...
LILITH DARK!

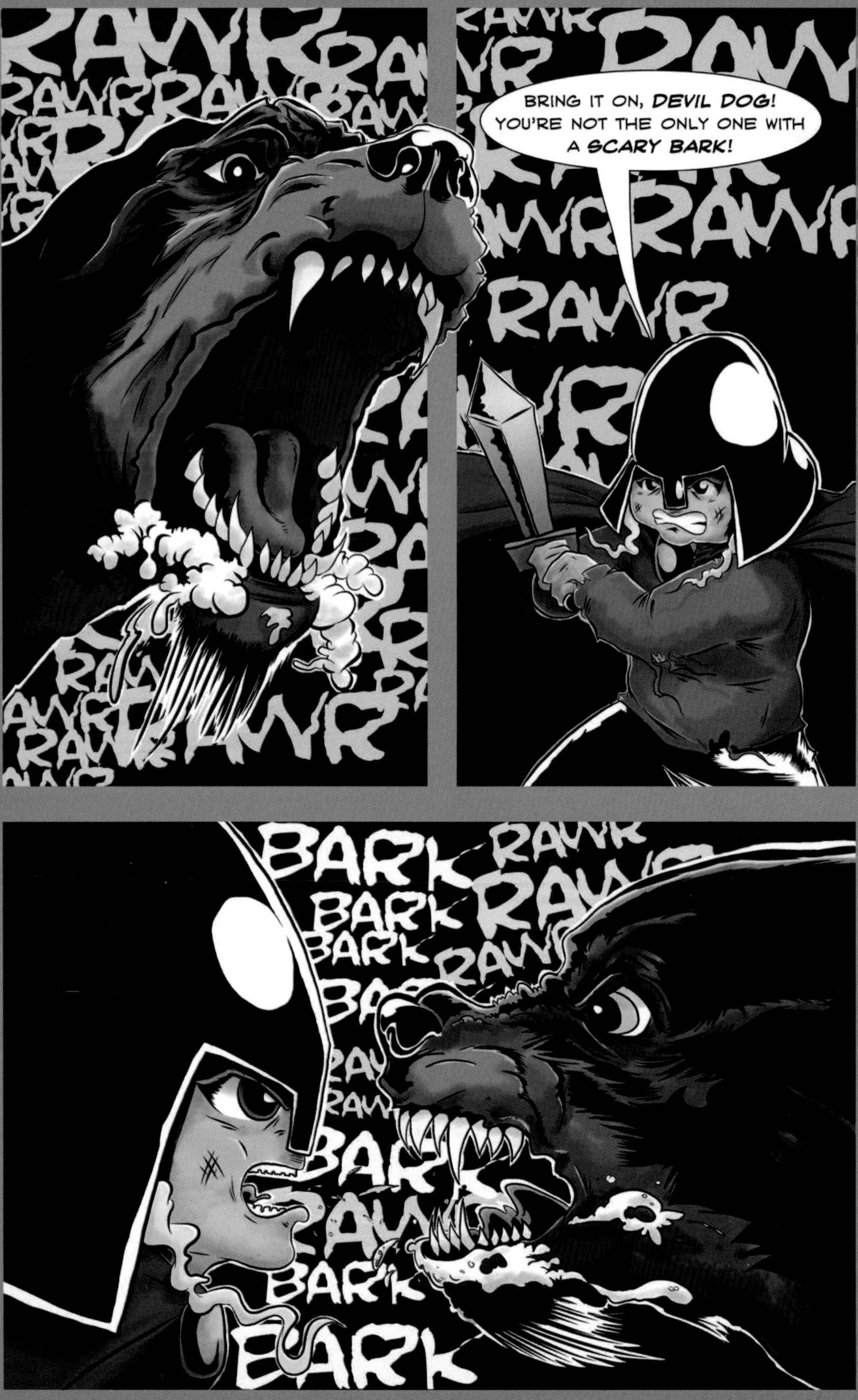
RAWR RAWR RAWR RAWR RAWR
BRING IT ON, DEVIL DOG! YOU'RE NOT THE ONLY ONE WITH A SCARY BARK!
RAWR RAWR RAWR RAWR
BARK RAWR
BARK RAWR
BARK RAWR
BARK BARK BARK BARK

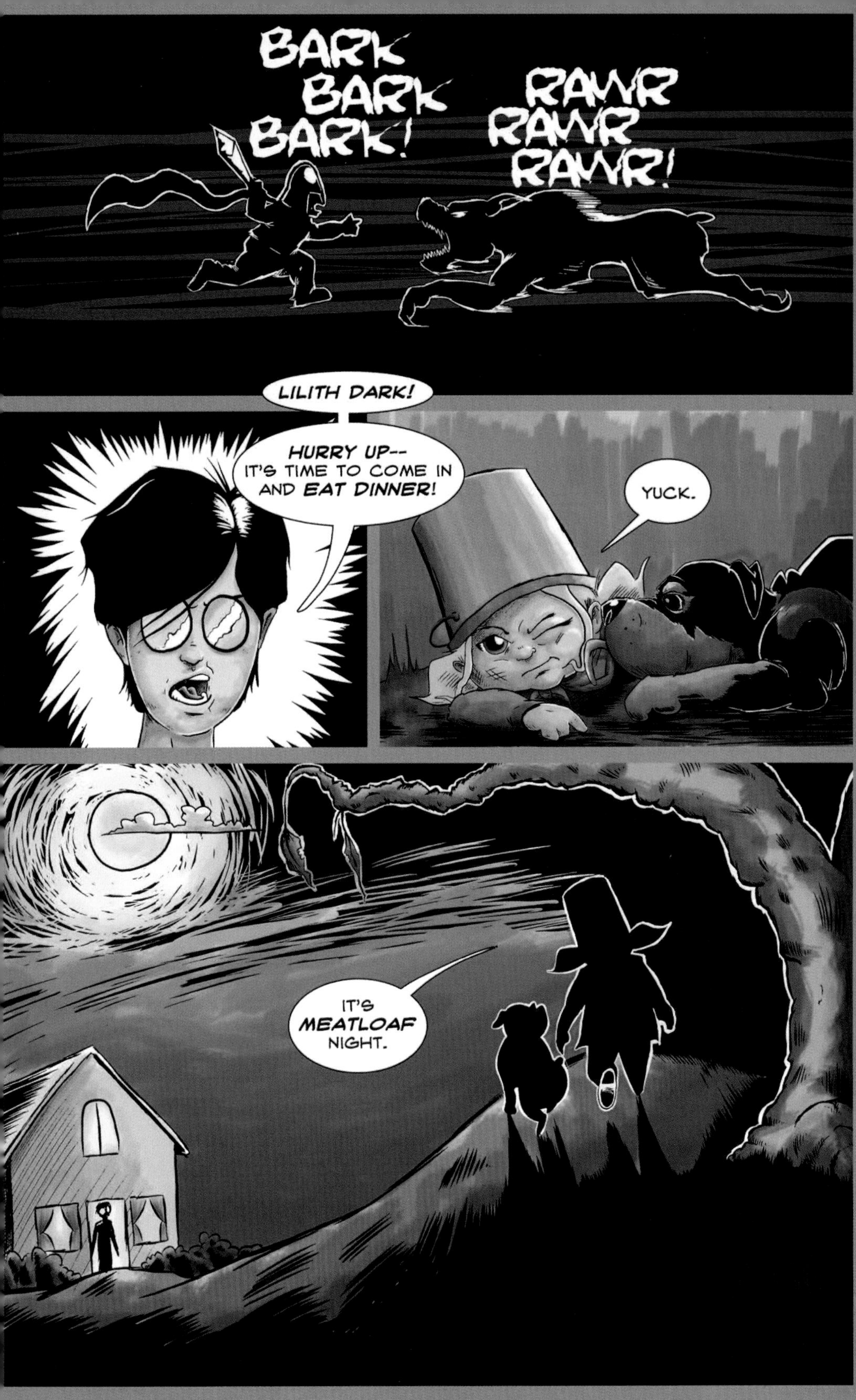
BARK
BARK
BARK!
RAWR
RAWR
RAWR!
LILITH DARK!
HURRY UP-- IT'S TIME TO COME IN AND EAT DINNER!
YUCK.
IT'S MEATLOAF NIGHT.

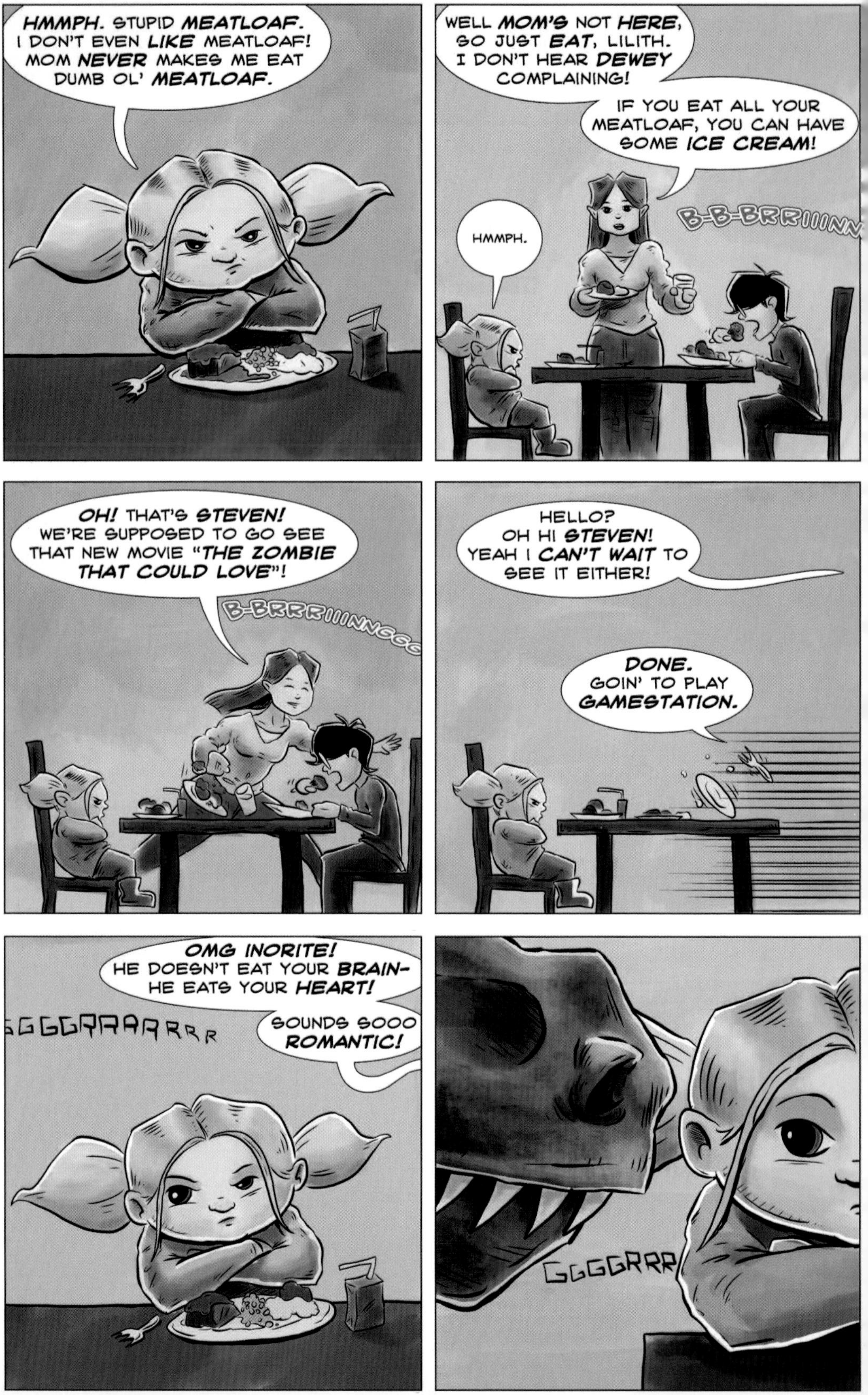
HMMPH. STUPID MEATLOAF. I DON'T EVEN LIKE MEATLOAF! MOM NEVER MAKES ME EAT DUMB OL' MEATLOAF.
WELL MOM'S NOT HERE, SO JUST EAT, LILITH. I DON'T HEAR DEWEY COMPLAINING!
IF YOU EAT ALL YOUR MEATLOAF, YOU CAN HAVE SOME ICE CREAM!
HMMPH.
B-B-BRRRIIIINN
OH! THAT'S STEVEN! WE'RE SUPPOSED TO GO SEE THAT NEW MOVIE "THE ZOMBIE THAT COULD LOVE"!
B-BRRRIIIINNGGG
HELLO? OH HI STEVEN! YEAH I CAN'T WAIT TO SEE IT EITHER!
DONE. GOIN' TO PLAY GAMESTATION.
OMG INORITE! HE DOESN'T EAT YOUR BRAIN- HE EATS YOUR HEART!
SOUNDS SOOO ROMANTIC!
GGGGRRRRRRRR
GGGGRRR

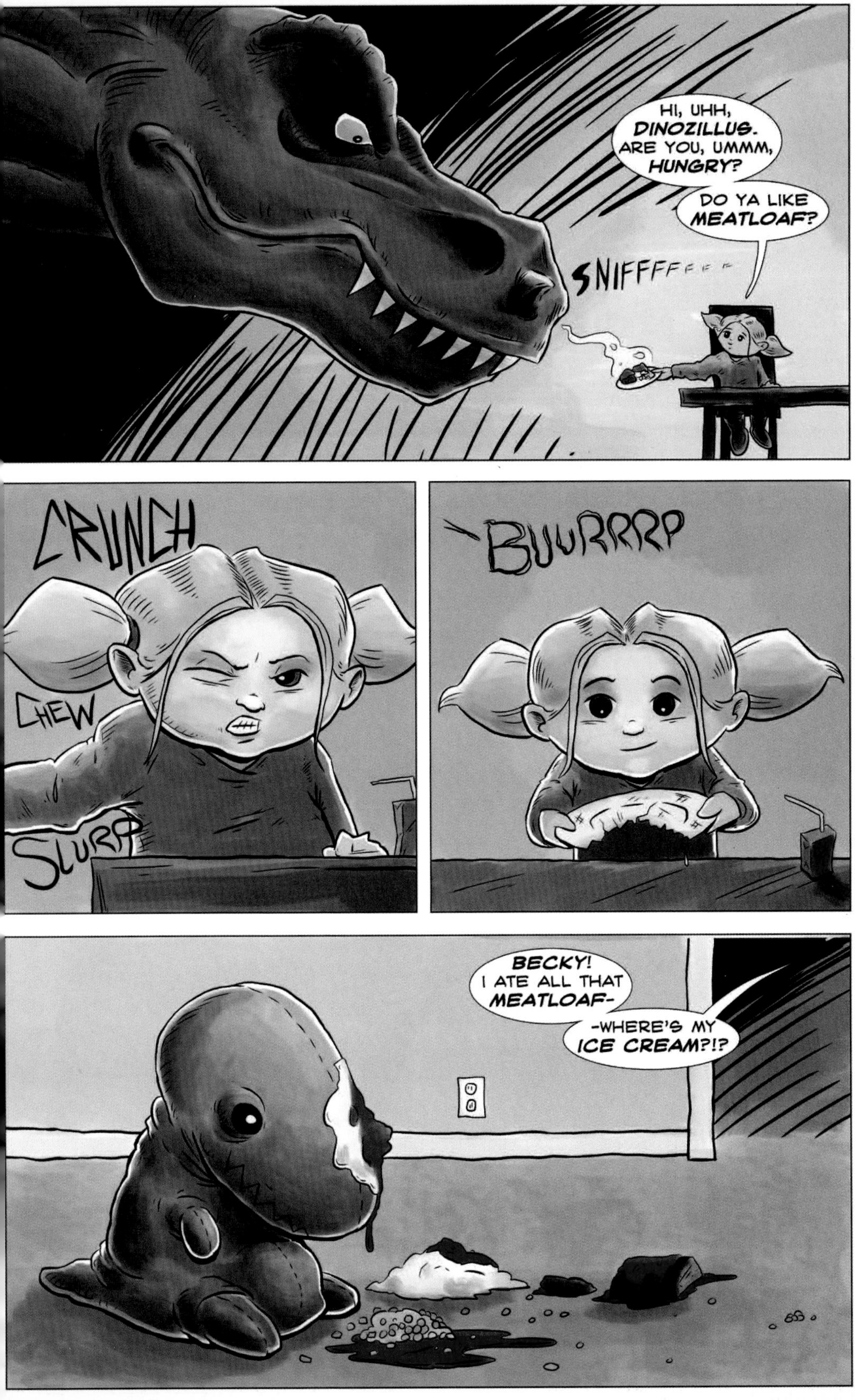

HI, UHH, DINOZILLUS. ARE YOU, UMMM, HUNGRY?
DO YA LIKE MEATLOAF?
SNIFFFFFFF
CRUNCH
CHEW
SLURP
BUUURRRP
BECKY! I ATE ALL THAT MEATLOAF-
-WHERE'S MY ICE CREAM?!?

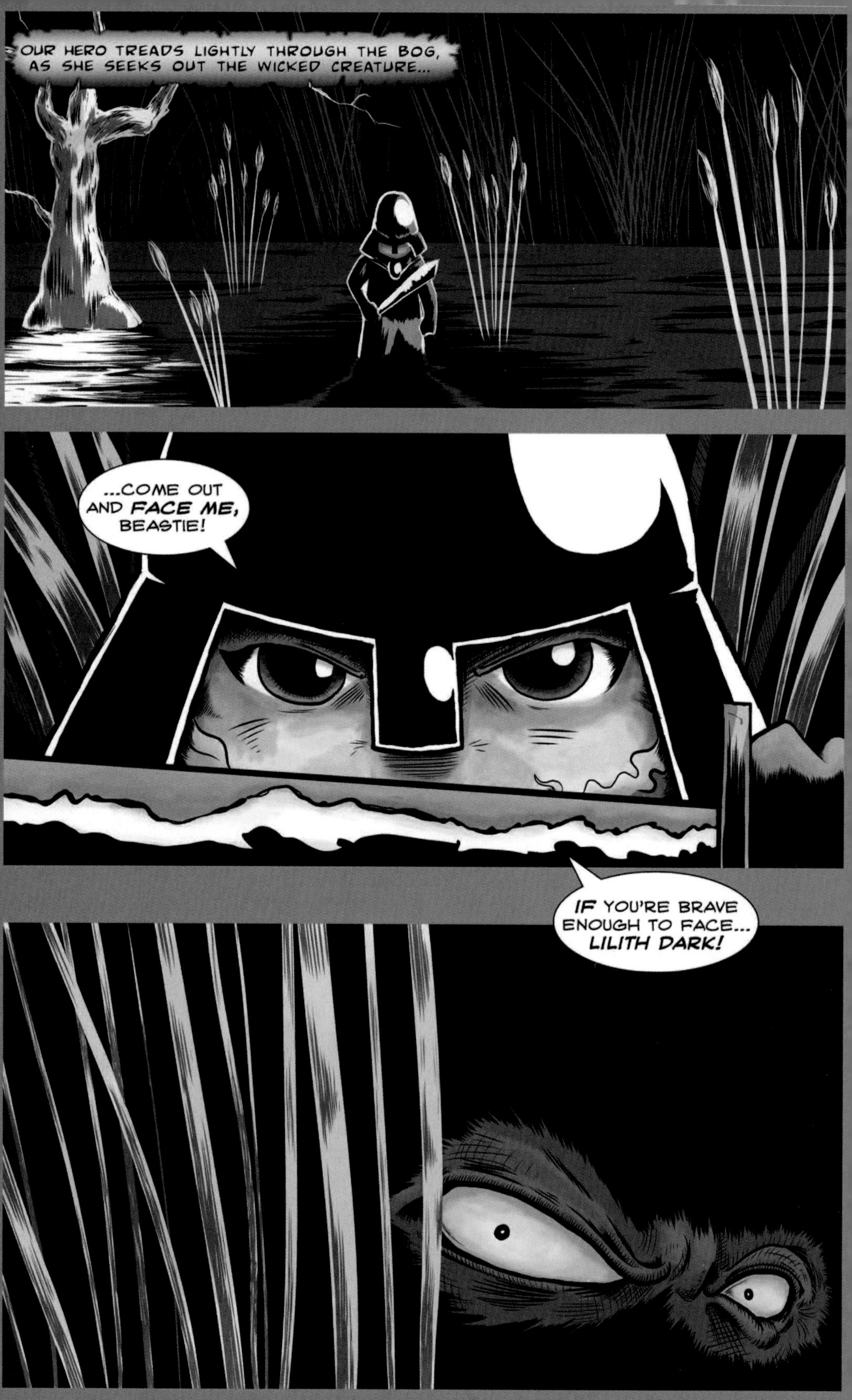
OUR HERO TREADS LIGHTLY THROUGH THE BOG, AS SHE SEEKS OUT THE WICKED CREATURE...
...COME OUT AND FACE ME, BEASTIE!
IF YOU'RE BRAVE ENOUGH TO FACE... LILITH DARK!

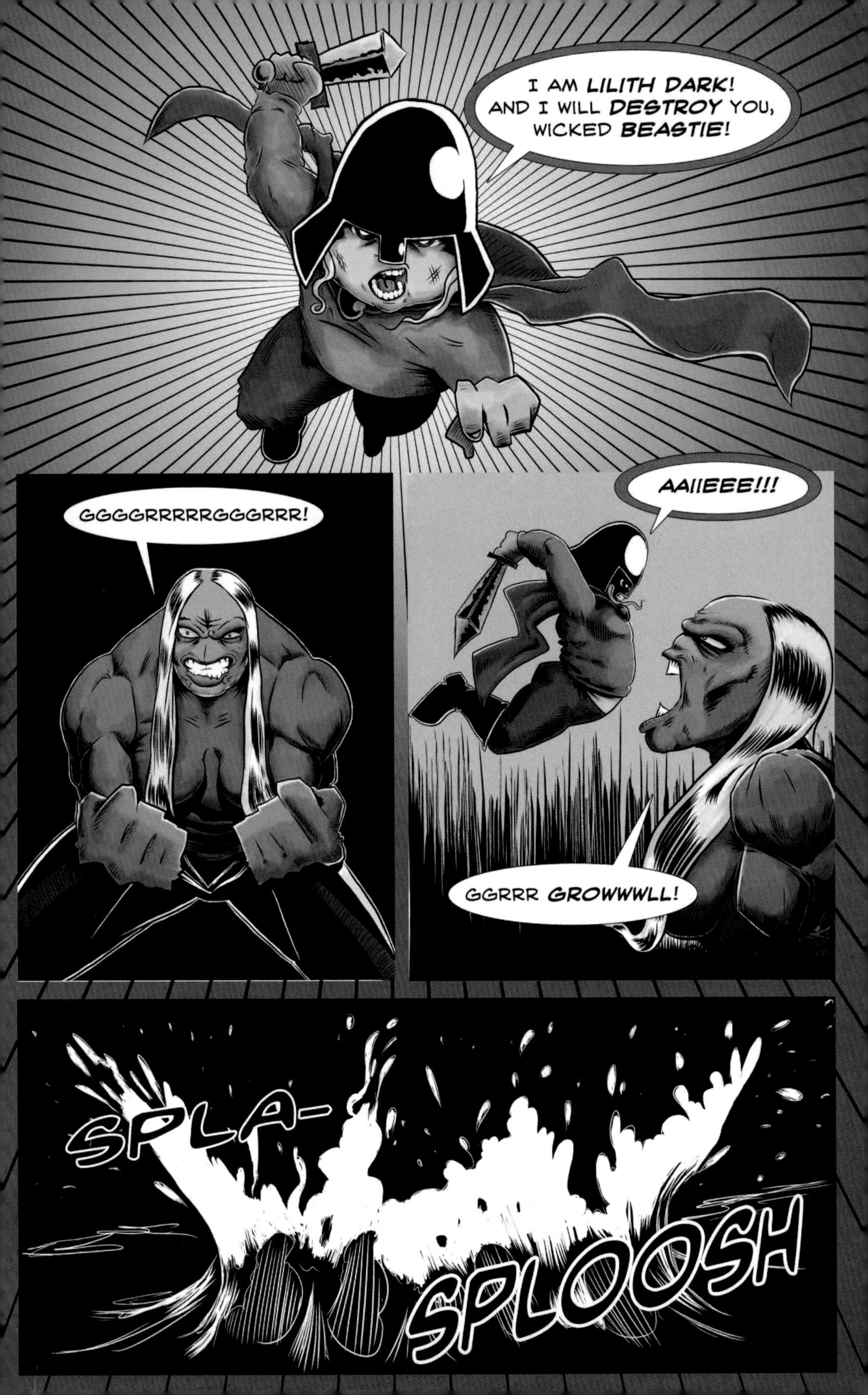
I AM LILITH DARK! AND I WILL DESTROY YOU, WICKED BEASTIE!
GGGGRRRRRGGGRRR!
AAIIEEE!!!
GGRRR GROWWWLL!
SPLA-
SPLOOSH

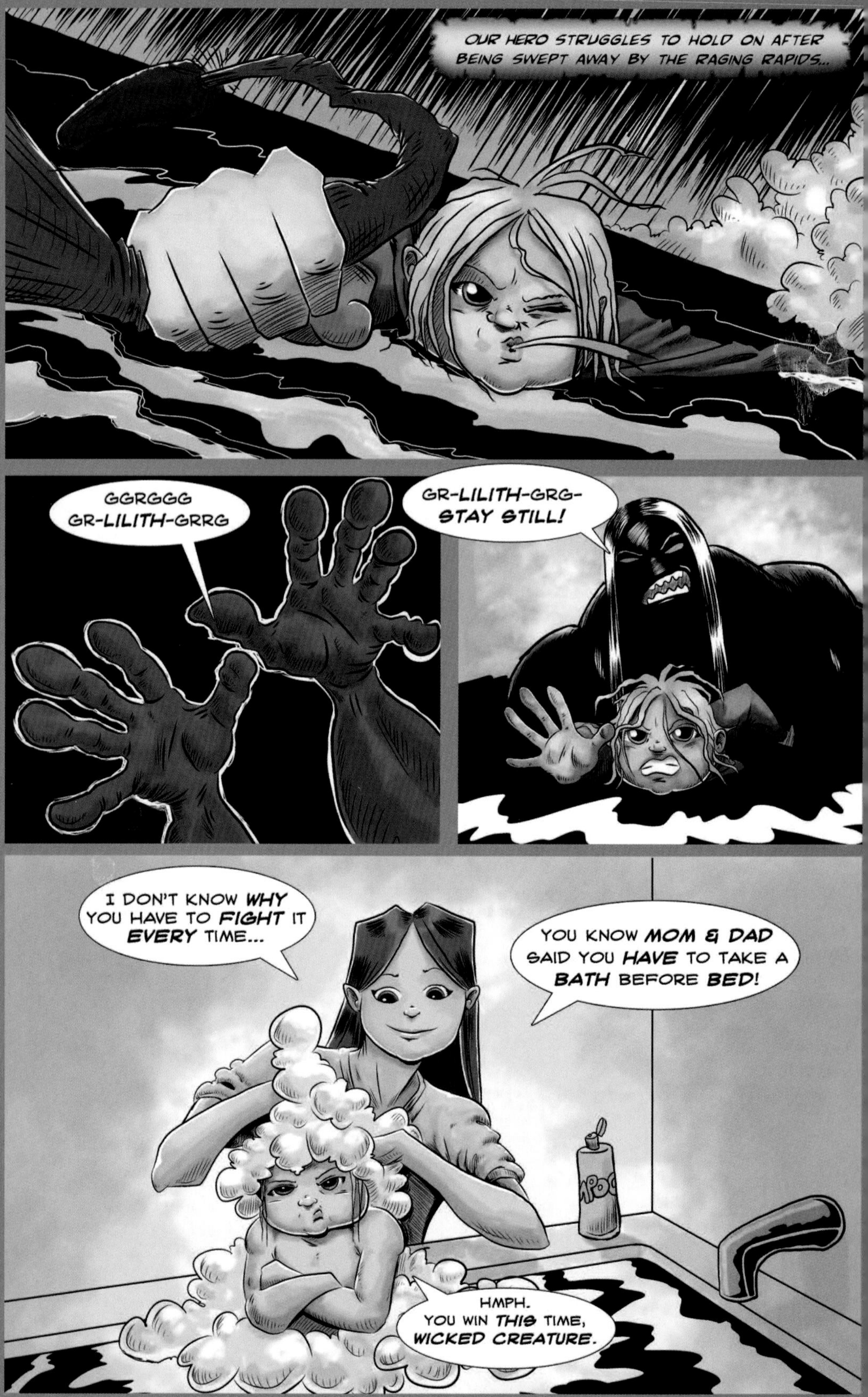
OUR HERO STRUGGLES TO HOLD ON AFTER BEING SWEPT AWAY BY THE RAGING RAPIDS...
GGRGGG GR-LILITH-GRRG
GR-LILITH-GRG- STAY STILL!
I DON'T KNOW WHY YOU HAVE TO FIGHT IT EVERY TIME...
YOU KNOW MOM & DAD SAID YOU HAVE TO TAKE A BATH BEFORE BED!
HMPH. YOU WIN THIS TIME, WICKED CREATURE.

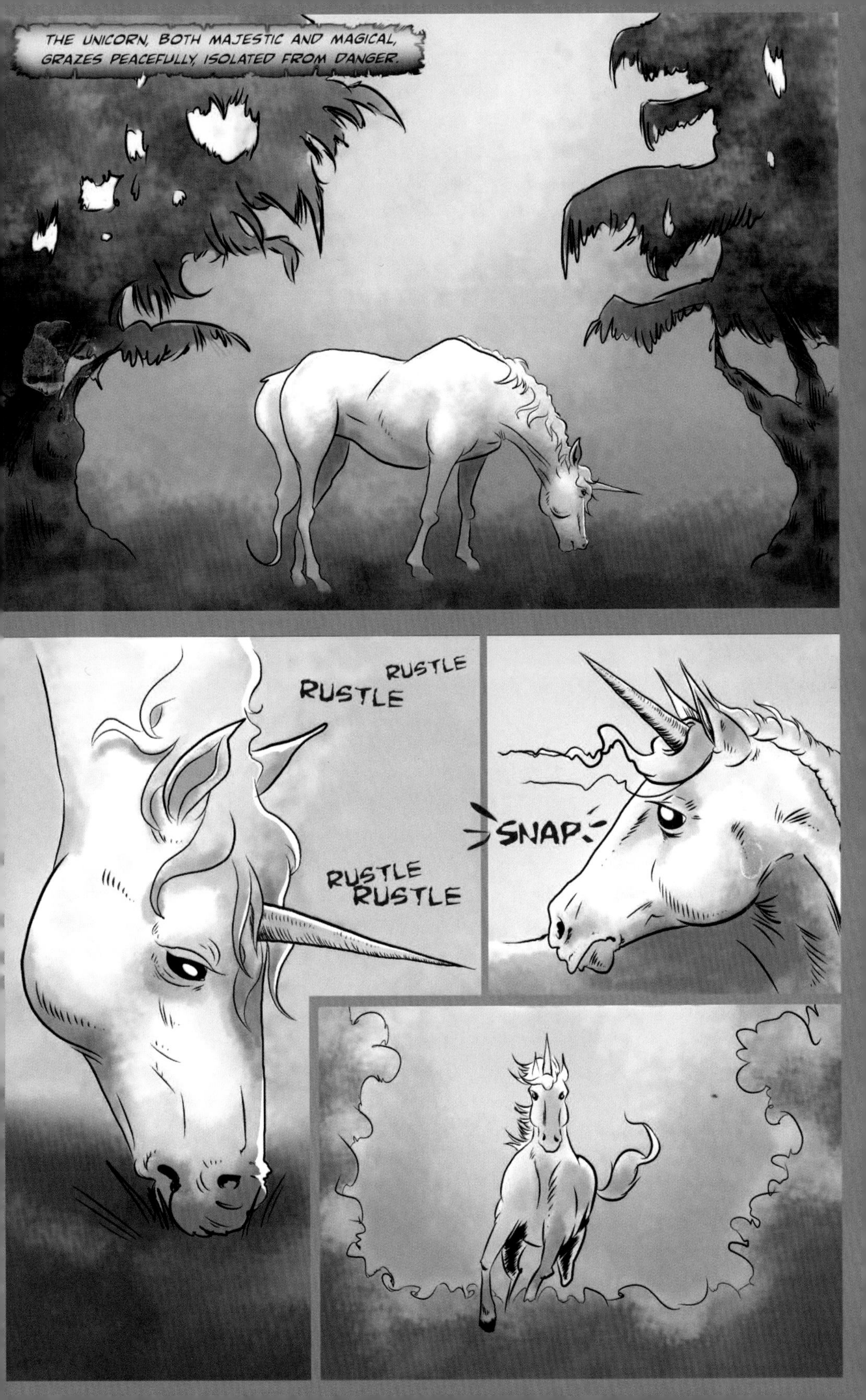
THE UNICORN, BOTH MAJESTIC AND MAGICAL, GRAZES PEACEFULLY, ISOLATED FROM DANGER.
RUSTLE
RUSTLE
RUSTLE
RUSTLE
SNAP

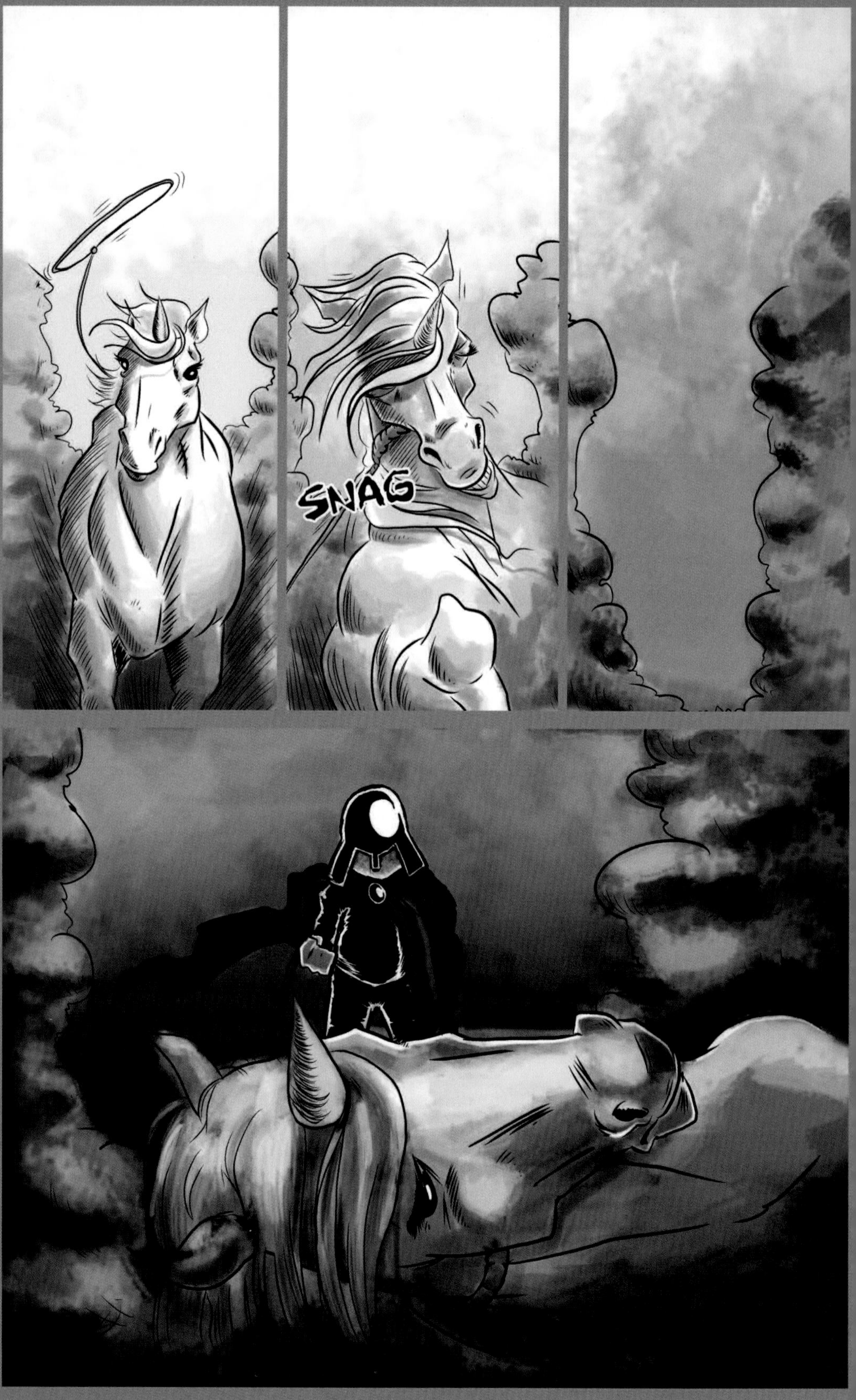
SNAG

THE SCOUNDREL RAISES HER SWORD, READY TO CLAIM THE HORN & ALL OF IT'S POWER AS HER OWN...

RRRGGGG! GET **OFF** OF ME!

STAY **STILL!** I ALMOST **GOTS** IT!

NNNNNGGGGG!

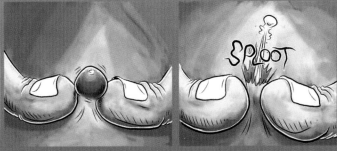

SPLOOT

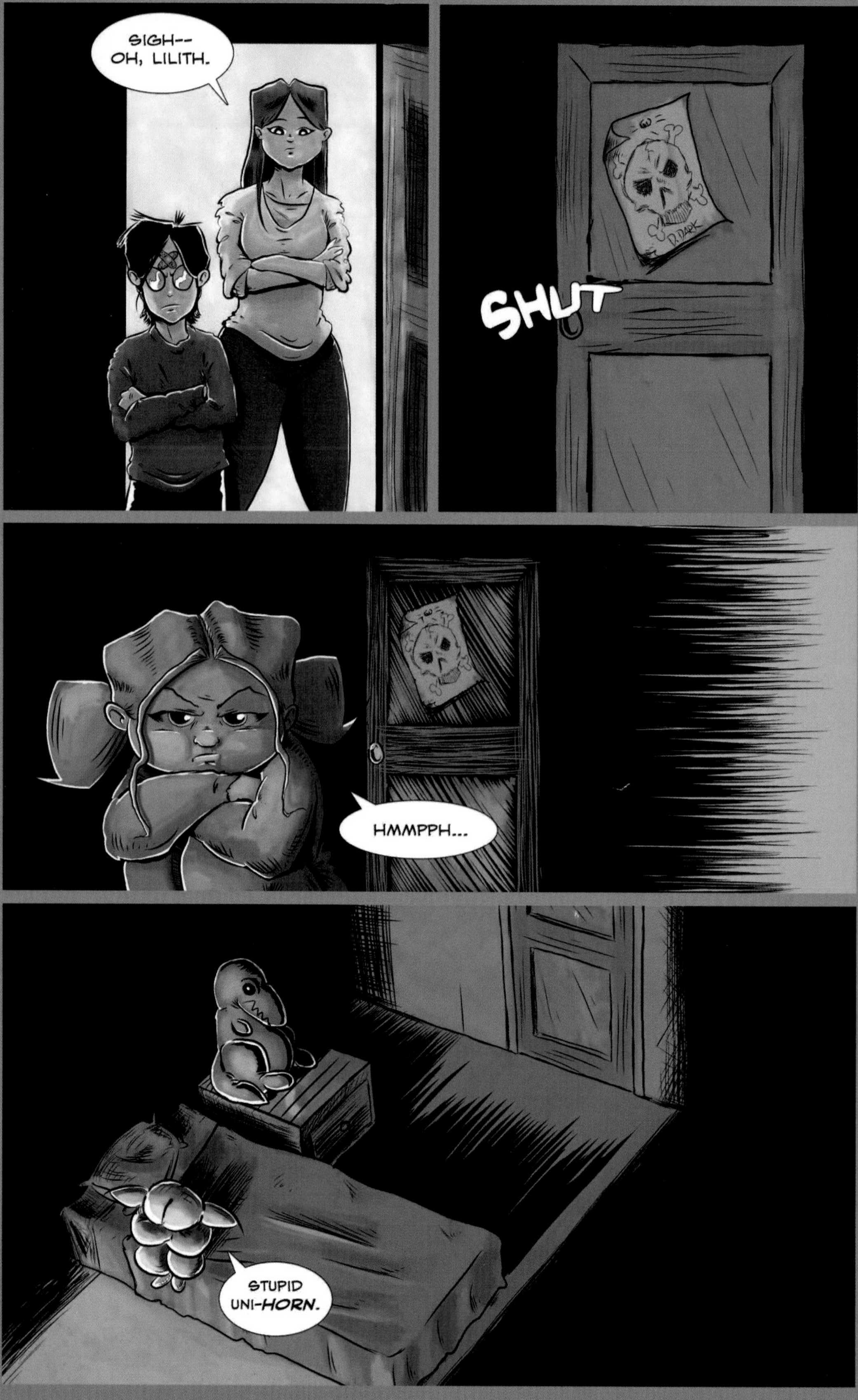
SIGH--
OH, LILITH.
D. DARK
SHUT
HMMPPH...
STUPID
UNI-*HORN*.

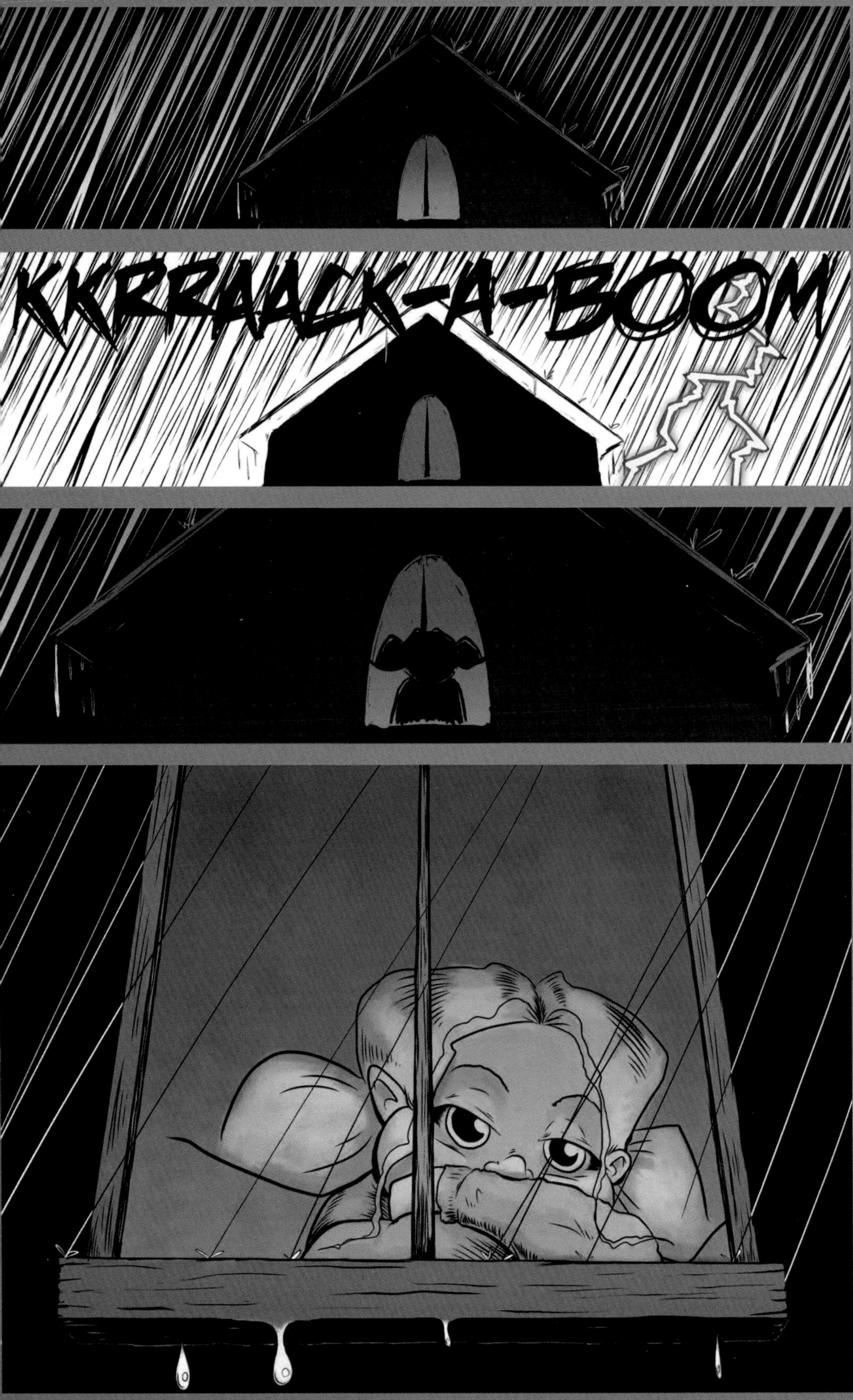
KKRRAACK-A-BOOM

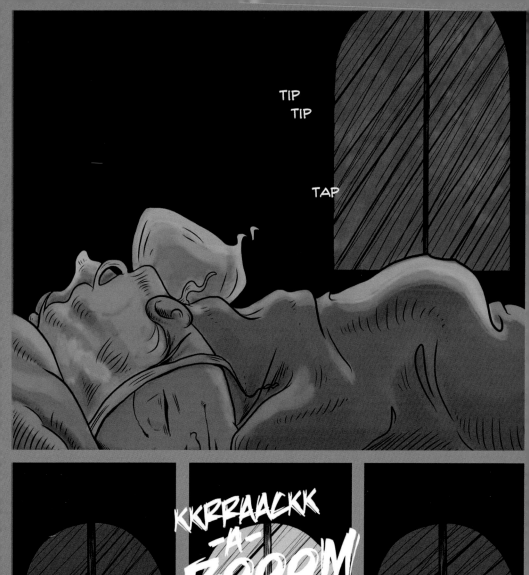

TIP
TIP

TAP

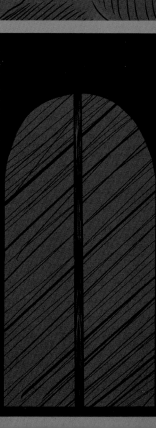

KKRRAACKK
-A-
BOOOM

OUR HERO BEGINS TO DREAM OF TIMES GONE BY...
CRUNCH
CRUNCH
AAAIIIEEEEE!
FFFZZZZOOOOWWWNNNN

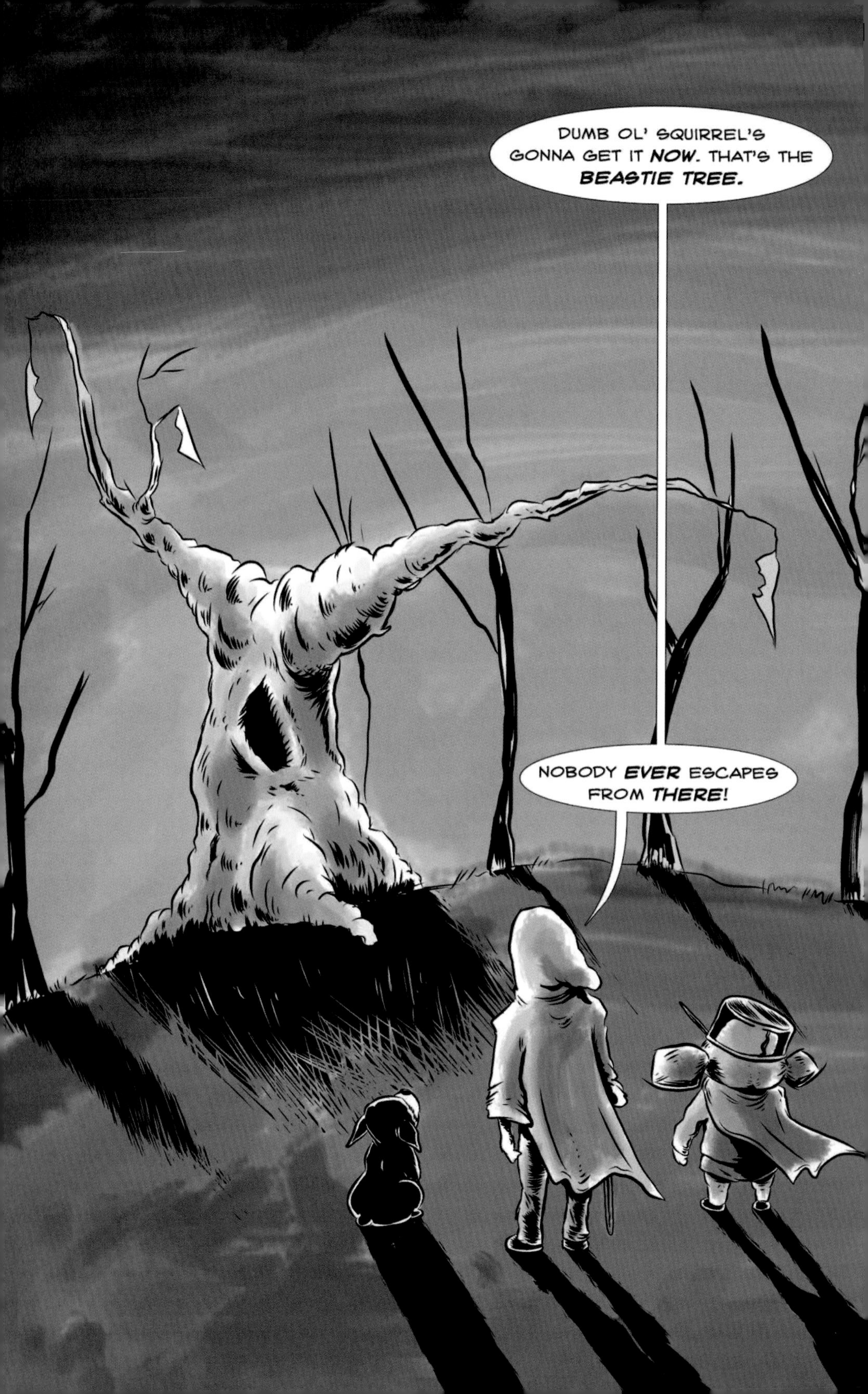
DUMB OL' SQUIRREL'S GONNA GET IT ***NOW***. THAT'S THE ***BEASTIE TREE.***
NOBODY ***EVER*** ESCAPES FROM ***THERE!***

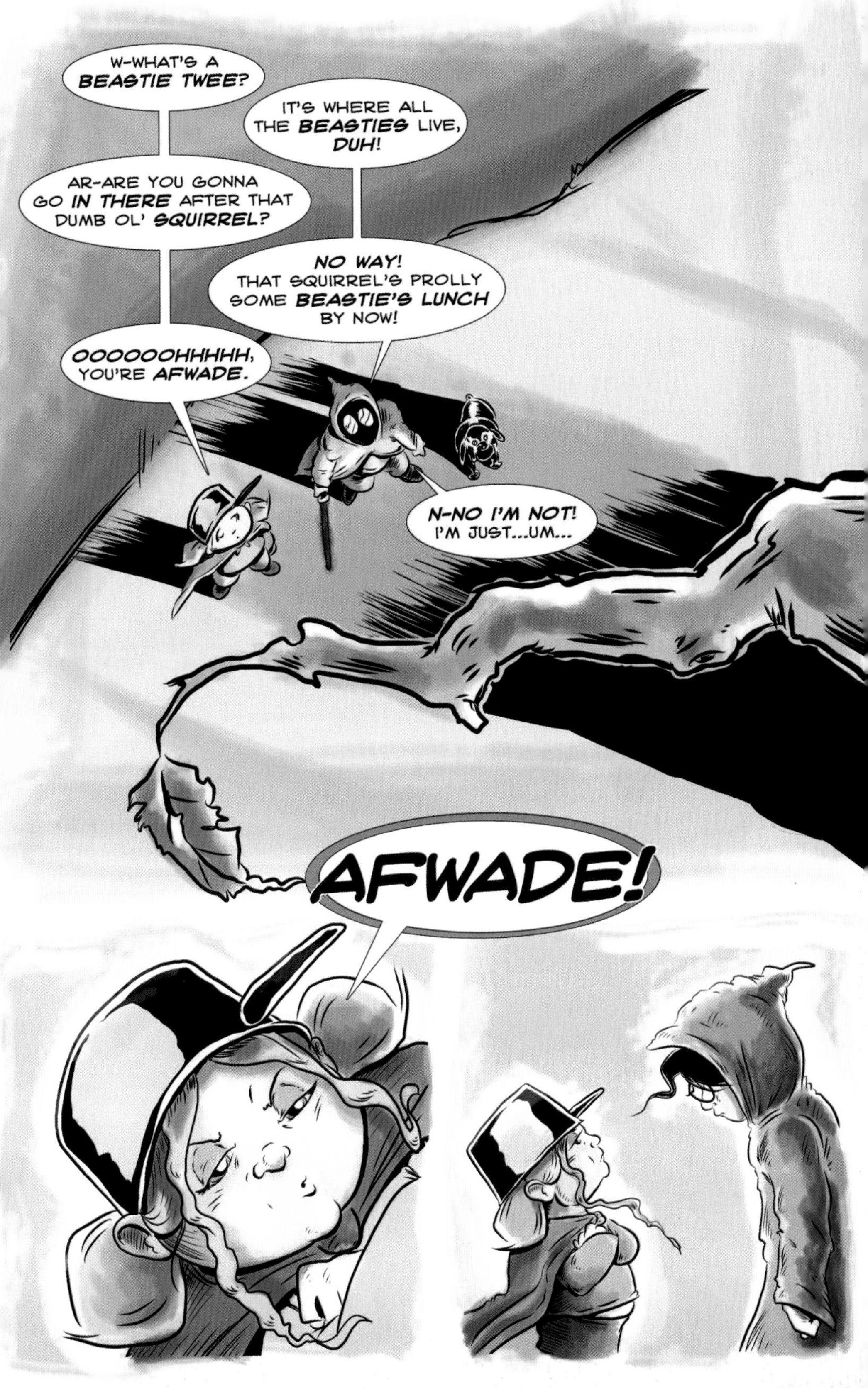
W-WHAT'S A BEASTIE TWEE?
IT'S WHERE ALL THE BEASTIES LIVE, DUH!
AR-ARE YOU GONNA GO IN THERE AFTER THAT DUMB OL' SQUIRREL?
NO WAY! THAT SQUIRREL'S PROLLY SOME BEASTIE'S LUNCH BY NOW!
OOOOOOHHHHH, YOU'RE AFWADE.
N-NO I'M NOT! I'M JUST...UM...
AFWADE!

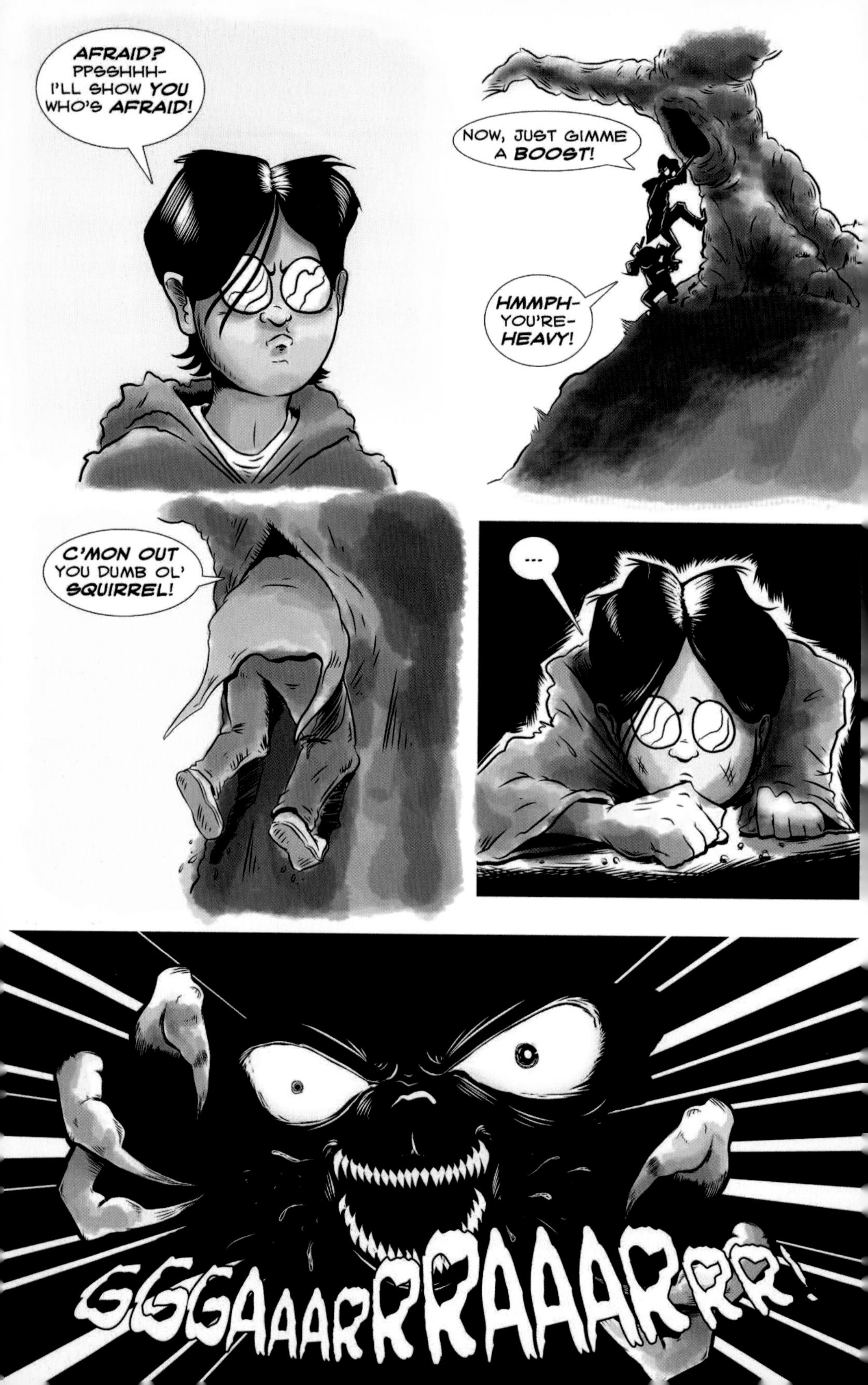
AFRAID? PPSSHHH- I'LL SHOW YOU WHO'S AFRAID!
NOW, JUST GIMME A BOOST!
HMMPH- YOU'RE- HEAVY!
C'MON OUT YOU DUMB OL' SQUIRREL!
...
GGGAAARRRAAARRR!

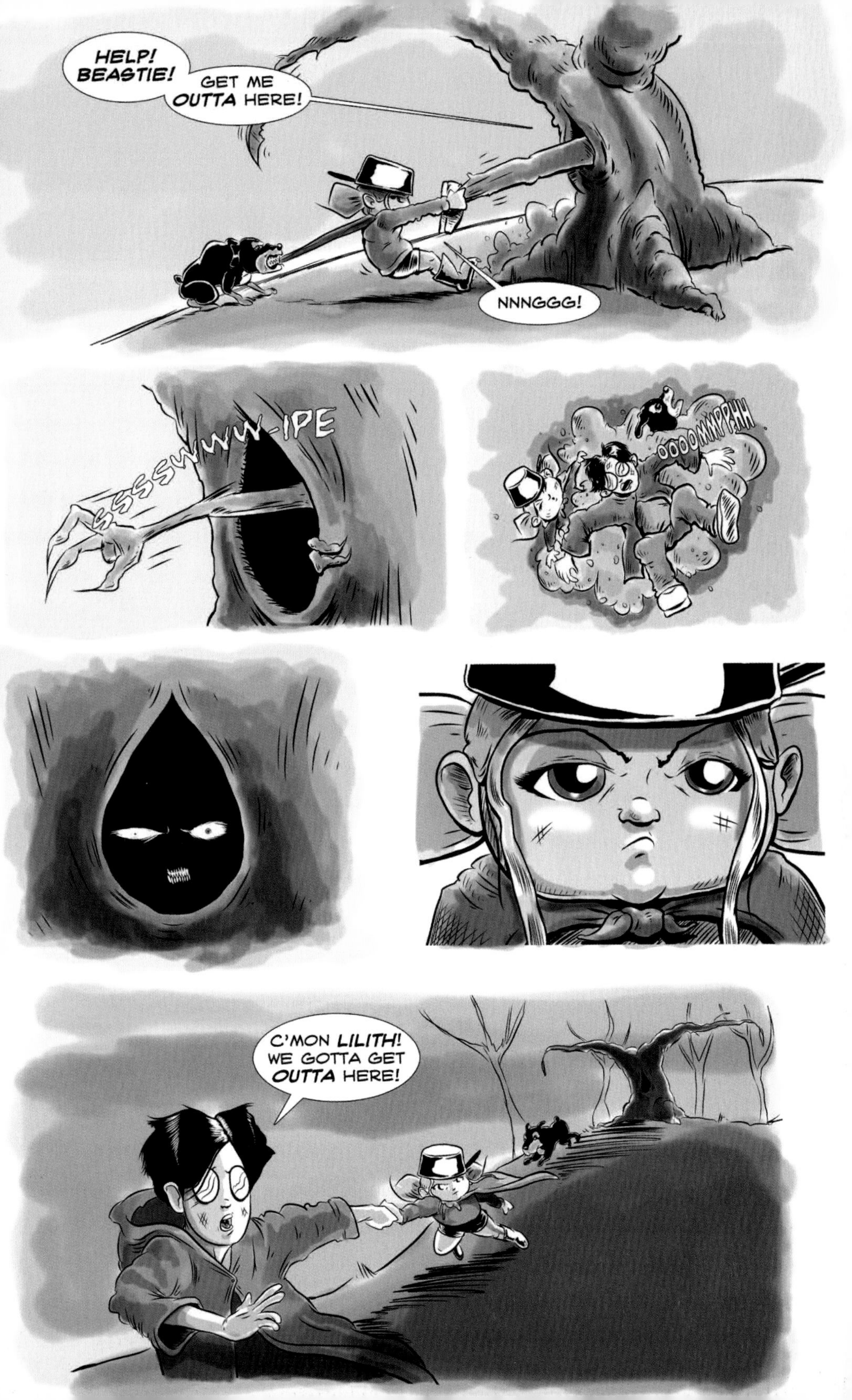
HELP! BEASTIE!
GET ME OUTTA HERE!
NNNGGG!
SSSSWWW-IPE
OOOOMMPPHH
C'MON LILITH! WE GOTTA GET OUTTA HERE!

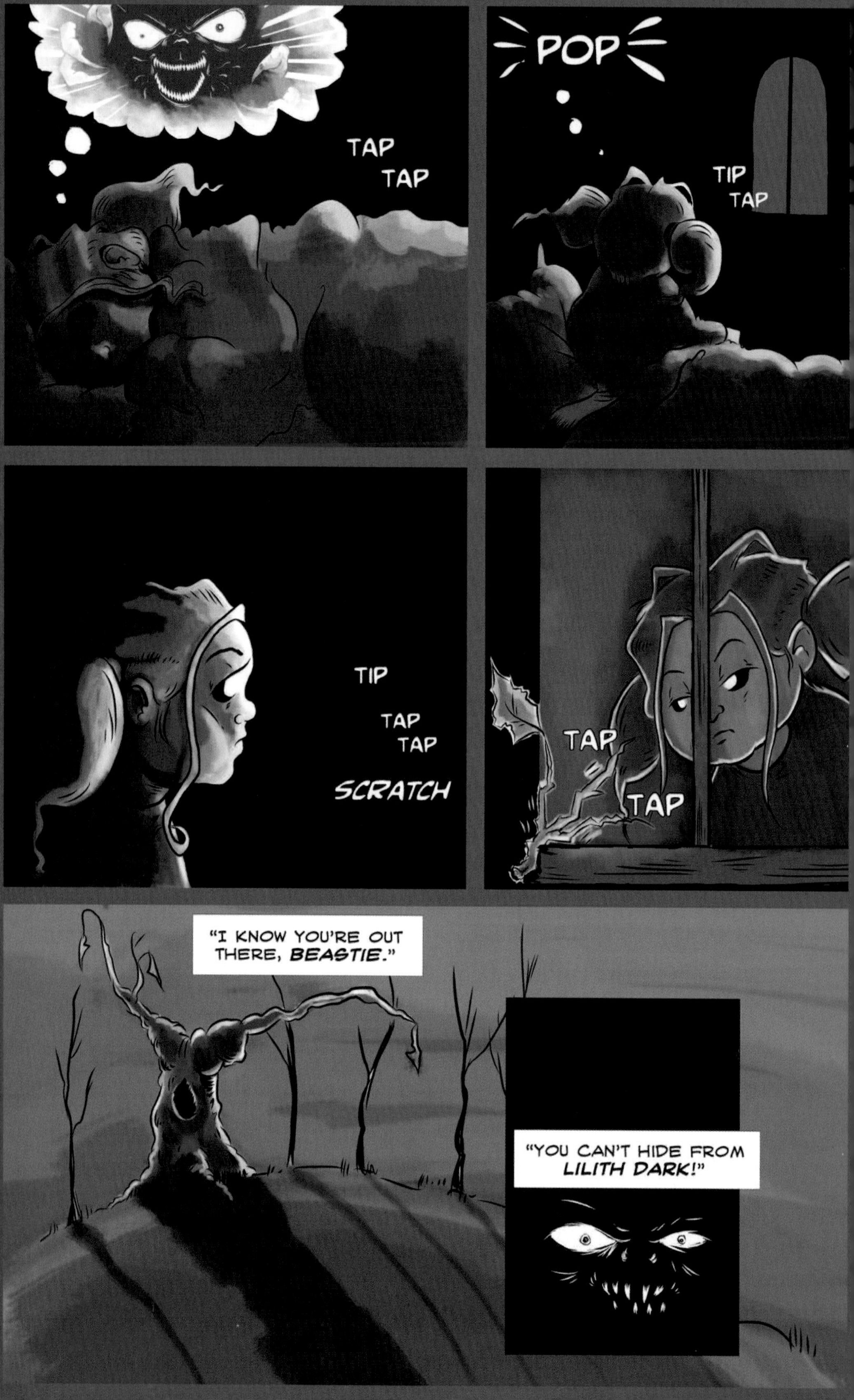
TAP
TAP
POP
TIP
TAP
TIP
TAP
TAP
SCRATCH
TAP
TAP
"I KNOW YOU'RE OUT THERE, BEASTIE."
"YOU CAN'T HIDE FROM LILITH DARK!"

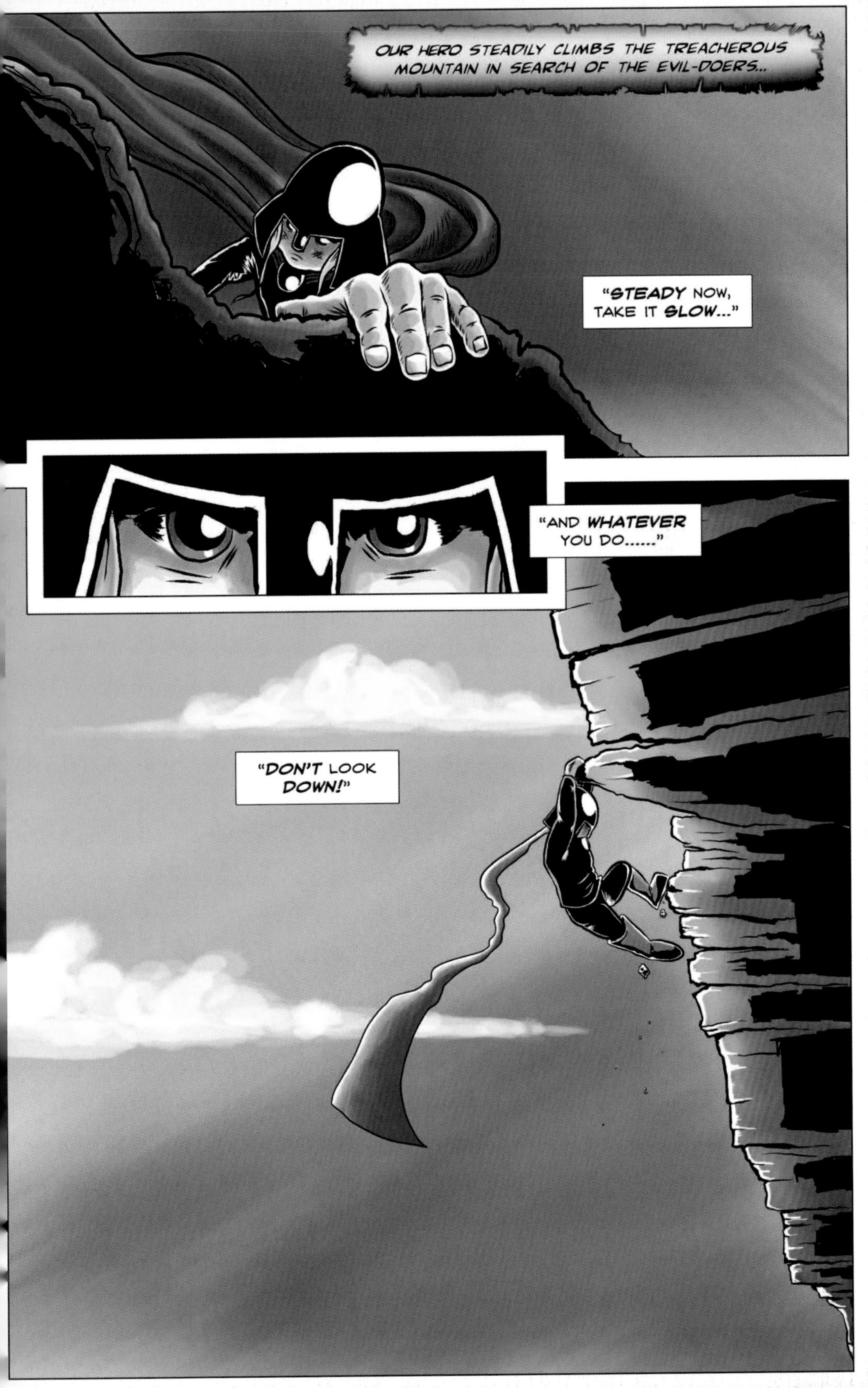
OUR HERO STEADILY CLIMBS THE TREACHEROUS MOUNTAIN IN SEARCH OF THE EVIL-DOERS...
"STEADY NOW, TAKE IT SLOW..."
"AND WHATEVER YOU DO......"
"DON'T LOOK DOWN!"

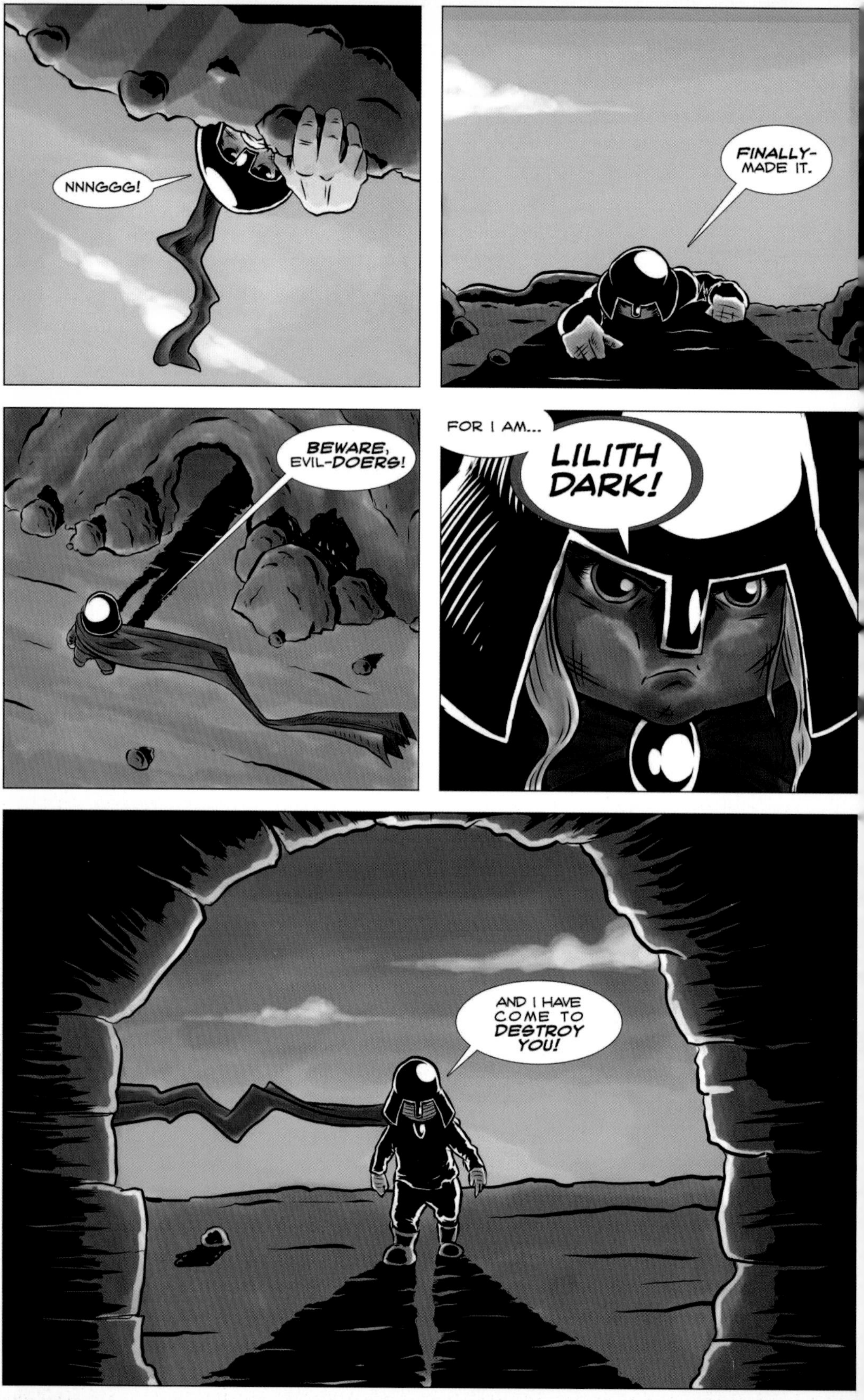
NNNGGG!
FINALLY- MADE IT.
BEWARE, EVIL-DOERS!
FOR I AM...
LILITH DARK!
AND I HAVE COME TO DESTROY YOU!

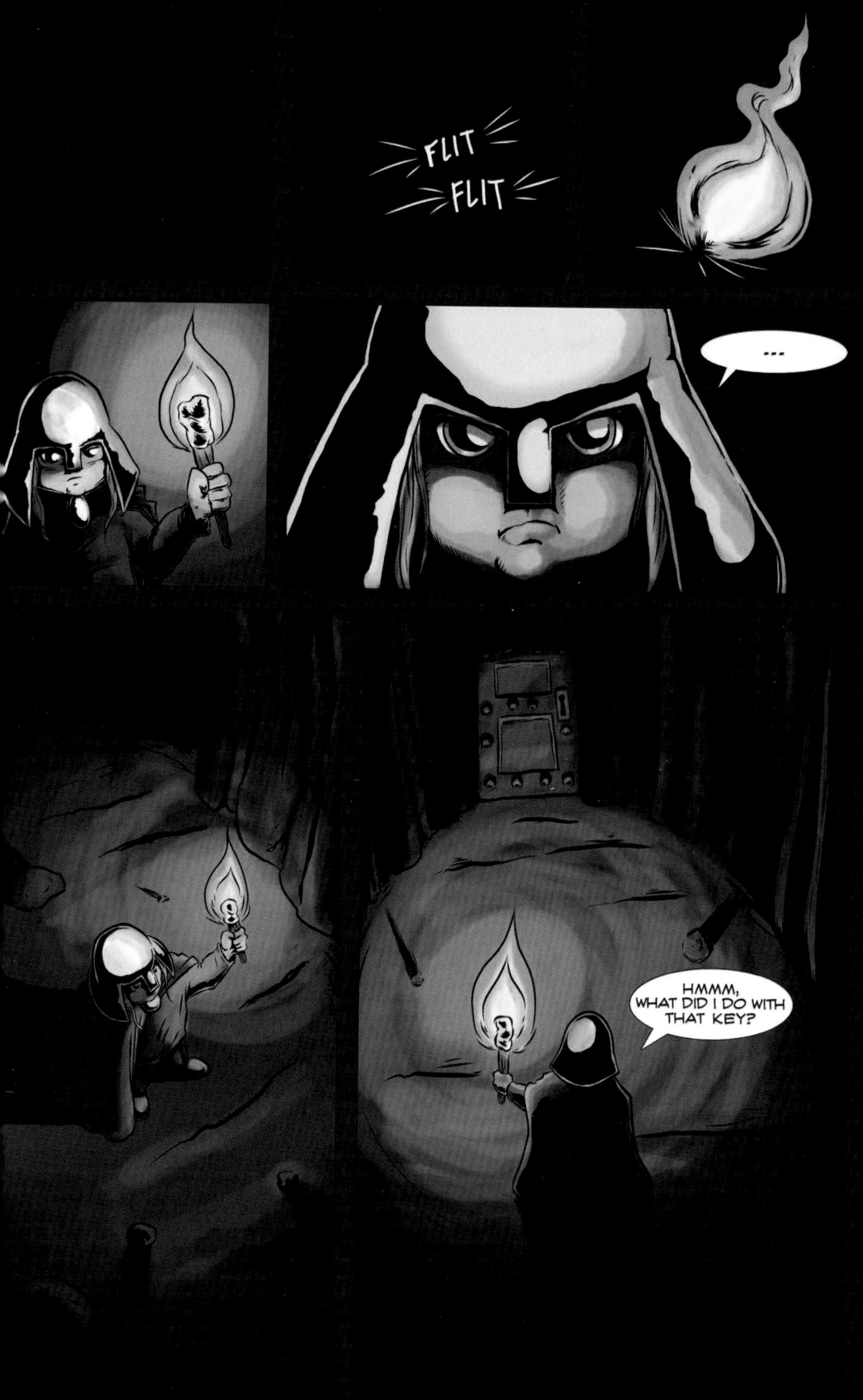
FLIT
FLIT
...
HMMM, WHAT DID I DO WITH THAT KEY?

CH-
CLICK

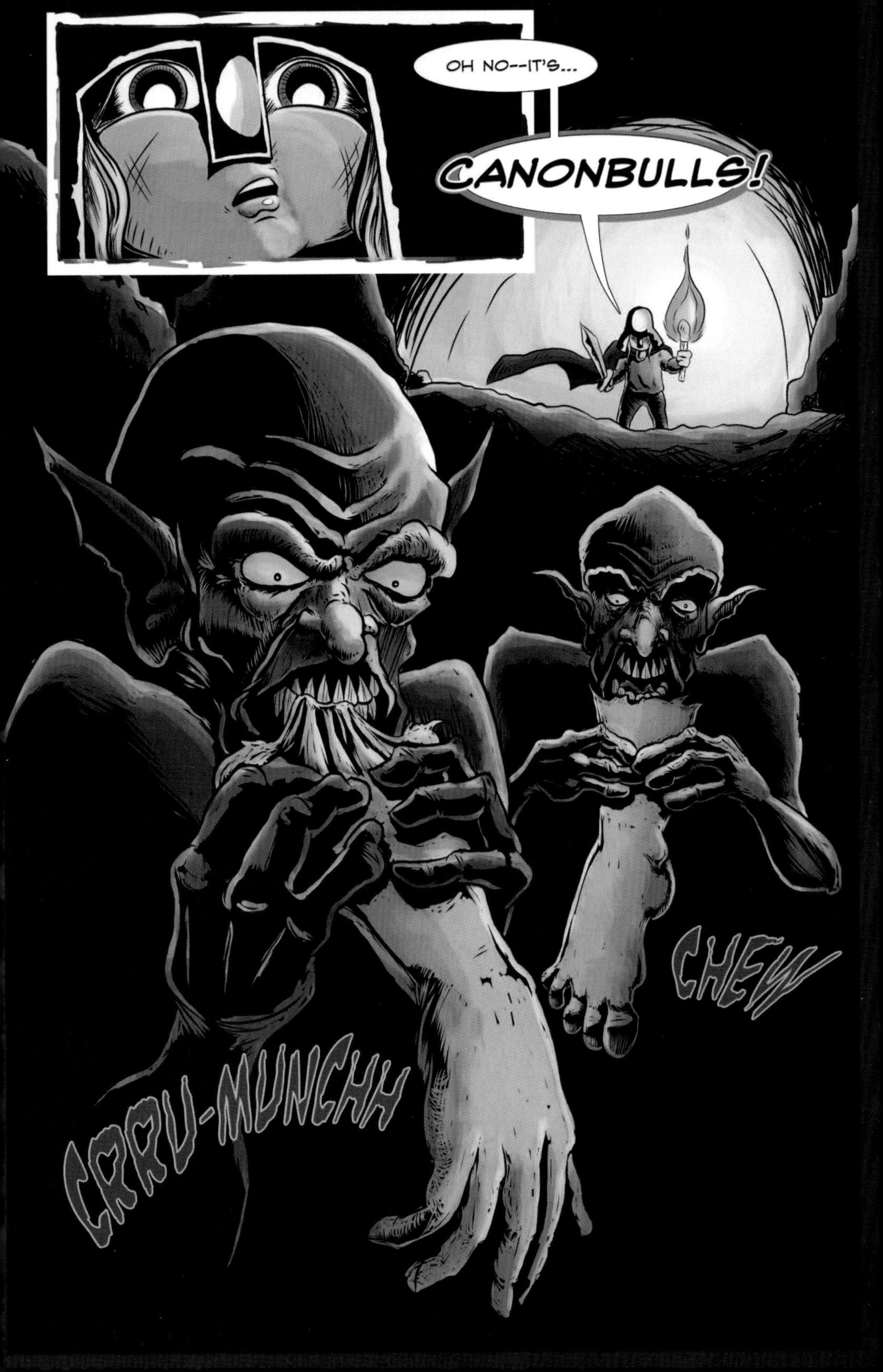
OH NO--IT'S...
CANONBULLS!
CHEW
CRRU-MUNCHH

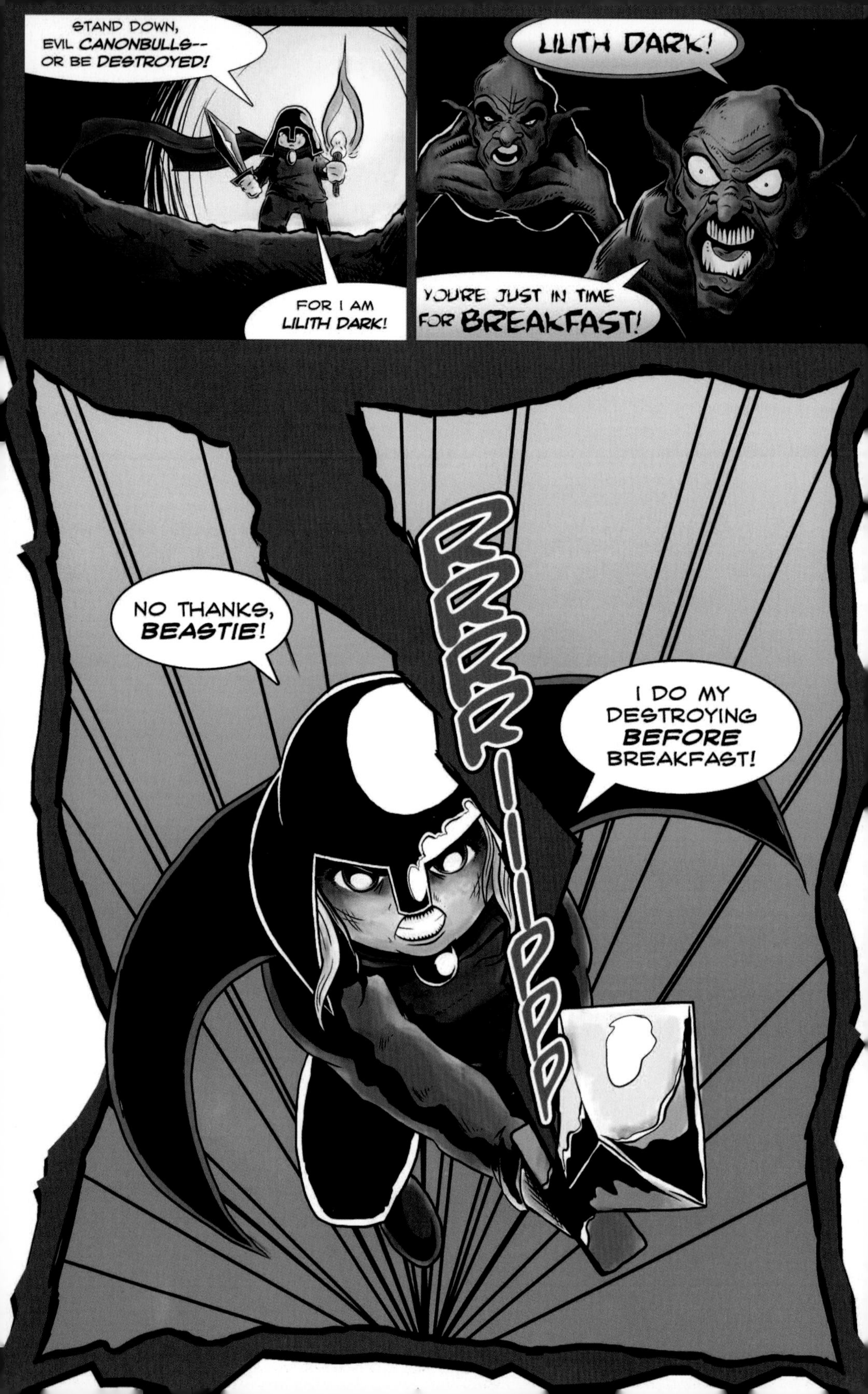
STAND DOWN, EVIL CANONBULLS-- OR BE DESTROYED!
FOR I AM LILITH DARK!
LILITH DARK!
YOU'RE JUST IN TIME FOR BREAKFAST!
NO THANKS, BEASTIE!
RRRRR-I-I-I-PPPP
I DO MY DESTROYING BEFORE BREAKFAST!

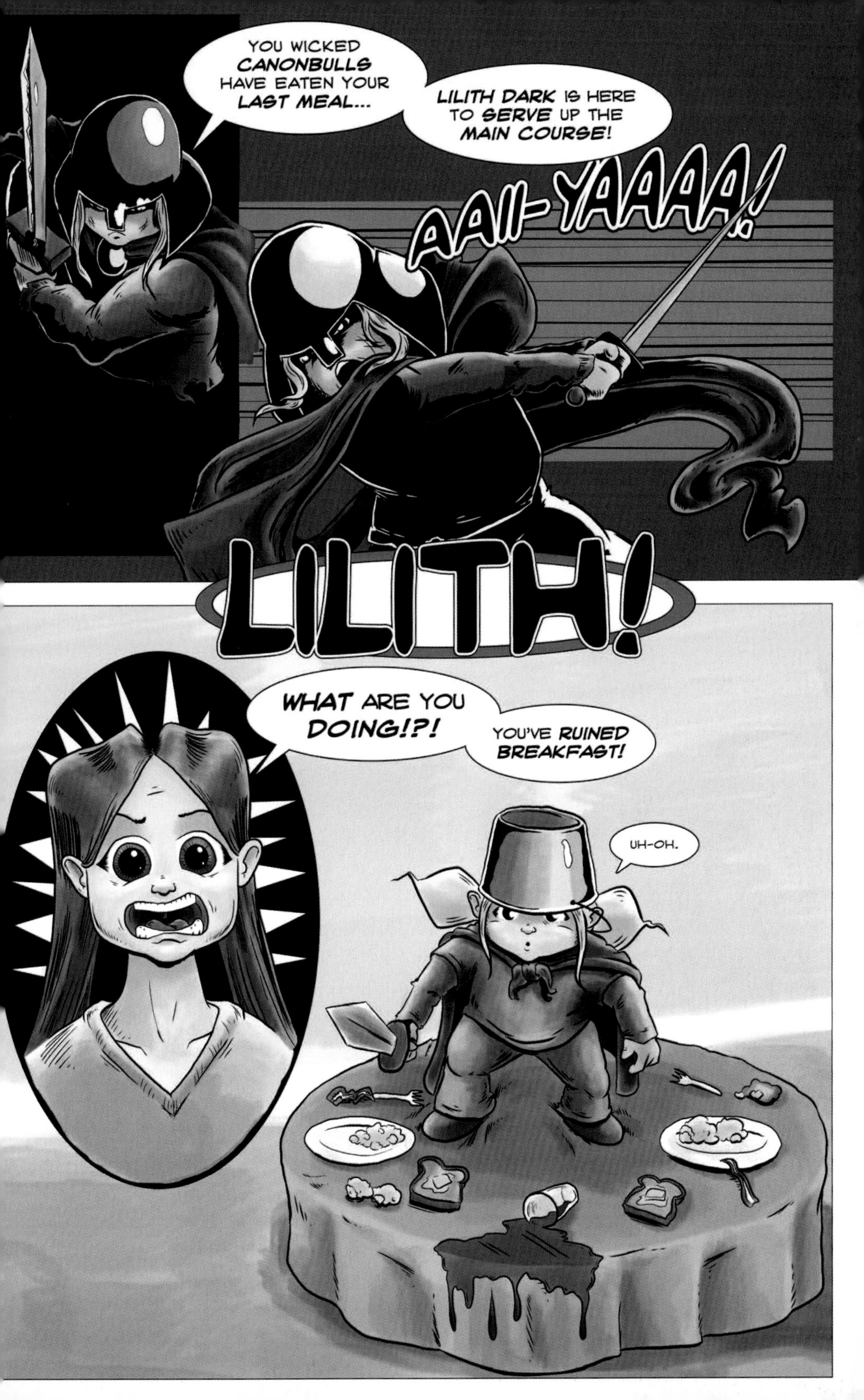
YOU WICKED CANONBULLS HAVE EATEN YOUR LAST MEAL...
LILITH DARK IS HERE TO SERVE UP THE MAIN COURSE!
AAII-YAAAAA!
LILITH!
WHAT ARE YOU DOING!?!
YOU'VE RUINED BREAKFAST!
UH-OH.

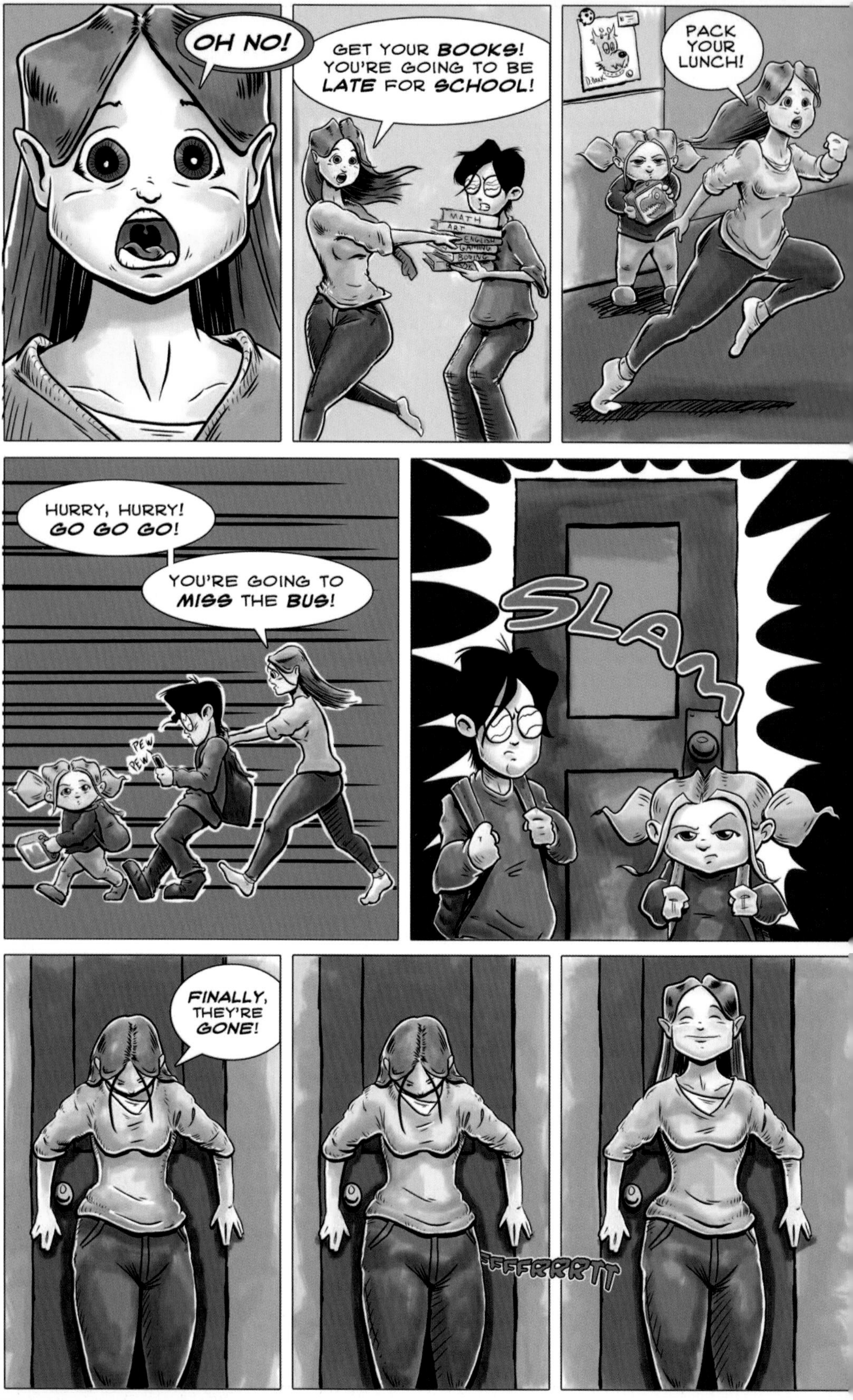
OH NO!
GET YOUR BOOKS! YOU'RE GOING TO BE LATE FOR SCHOOL!
MATH
ART
ENGLISH
GAMING
PACK YOUR LUNCH!
HURRY, HURRY! GO GO GO!
YOU'RE GOING TO MISS THE BUS!
PEW PEW
SLAM
FINALLY, THEY'RE GONE!
FFFRRRTT

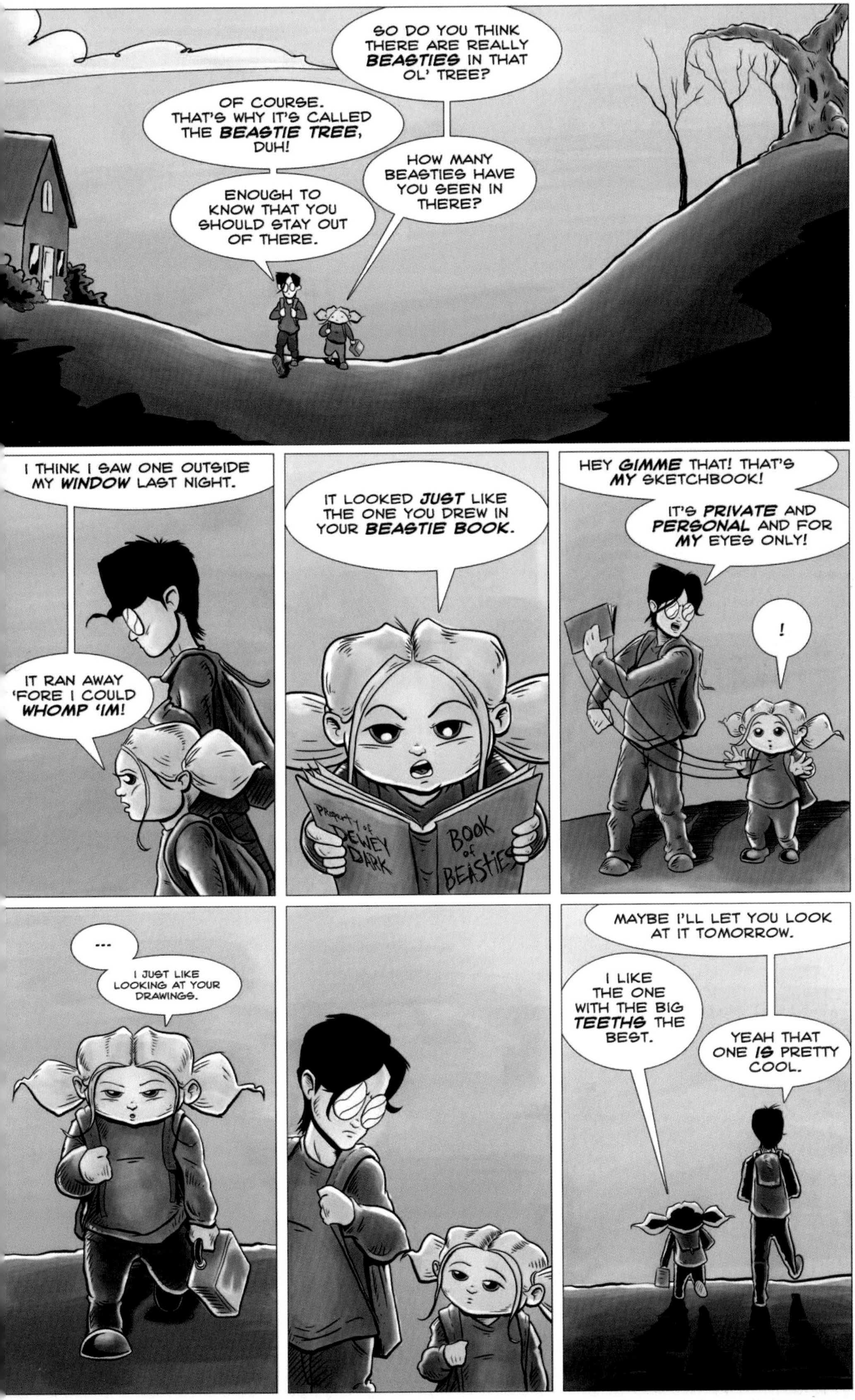
SO DO YOU THINK THERE ARE REALLY BEASTIES IN THAT OL' TREE?
OF COURSE. THAT'S WHY IT'S CALLED THE BEASTIE TREE, DUH!
HOW MANY BEASTIES HAVE YOU SEEN IN THERE?
ENOUGH TO KNOW THAT YOU SHOULD STAY OUT OF THERE.
I THINK I SAW ONE OUTSIDE MY WINDOW LAST NIGHT.
IT RAN AWAY 'FORE I COULD WHOMP 'IM!
IT LOOKED JUST LIKE THE ONE YOU DREW IN YOUR BEASTIE BOOK.
Property of DEWEY DARK
BOOK of BEASTIES
HEY GIMME THAT! THAT'S MY SKETCHBOOK!
IT'S PRIVATE AND PERSONAL AND FOR MY EYES ONLY!
!
...
I JUST LIKE LOOKING AT YOUR DRAWINGS.
MAYBE I'LL LET YOU LOOK AT IT TOMORROW.
I LIKE THE ONE WITH THE BIG TEETHS THE BEST.
YEAH THAT ONE IS PRETTY COOL.

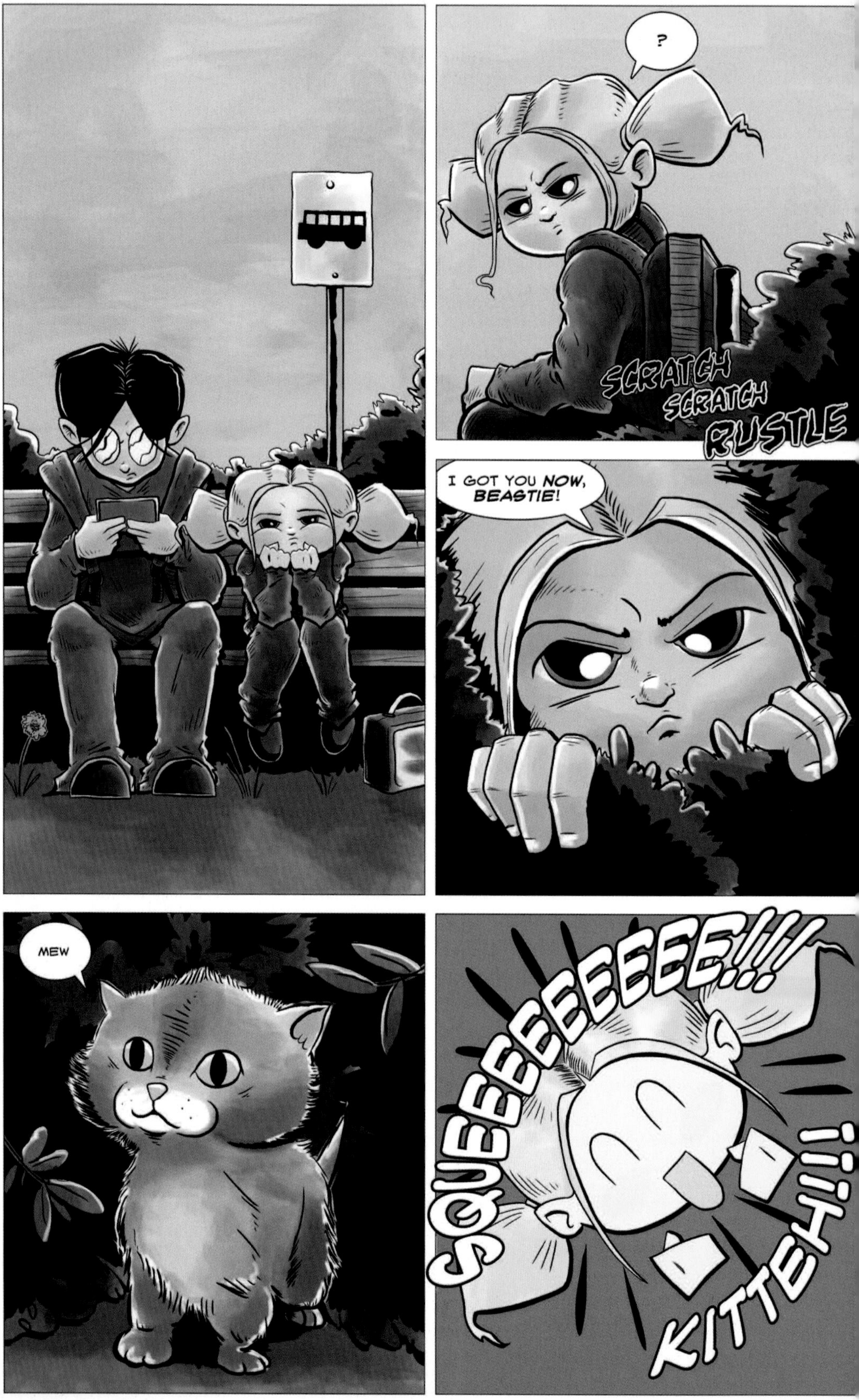
?
SCRATCH
SCRATCH
RUSTLE
I GOT YOU NOW, BEASTIE!
MEW
SQUEEEEEEEEEE!!!
KITTEH!!!!

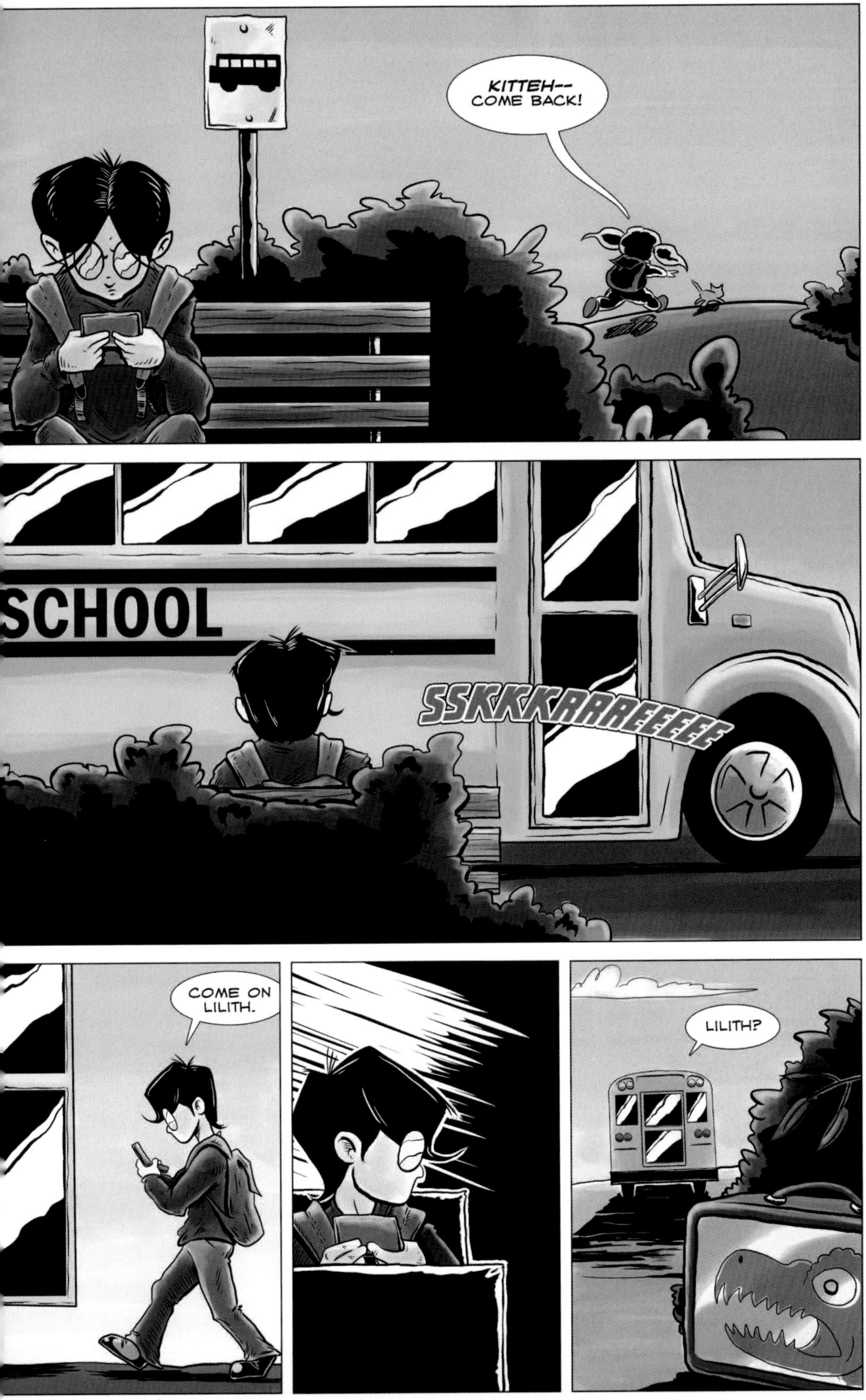
KITTEH--
COME BACK!
SCHOOL
SSKKKRRRREEEEEE
COME ON
LILITH.
LILITH?

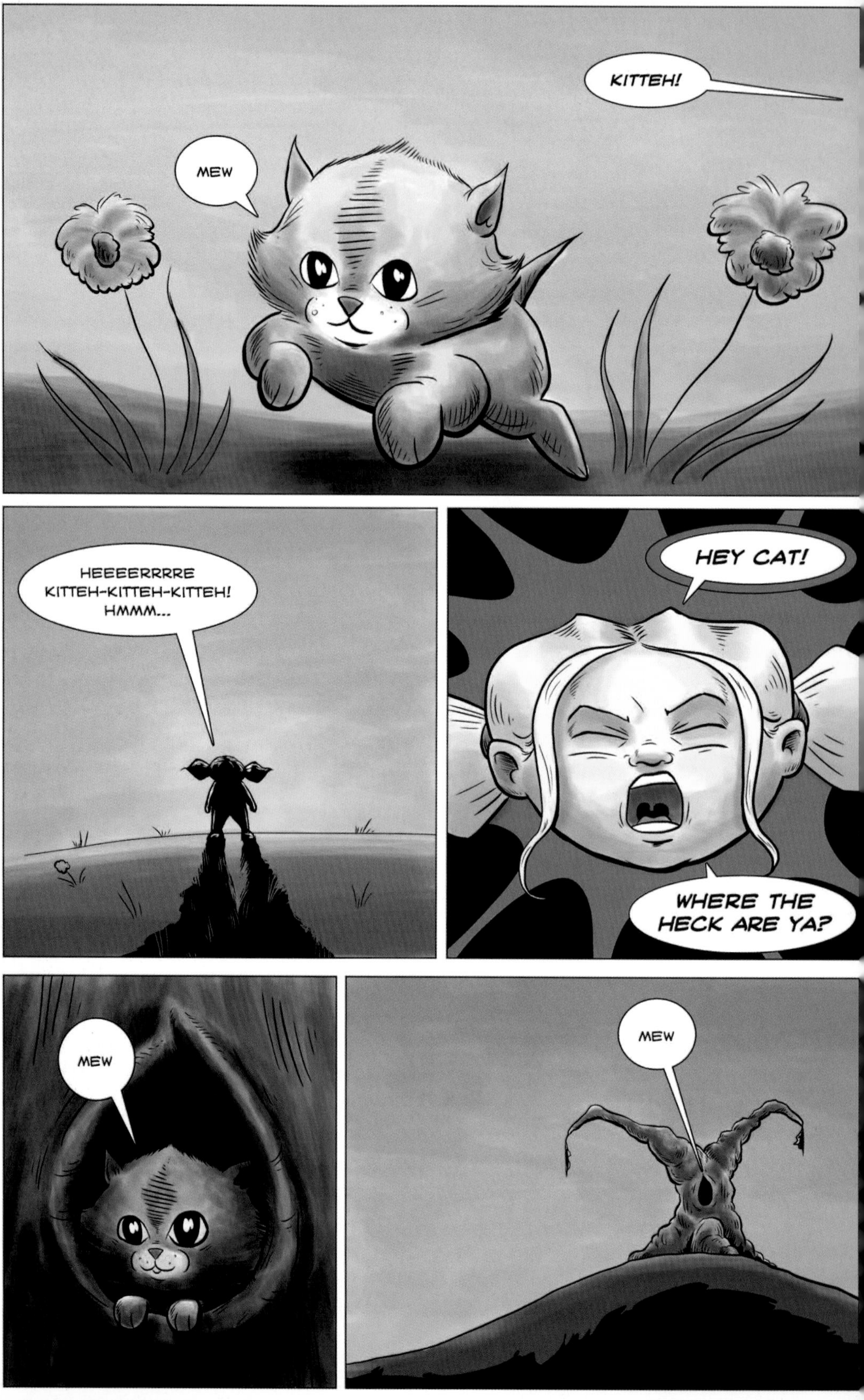
KITTEH!
MEW
HEEEERRRRE KITTEH-KITTEH-KITTEH! HMMM...
HEY CAT!
WHERE THE HECK ARE YA?
MEW
MEW

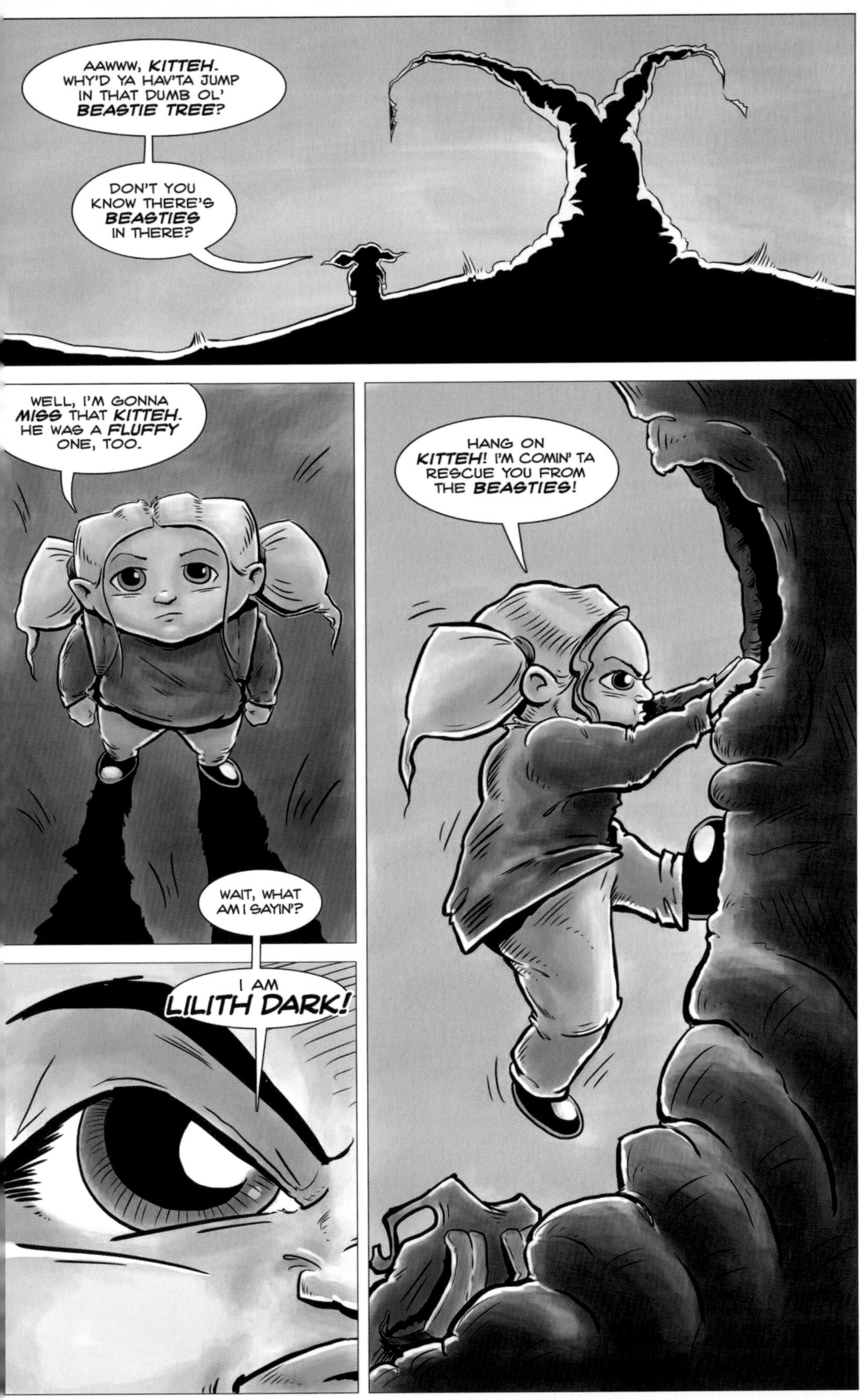
AAWWW, KITTEH. WHY'D YA HAV'TA JUMP IN THAT DUMB OL' BEASTIE TREE?
DON'T YOU KNOW THERE'S BEASTIES IN THERE?
WELL, I'M GONNA MISS THAT KITTEH. HE WAS A FLUFFY ONE, TOO.
WAIT, WHAT AM I SAYIN'?
I AM LILITH DARK!
HANG ON KITTEH! I'M COMIN' TA RESCUE YOU FROM THE BEASTIES!

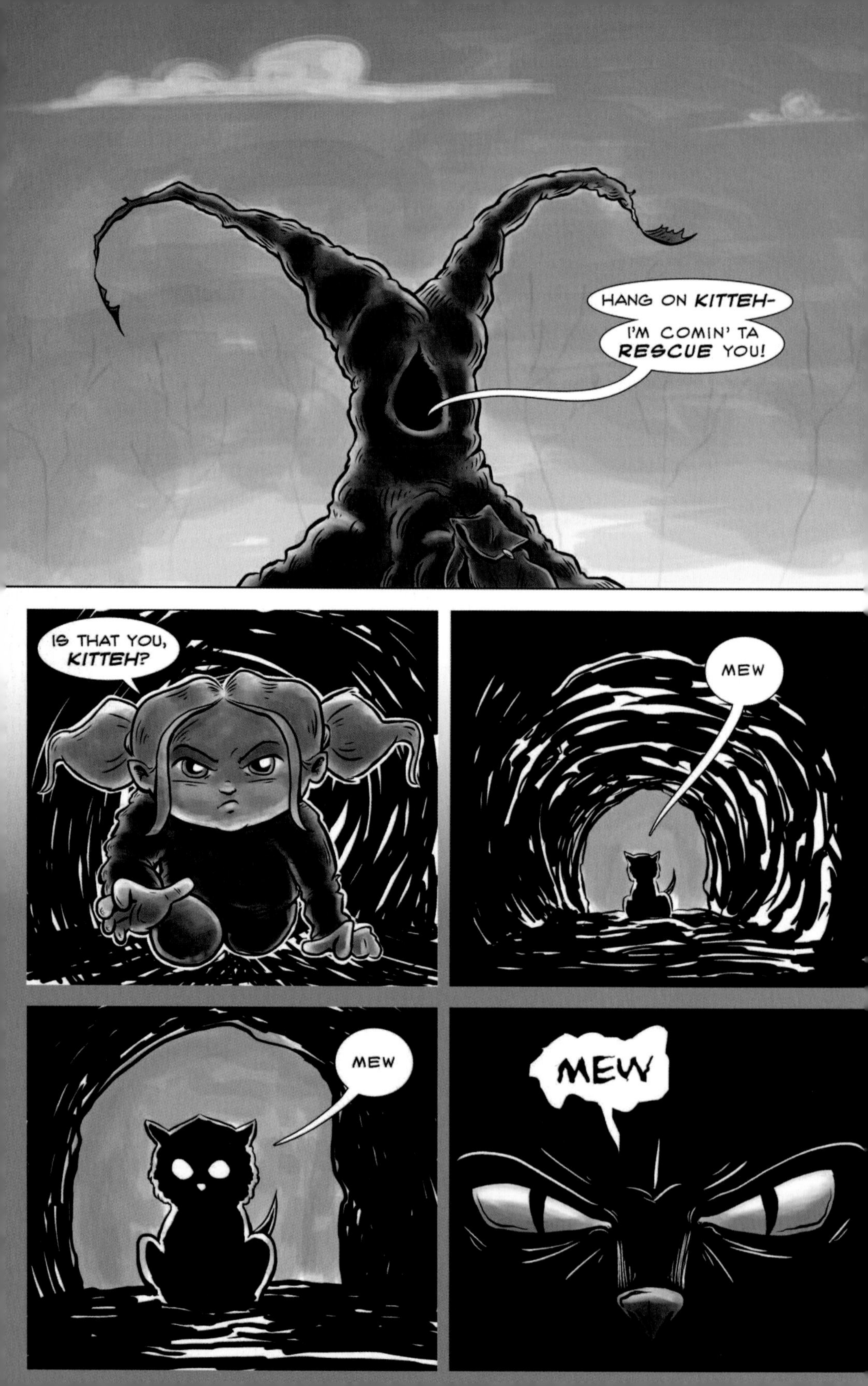
HANG ON KITTEH-
I'M COMIN' TA RESCUE YOU!
IS THAT YOU, KITTEH?
MEW
MEW
MEW

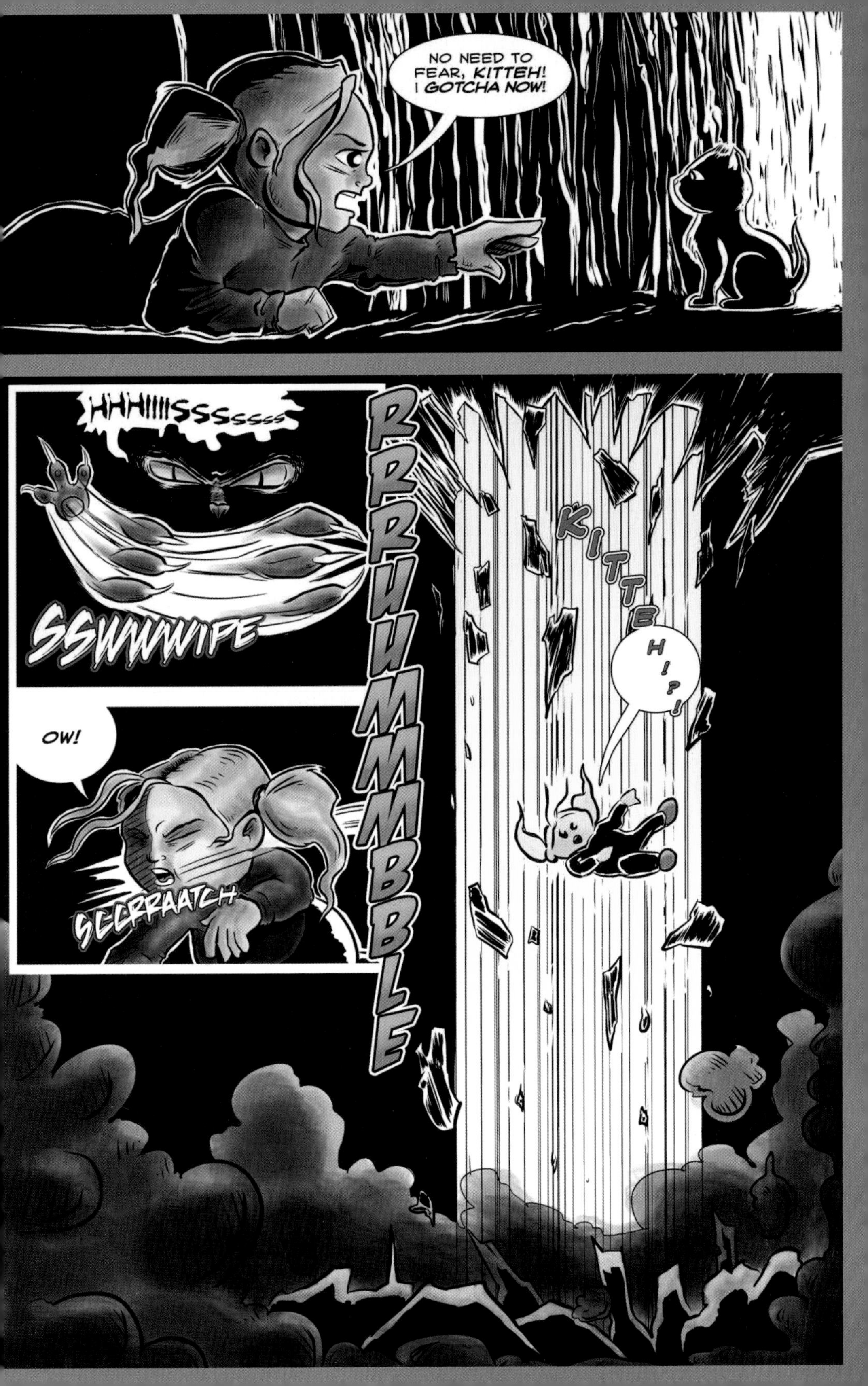
NO NEED TO FEAR, KITTEH! I GOTCHA NOW!
HHHIIIISSSsssss
SSWWWIPE
OW!
SCCRRAATCH
RRRUMMMBBLE
KITTEH!?!

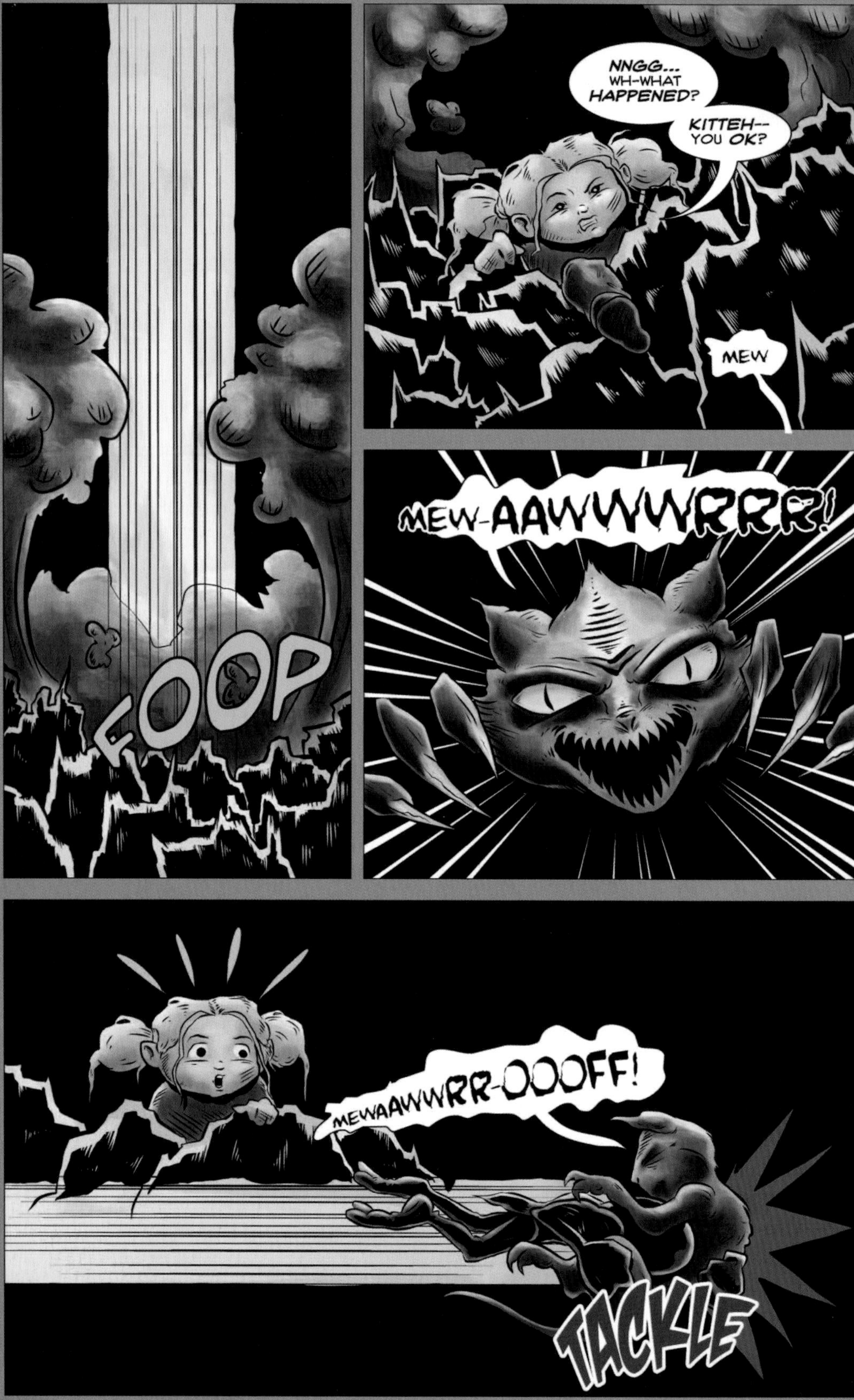
FOOP
NNGG... WH-WHAT HAPPENED?
KITTEH-- YOU OK?
MEW
MEW-AAWWWRRR!
MEWAAWWRR-OOOFF!
TACKLE

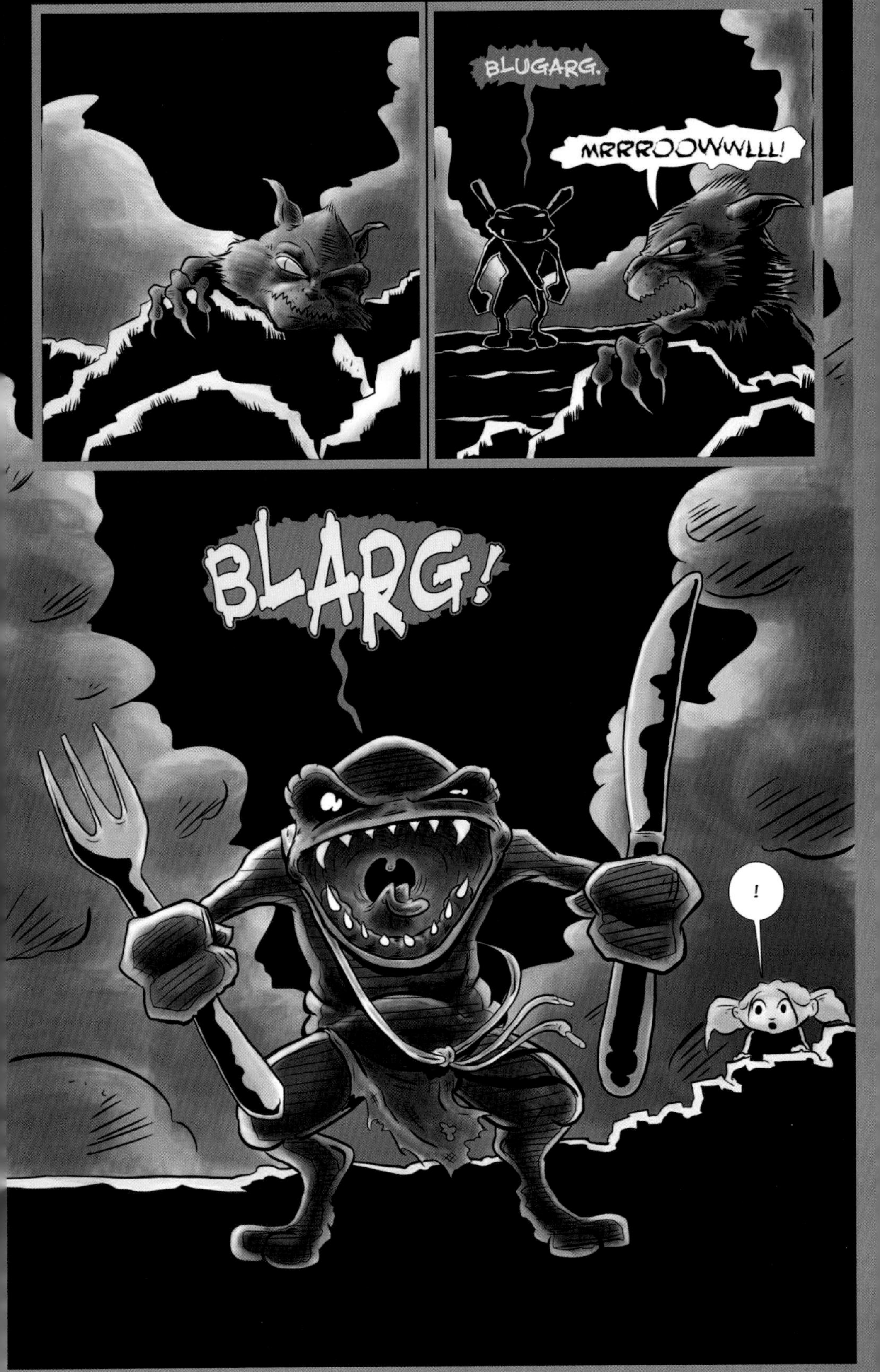
BLUGARG.
MRRROOWWLLL!
BLARG!
!

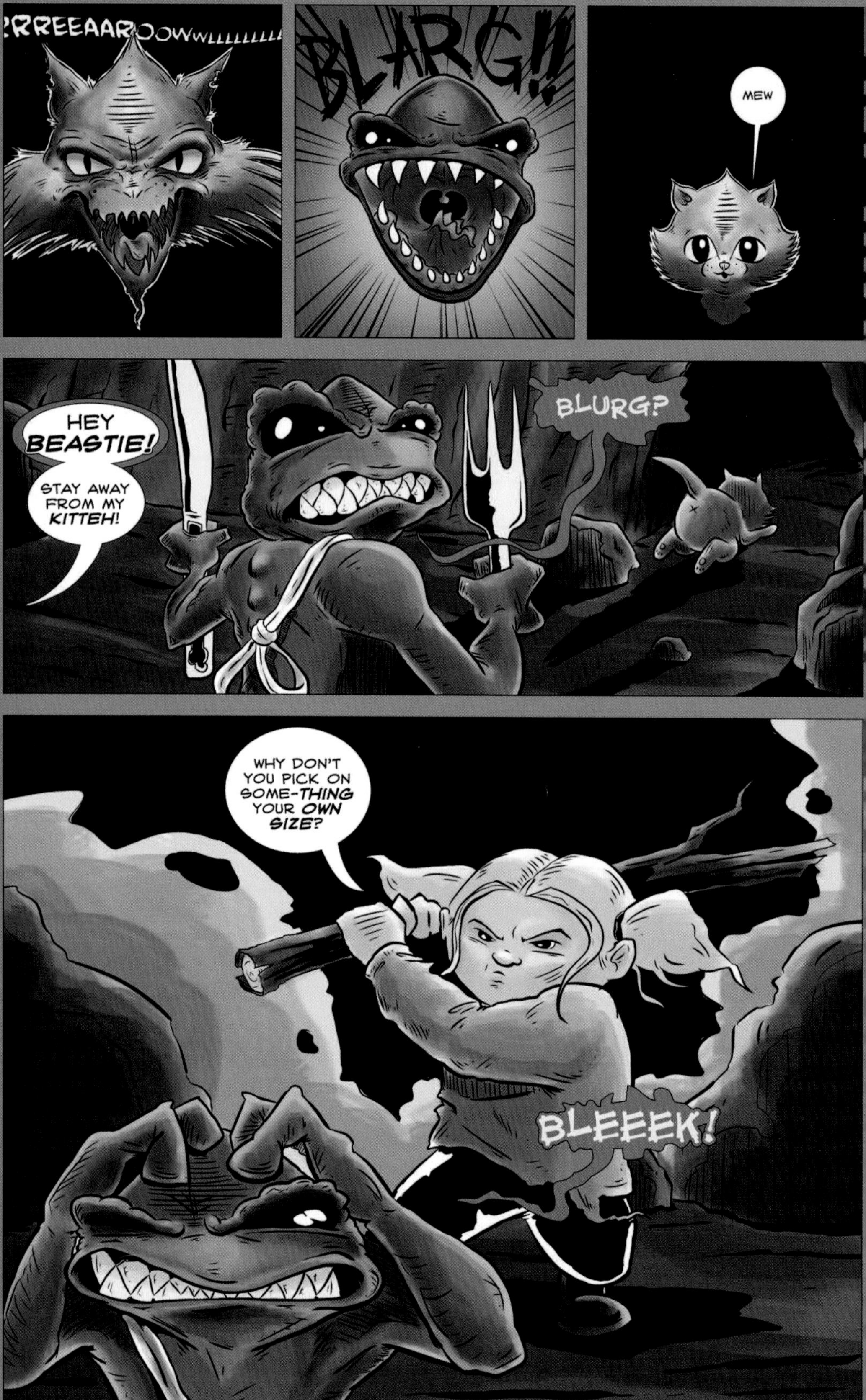
RRREEAAROOWWLLLLLLLL
BLARG!!
MEW
HEY BEASTIE!
STAY AWAY FROM MY KITTEH!
BLURG?
WHY DON'T YOU PICK ON SOME-THING YOUR OWN SIZE?
BLEEEK!

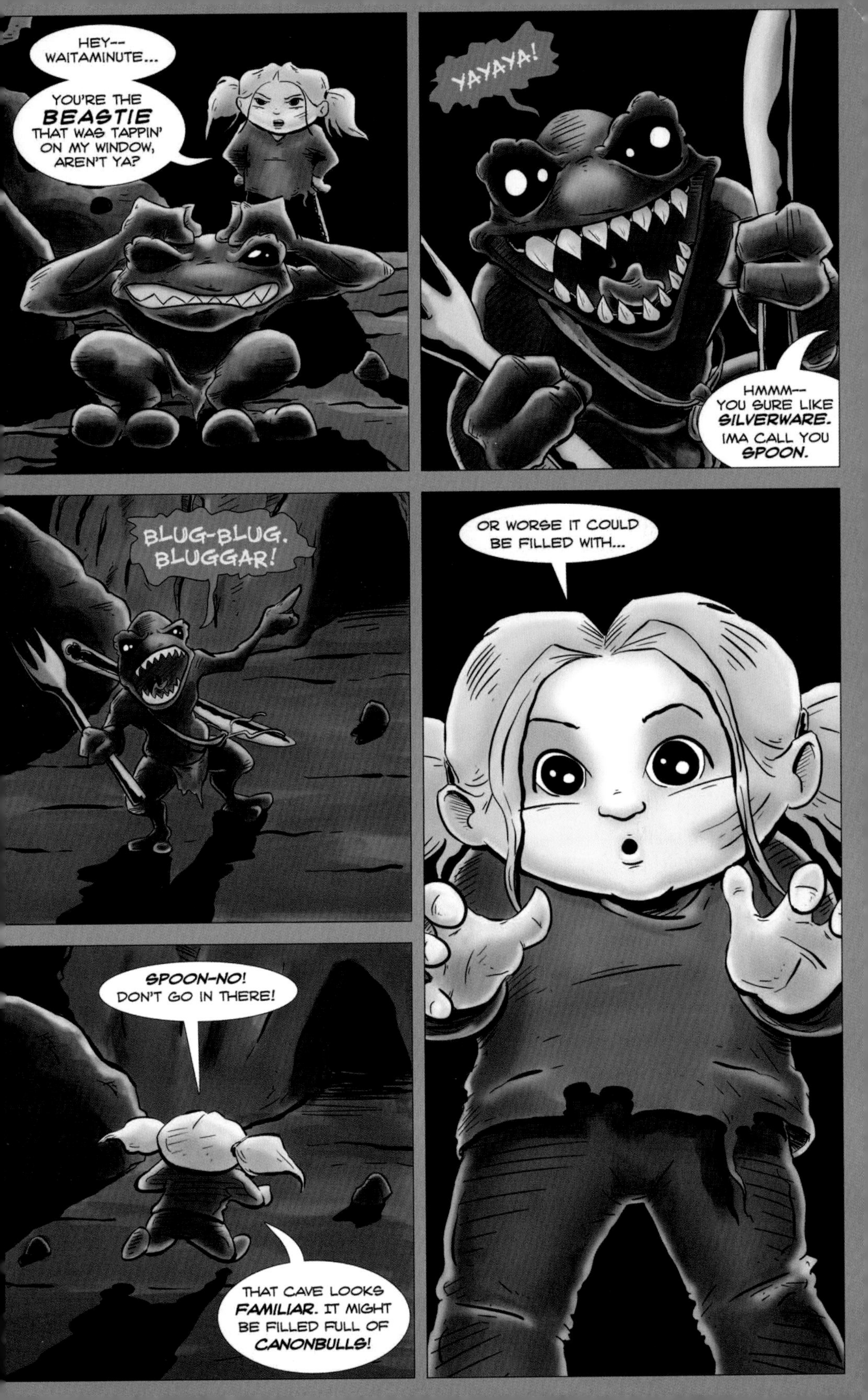
HEY-- WAITAMINUTE...
YOU'RE THE BEASTIE THAT WAS TAPPIN' ON MY WINDOW, AREN'T YA?
YAYAYA!
HMMM-- YOU SURE LIKE SILVERWARE. IMA CALL YOU SPOON.
BLUG-BLUG. BLUGGAR!
SPOON-NO! DON'T GO IN THERE!
THAT CAVE LOOKS FAMILIAR. IT MIGHT BE FILLED FULL OF CANONBULLS!
OR WORSE IT COULD BE FILLED WITH...

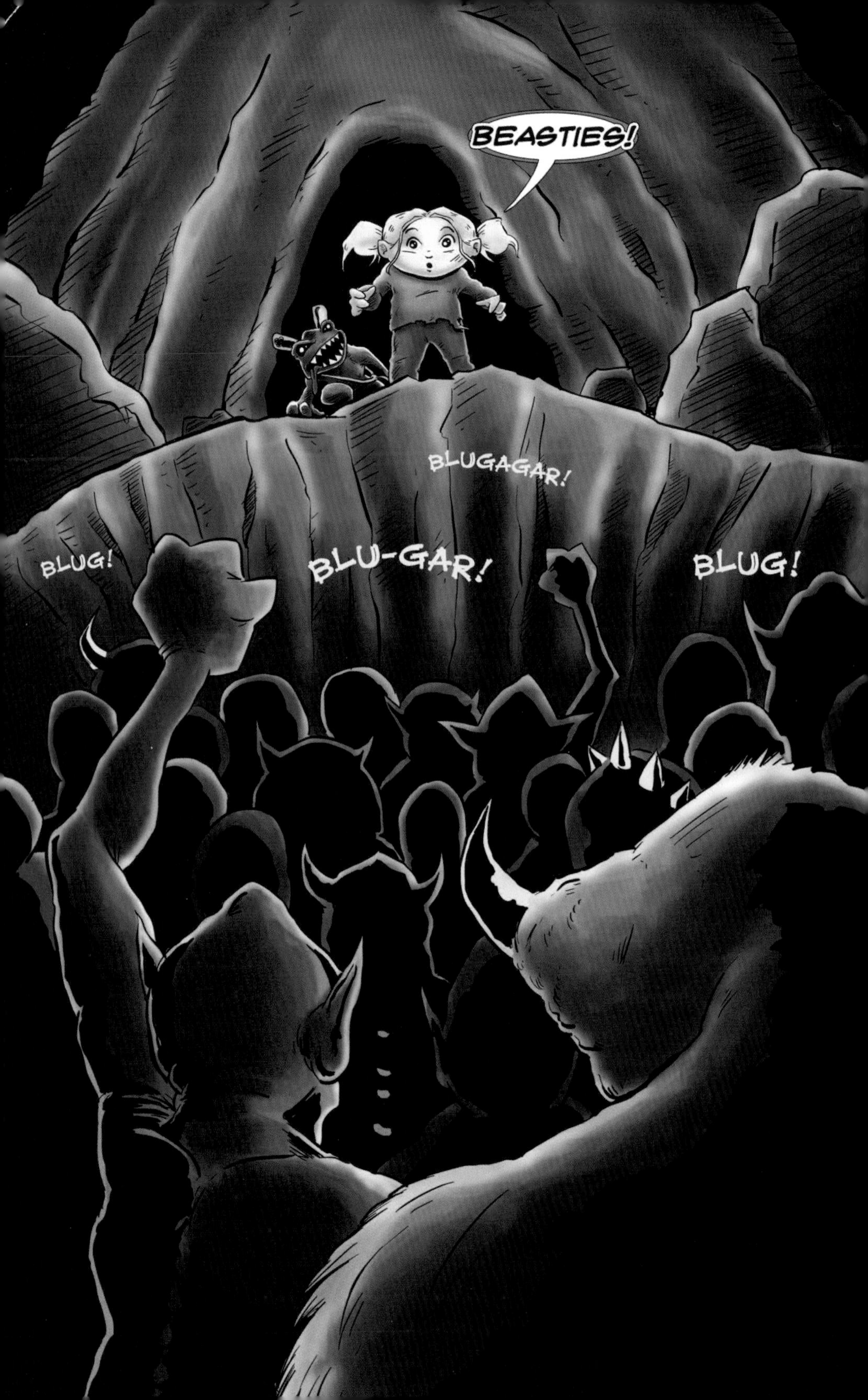
BEASTIES!
BLUGAGAR!
BLUG!
BLU-GAR!
BLUG!

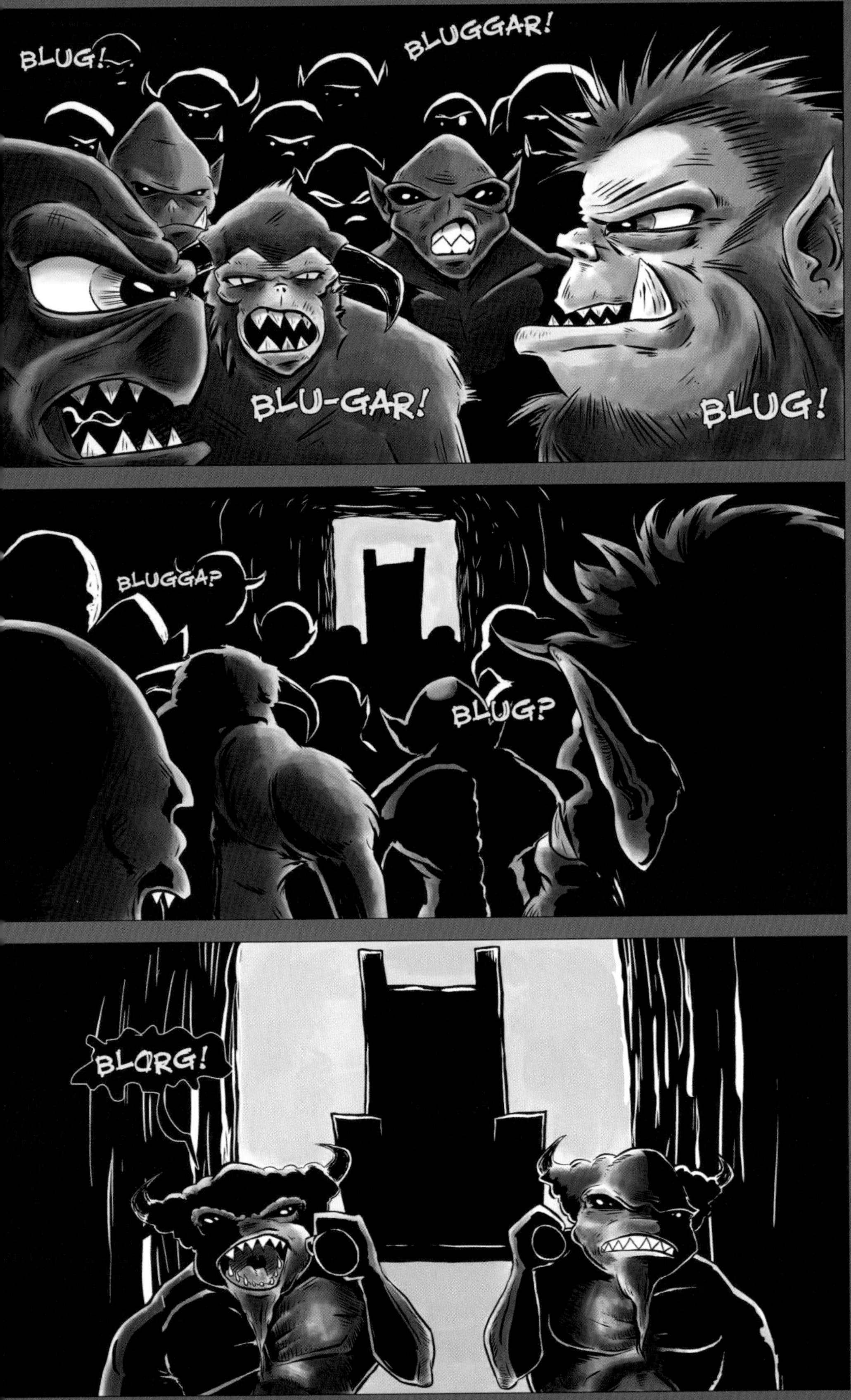
BLUG!
BLUGGAR!
BLU-GAR!
BLUG!
BLUGGA?
BLUG?
BLORG!

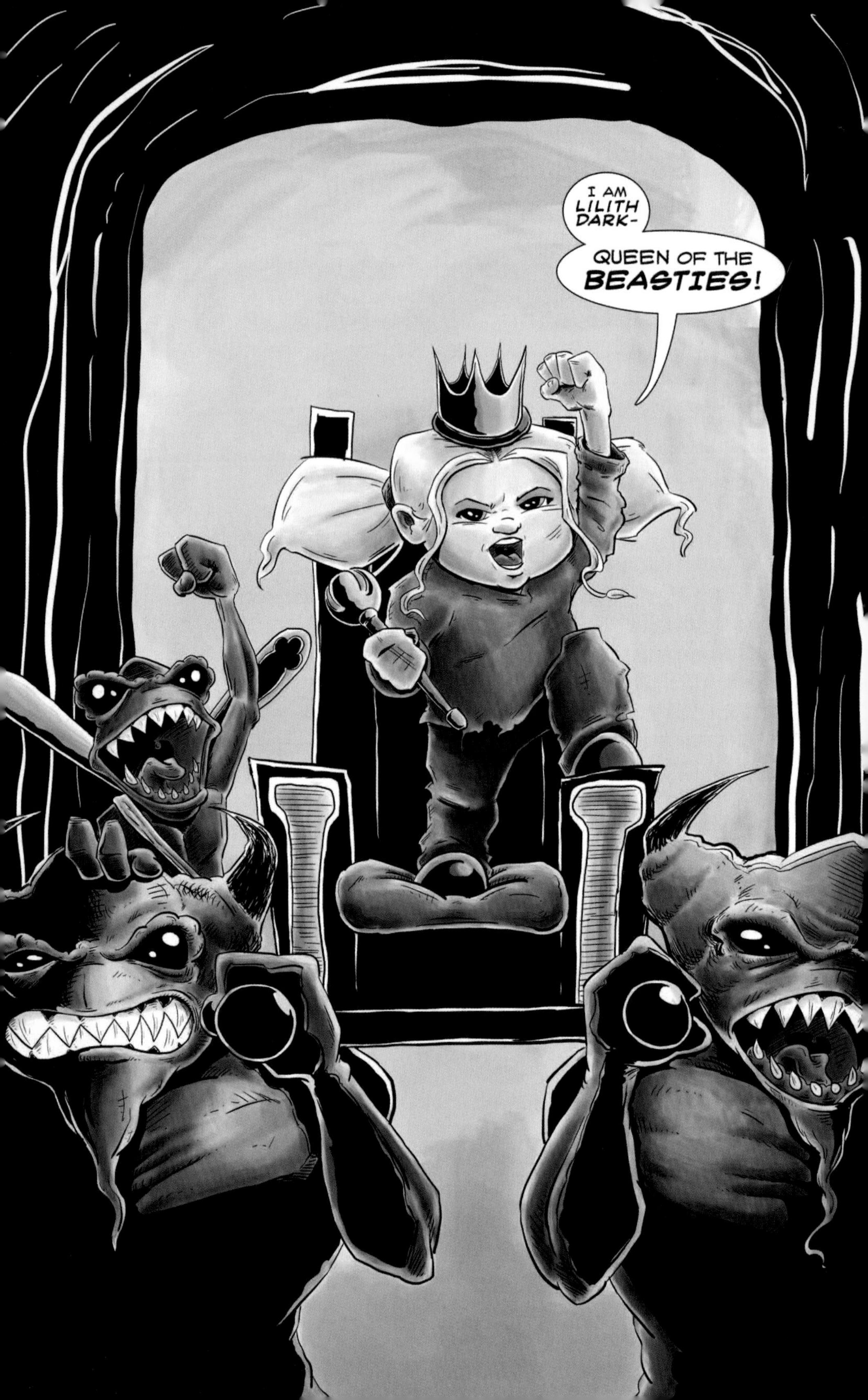
I AM LILITH DARK-
QUEEN OF THE BEASTIES!

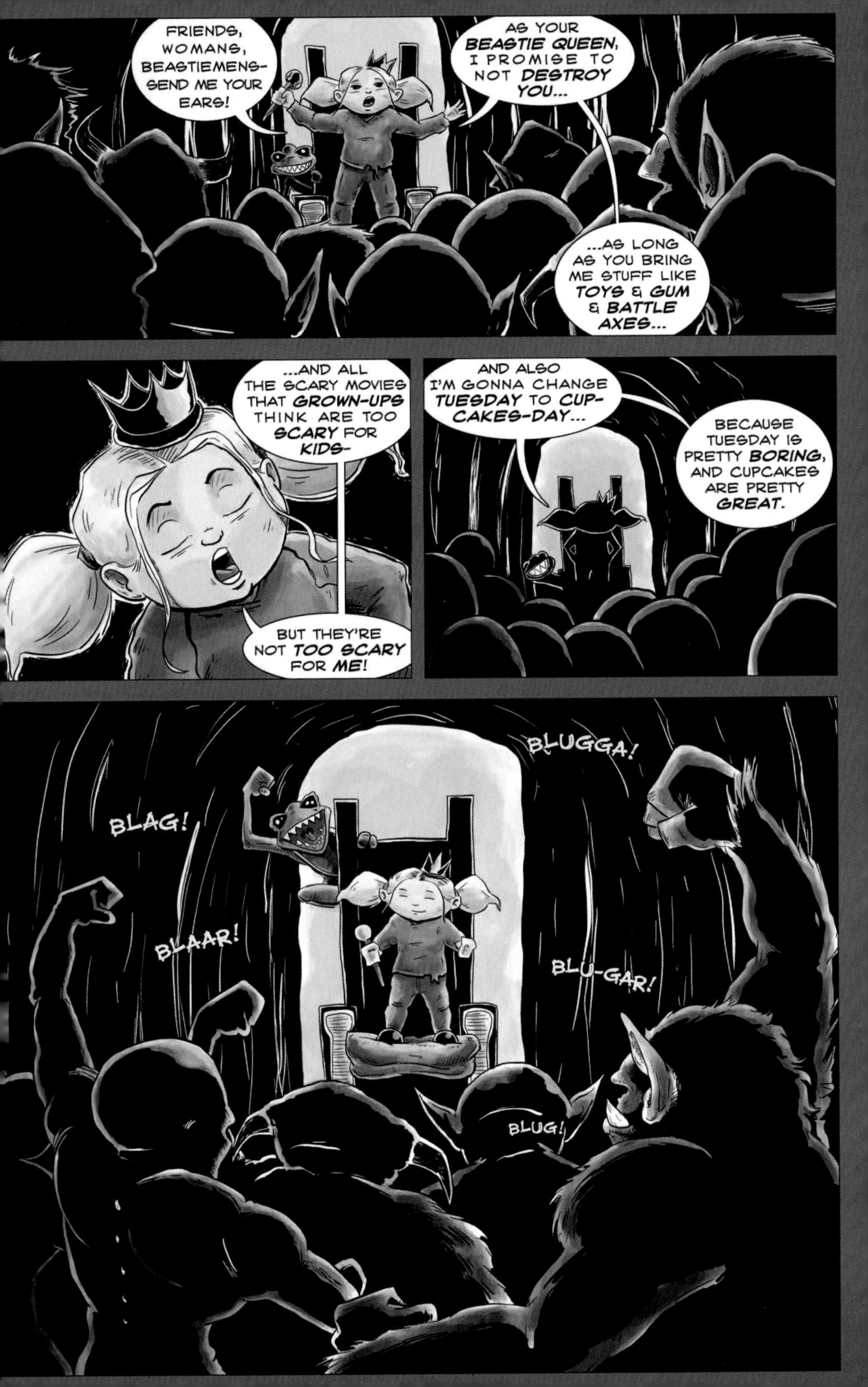
FRIENDS, WOMANS, BEASTIEMENS- SEND ME YOUR EARS!
AS YOUR BEASTIE QUEEN, I PROMISE TO NOT DESTROY YOU...
...AS LONG AS YOU BRING ME STUFF LIKE TOYS & GUM & BATTLE AXES...
...AND ALL THE SCARY MOVIES THAT GROWN-UPS THINK ARE TOO SCARY FOR KIDS-
BUT THEY'RE NOT TOO SCARY FOR ME!
AND ALSO I'M GONNA CHANGE TUESDAY TO CUP-CAKES-DAY...
BECAUSE TUESDAY IS PRETTY BORING, AND CUPCAKES ARE PRETTY GREAT.
BLUGGA!
BLAG!
BLAAR!
BLU-GAR!
BLUG!

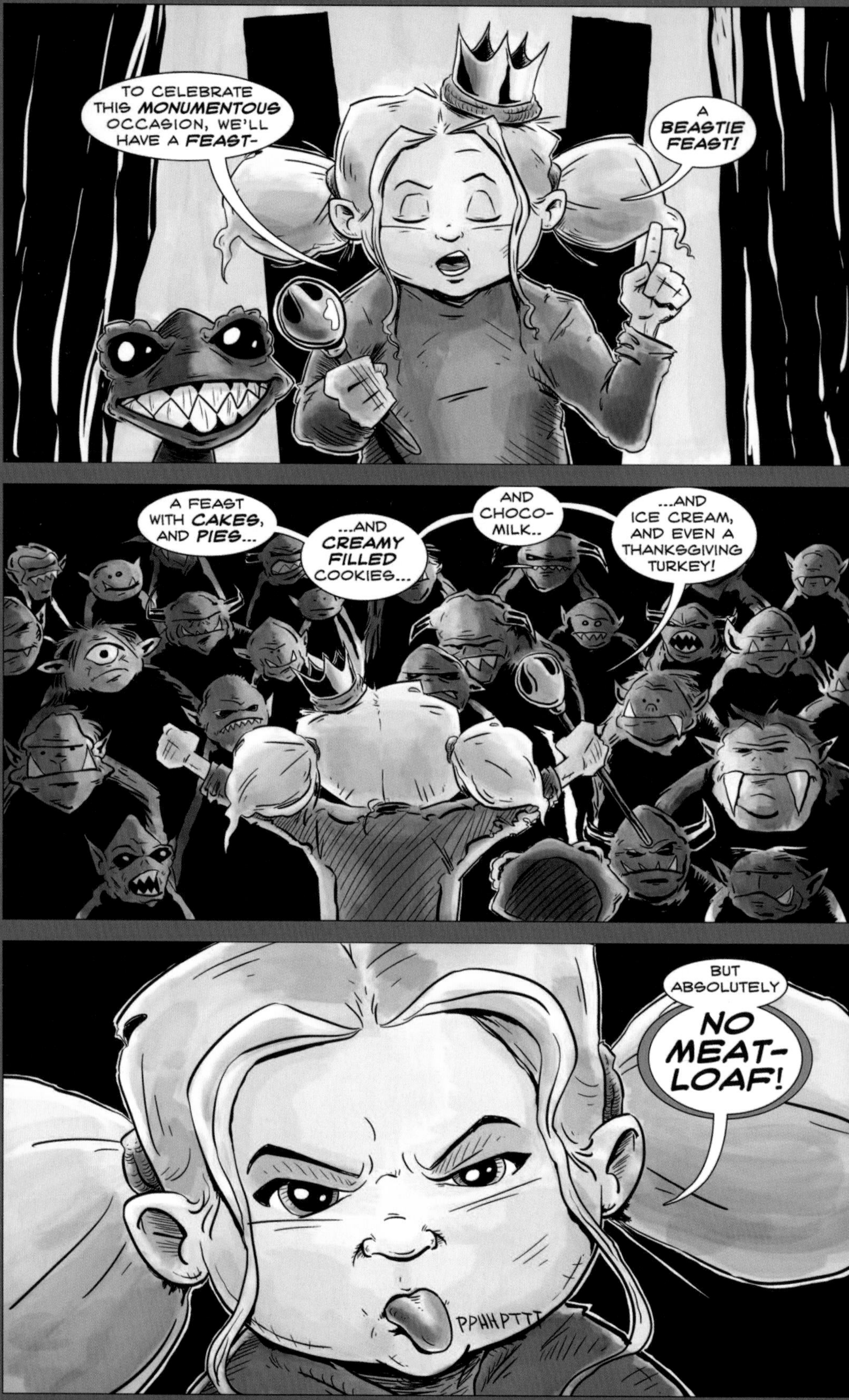
TO CELEBRATE THIS MONUMENTOUS OCCASION, WE'LL HAVE A FEAST-
A BEASTIE FEAST!
A FEAST WITH CAKES, AND PIES...
...AND CREAMY FILLED COOKIES...
AND CHOCO-MILK..
...AND ICE CREAM, AND EVEN A THANKSGIVING TURKEY!
BUT ABSOLUTELY
NO MEAT-LOAF!
PPHHPTTT

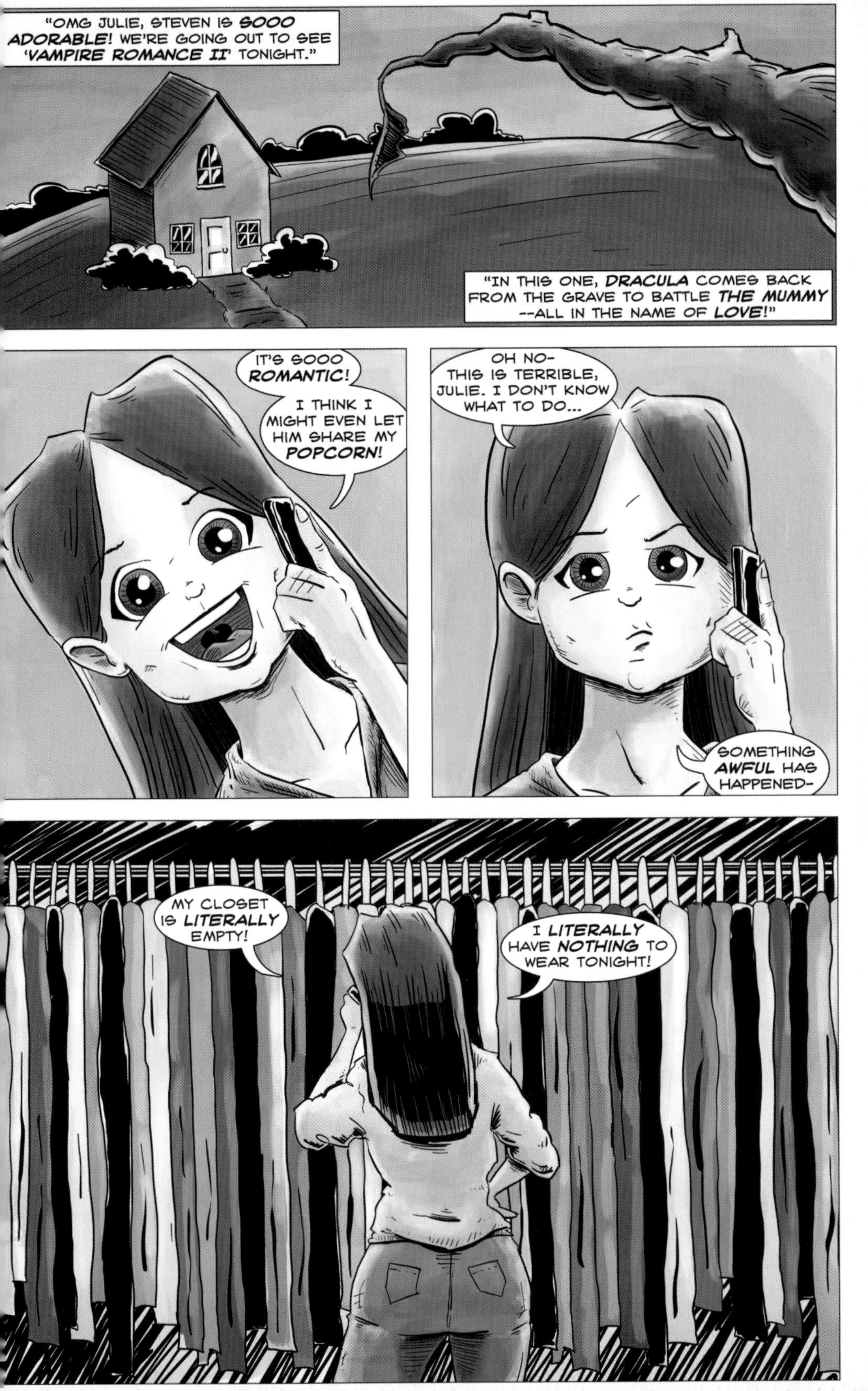
"OMG JULIE, STEVEN IS SOOO ADORABLE! WE'RE GOING OUT TO SEE 'VAMPIRE ROMANCE II' TONIGHT."
"IN THIS ONE, DRACULA COMES BACK FROM THE GRAVE TO BATTLE THE MUMMY --ALL IN THE NAME OF LOVE!"
IT'S SOOO ROMANTIC!
I THINK I MIGHT EVEN LET HIM SHARE MY POPCORN!
OH NO- THIS IS TERRIBLE, JULIE. I DON'T KNOW WHAT TO DO...
SOMETHING AWFUL HAS HAPPENED-
MY CLOSET IS LITERALLY EMPTY!
I LITERALLY HAVE NOTHING TO WEAR TONIGHT!

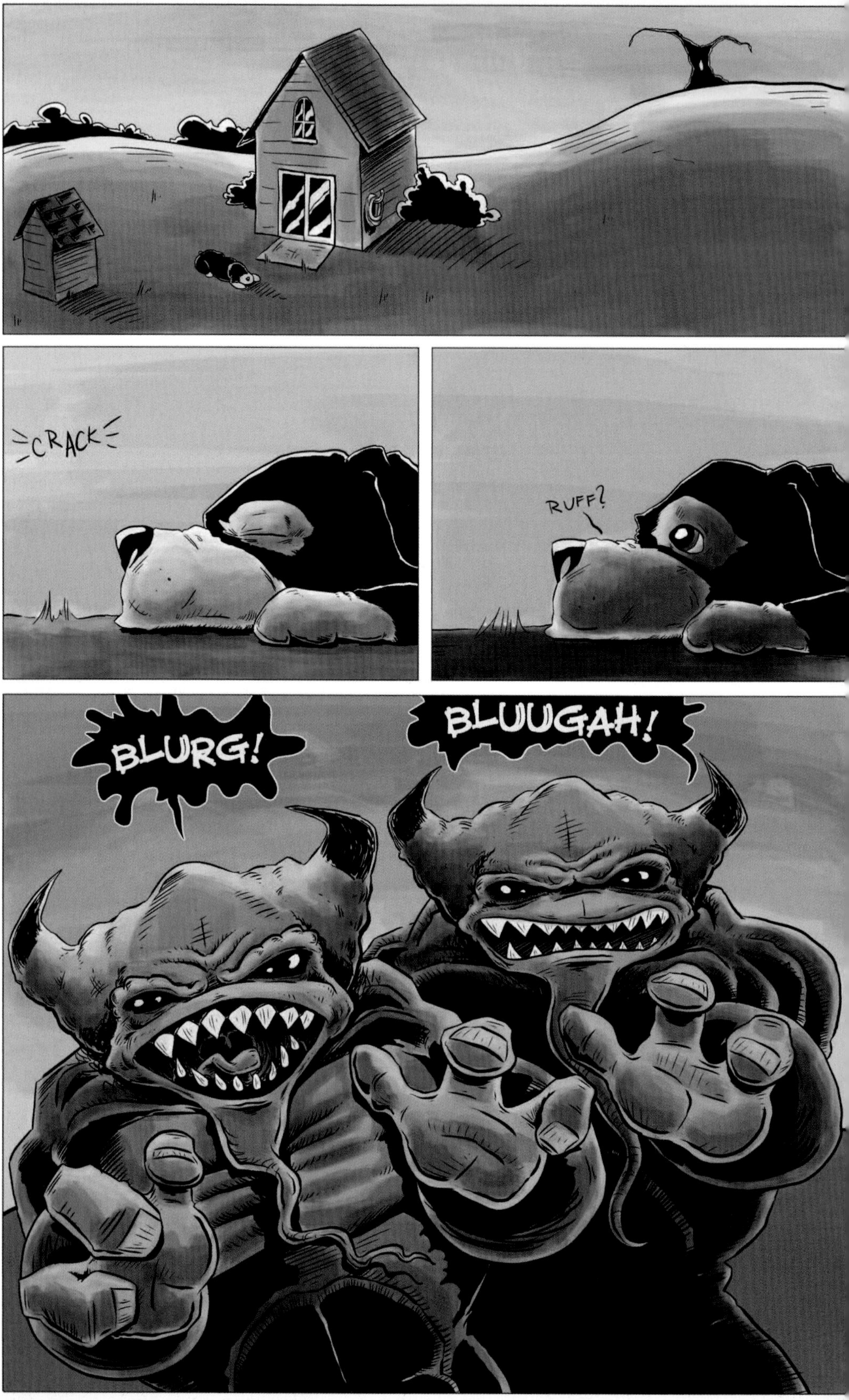
CRACK
RUFF?
BLURG!
BLUUGAH!

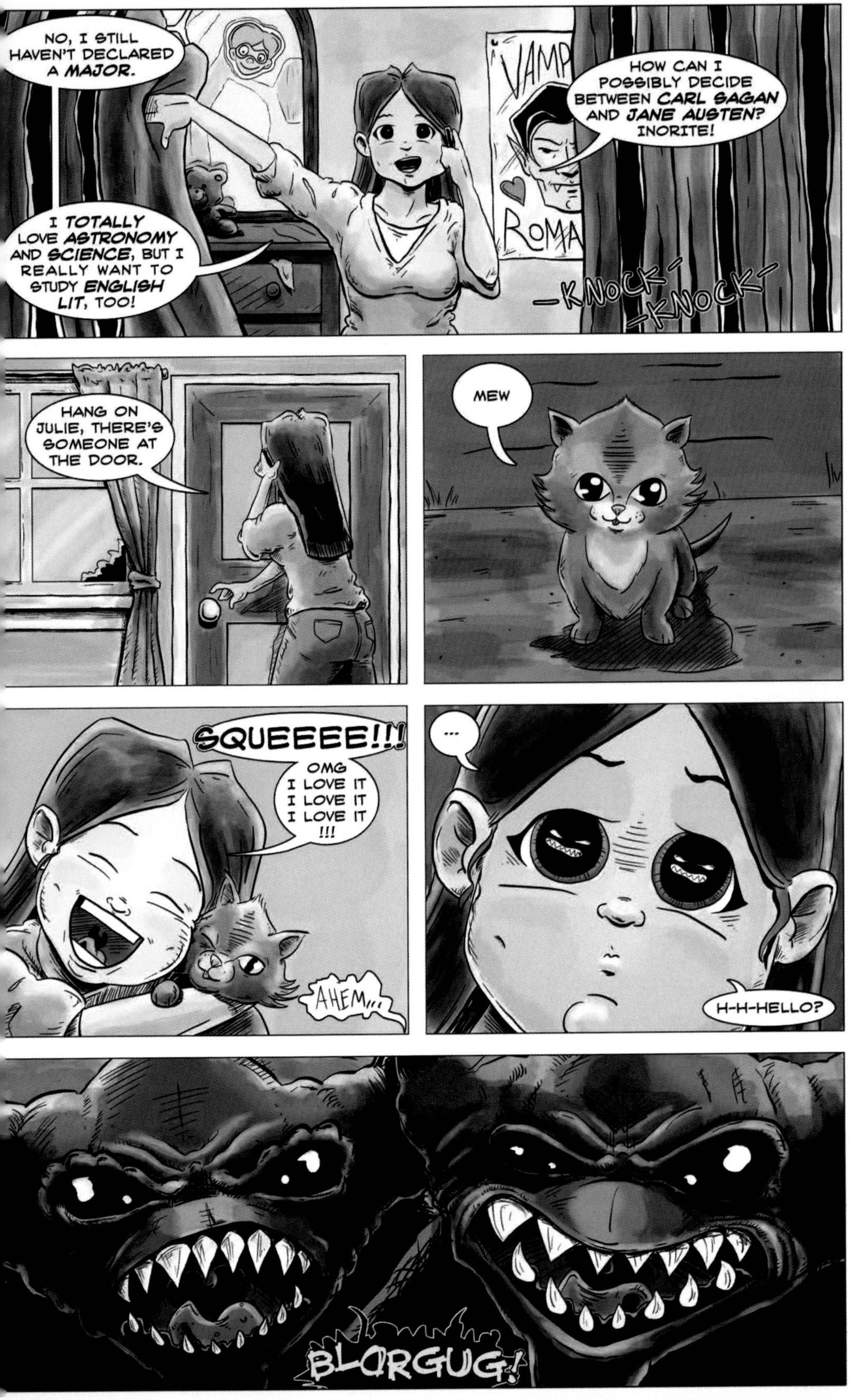
NO, I STILL HAVEN'T DECLARED A MAJOR.
I TOTALLY LOVE ASTRONOMY AND SCIENCE, BUT I REALLY WANT TO STUDY ENGLISH LIT, TOO!
VAMP
ROMA
HOW CAN I POSSIBLY DECIDE BETWEEN CARL SAGAN AND JANE AUSTEN? INORITE!
-KNOCK- -KNOCK-
HANG ON JULIE, THERE'S SOMEONE AT THE DOOR.
MEW
SQUEEEEE!!!
OMG I LOVE IT I LOVE IT I LOVE IT !!!
AHEM...
...
H-H-HELLO?
BLORGUG!

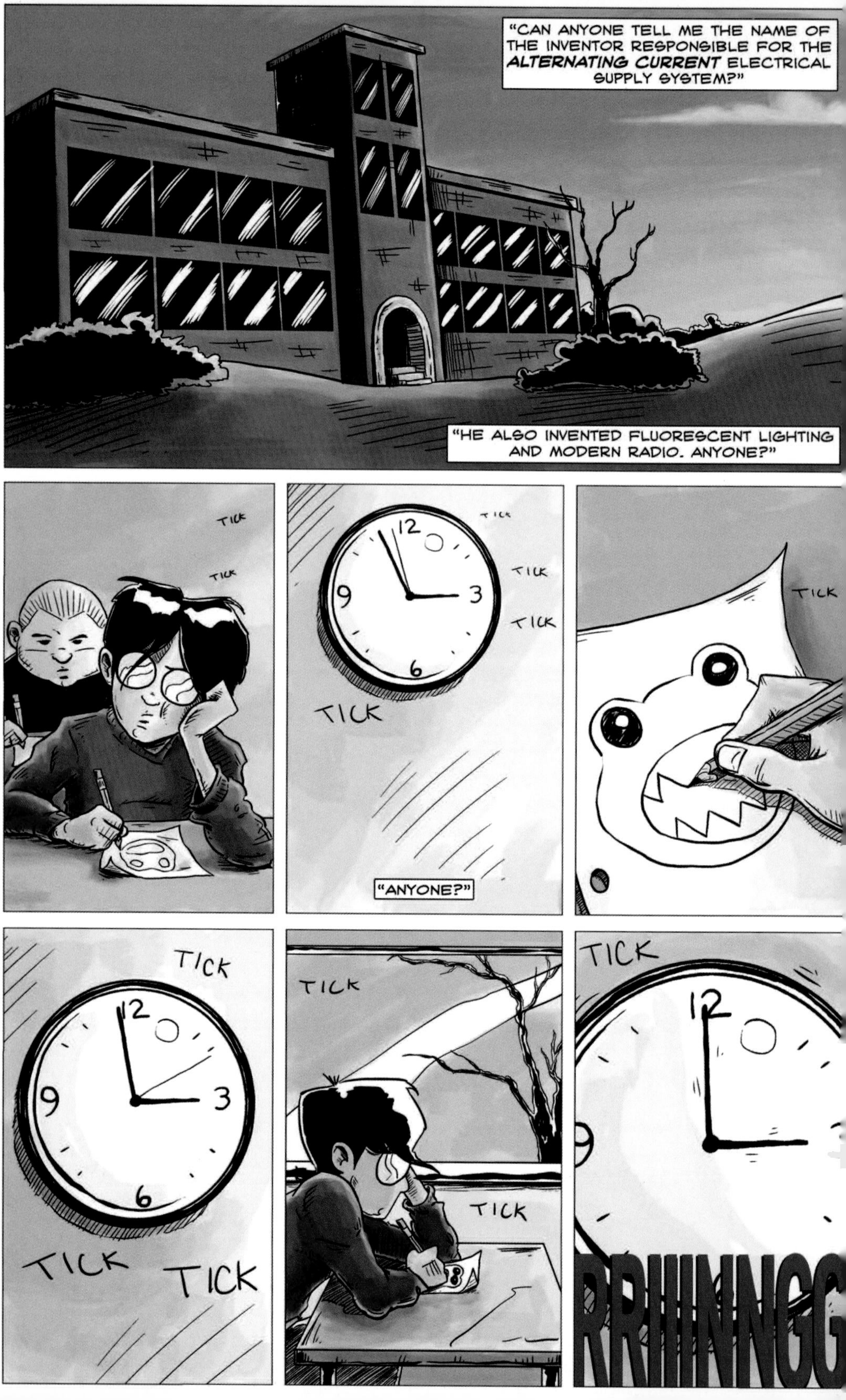

"CAN ANYONE TELL ME THE NAME OF THE INVENTOR RESPONSIBLE FOR THE ALTERNATING CURRENT ELECTRICAL SUPPLY SYSTEM?"
"HE ALSO INVENTED FLUORESCENT LIGHTING AND MODERN RADIO. ANYONE?"
TICK
TICK
TICK
TICK
TICK
TICK
"ANYONE?"
TICK
TICK
TICK
TICK
TICK
TICK
TICK
RRIIINNGG

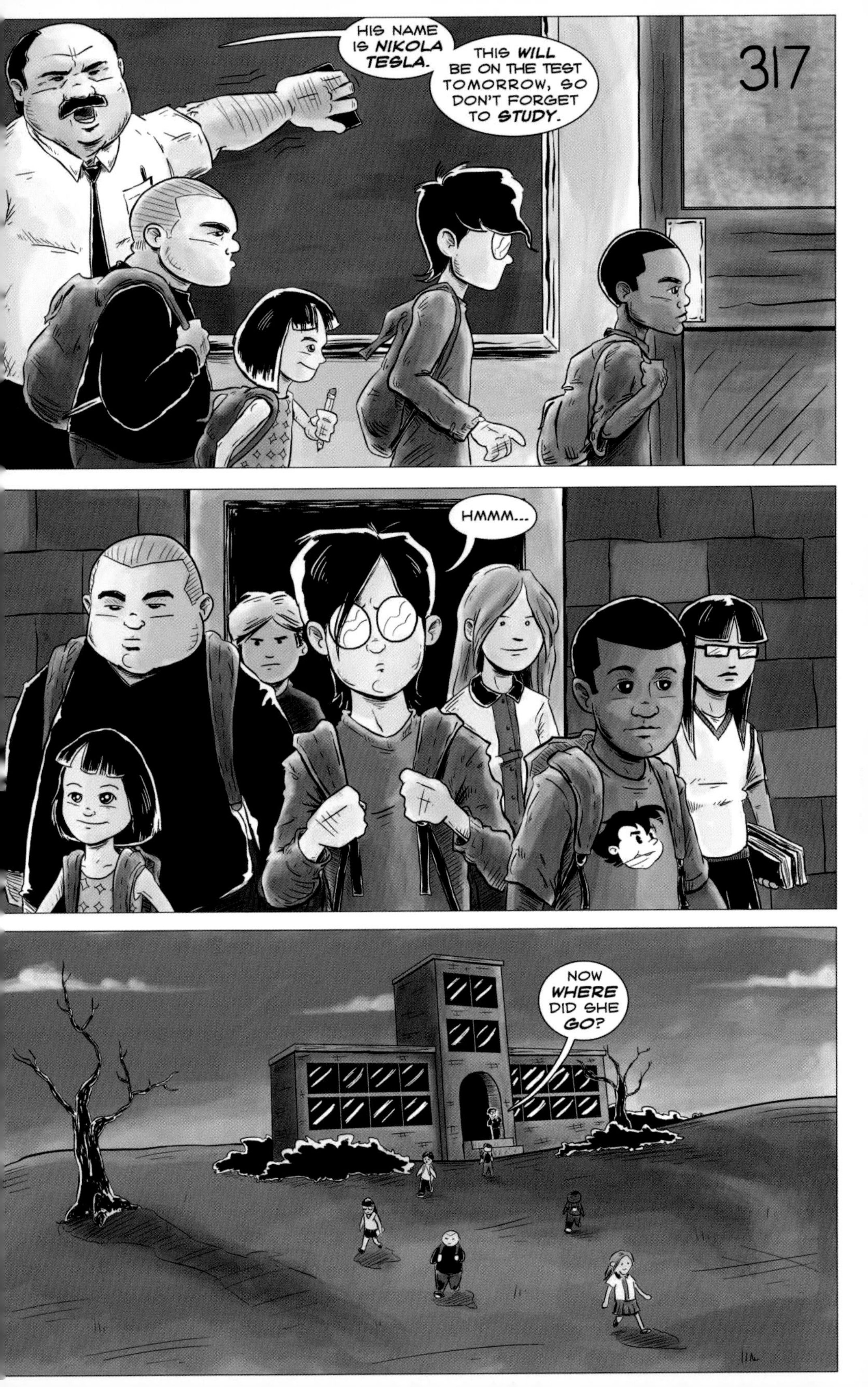
HIS NAME IS NIKOLA TESLA.
THIS WILL BE ON THE TEST TOMORROW, SO DON'T FORGET TO STUDY.
HMMM...
NOW WHERE DID SHE GO?

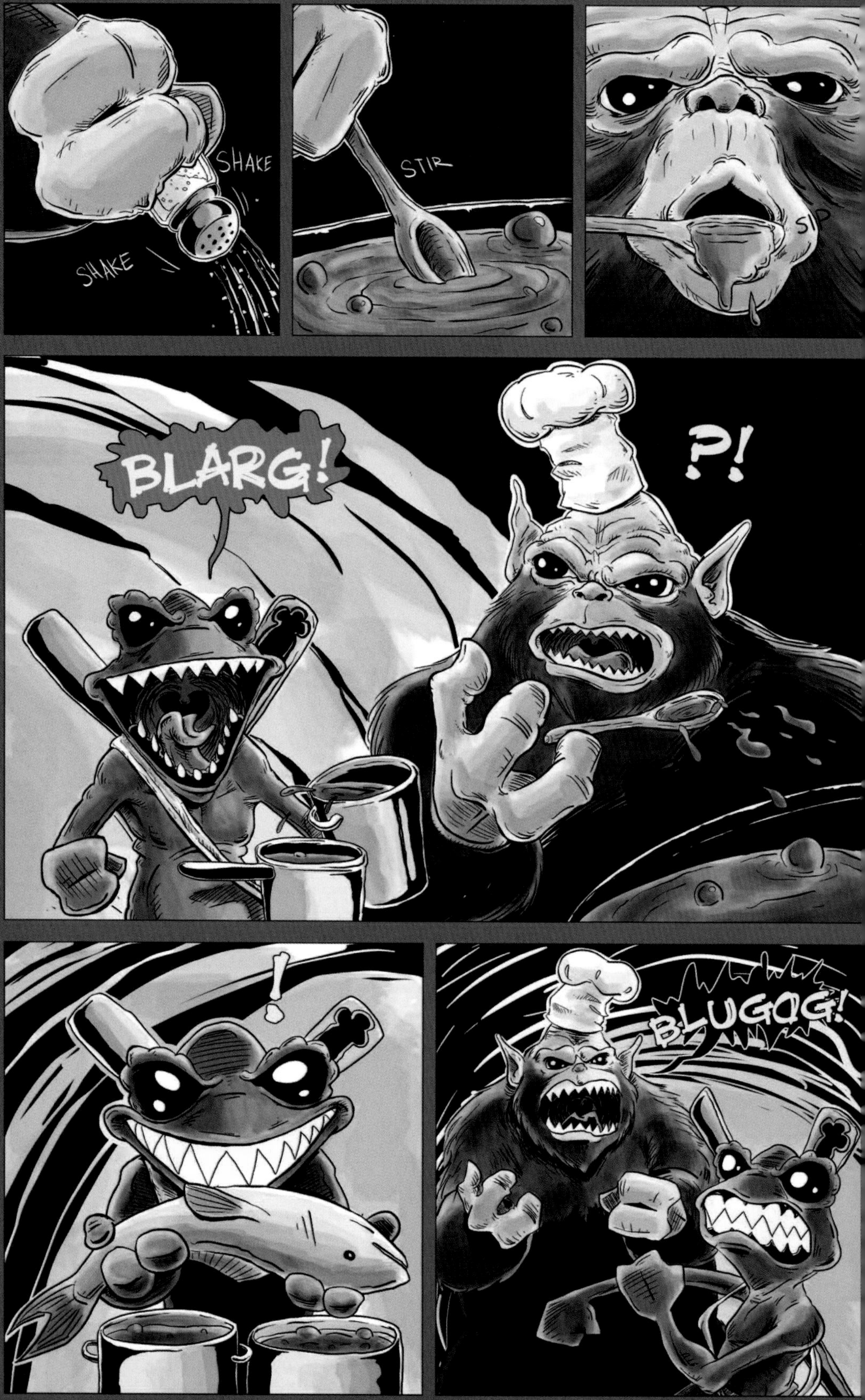
SHAKE
SHAKE
STIR
SIP
BLARG!
?!
!
BLUGOG!

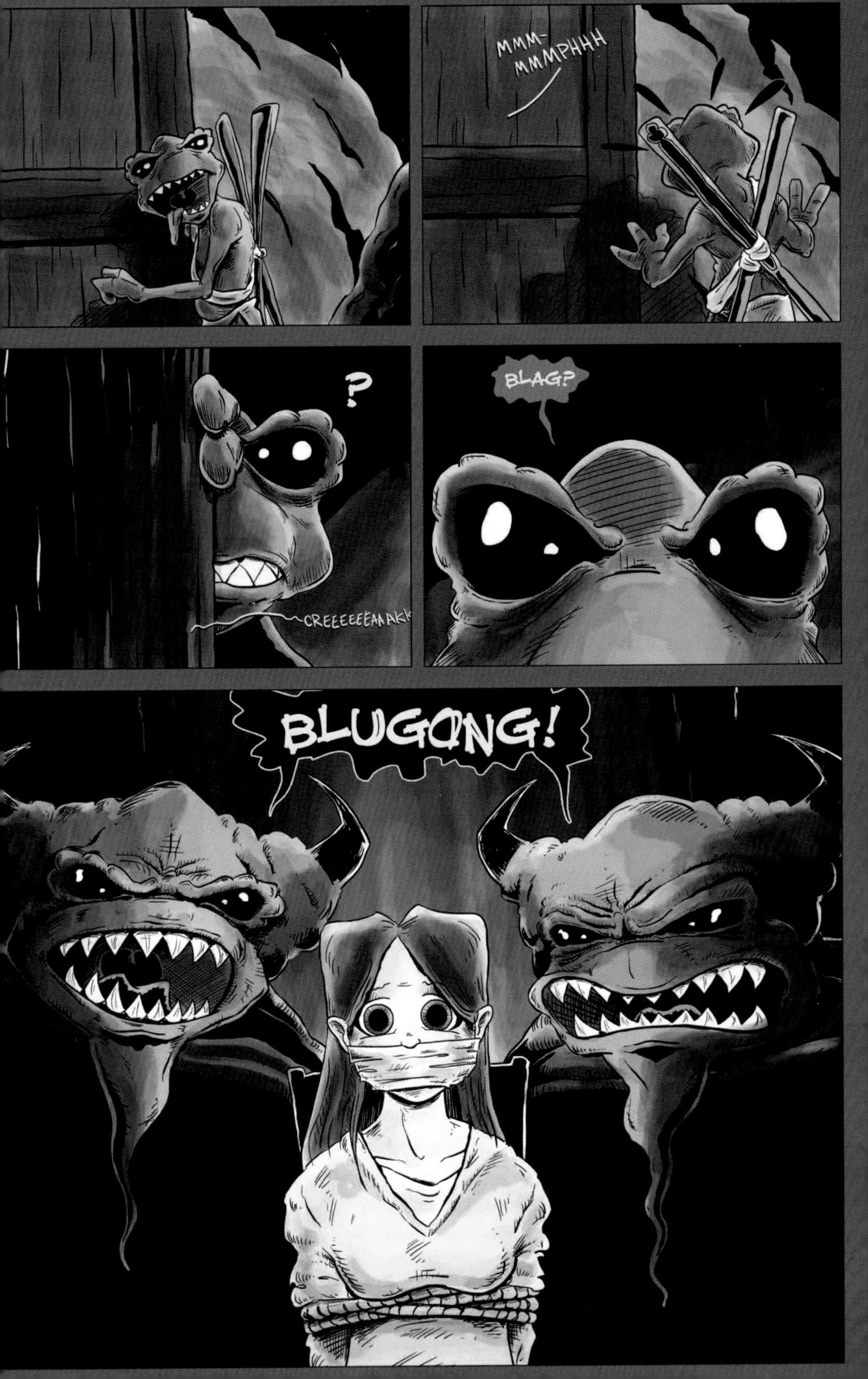
MMM-
MMMPHHH
?
CREEEEEEAAAKK
BLAG?
BLUGONG!

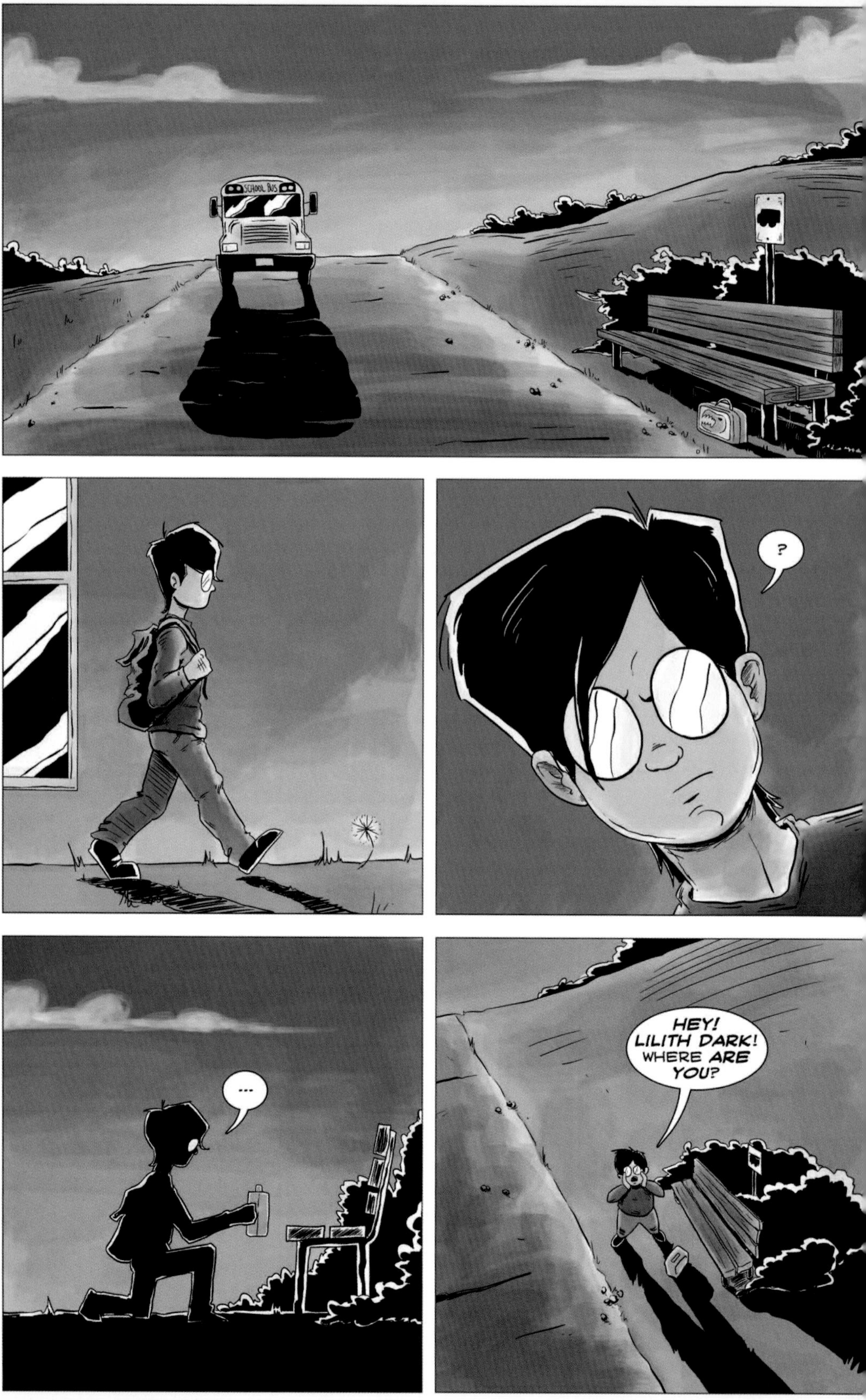
SCHOOL BUS
?
...
HEY! LILITH DARK! WHERE ARE YOU?

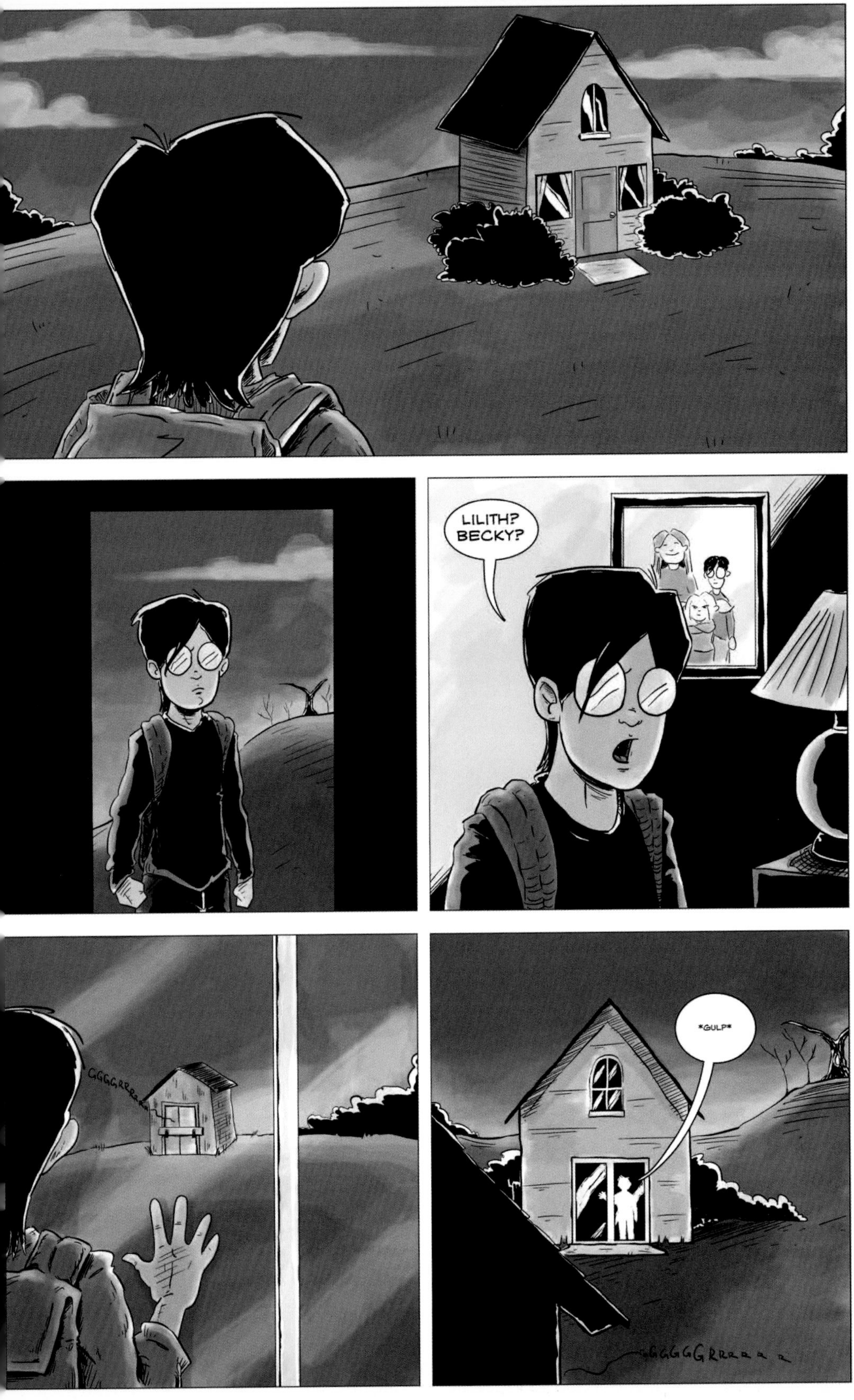
LILITH?
BECKY?
GGGGRRRRRR
GULP
GGGGGRRRRR R

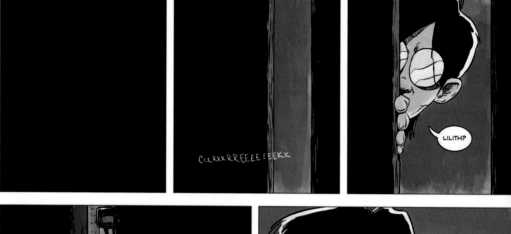

CCCRRRRREEEEEEEKK

LILITH?

GGGGGRRRRRR

K-K-KITTY? IS THAT YOU?

AAAHHHHHHH!

HA HA— I KNEW IT WAS YOU!

LICK

WHERE ARE YOU GOIN', BOY?

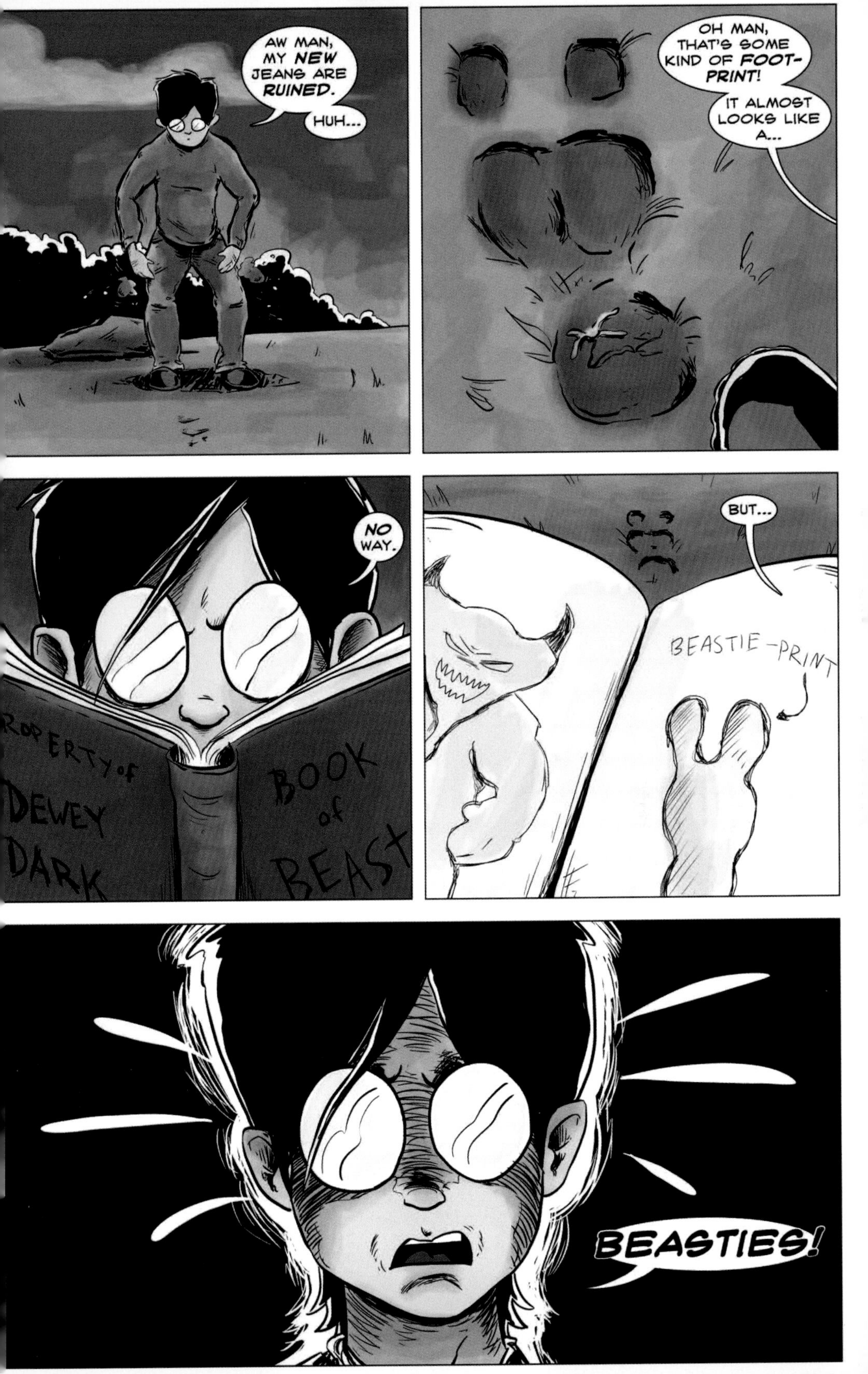
AW MAN, MY NEW JEANS ARE RUINED.
HUH...
OH MAN, THAT'S SOME KIND OF FOOT-PRINT!
IT ALMOST LOOKS LIKE A...
NO WAY.
PROPERTY of DEWEY DARK
BOOK of BEAST
BUT...
BEASTIE-PRINT
BEASTIES!

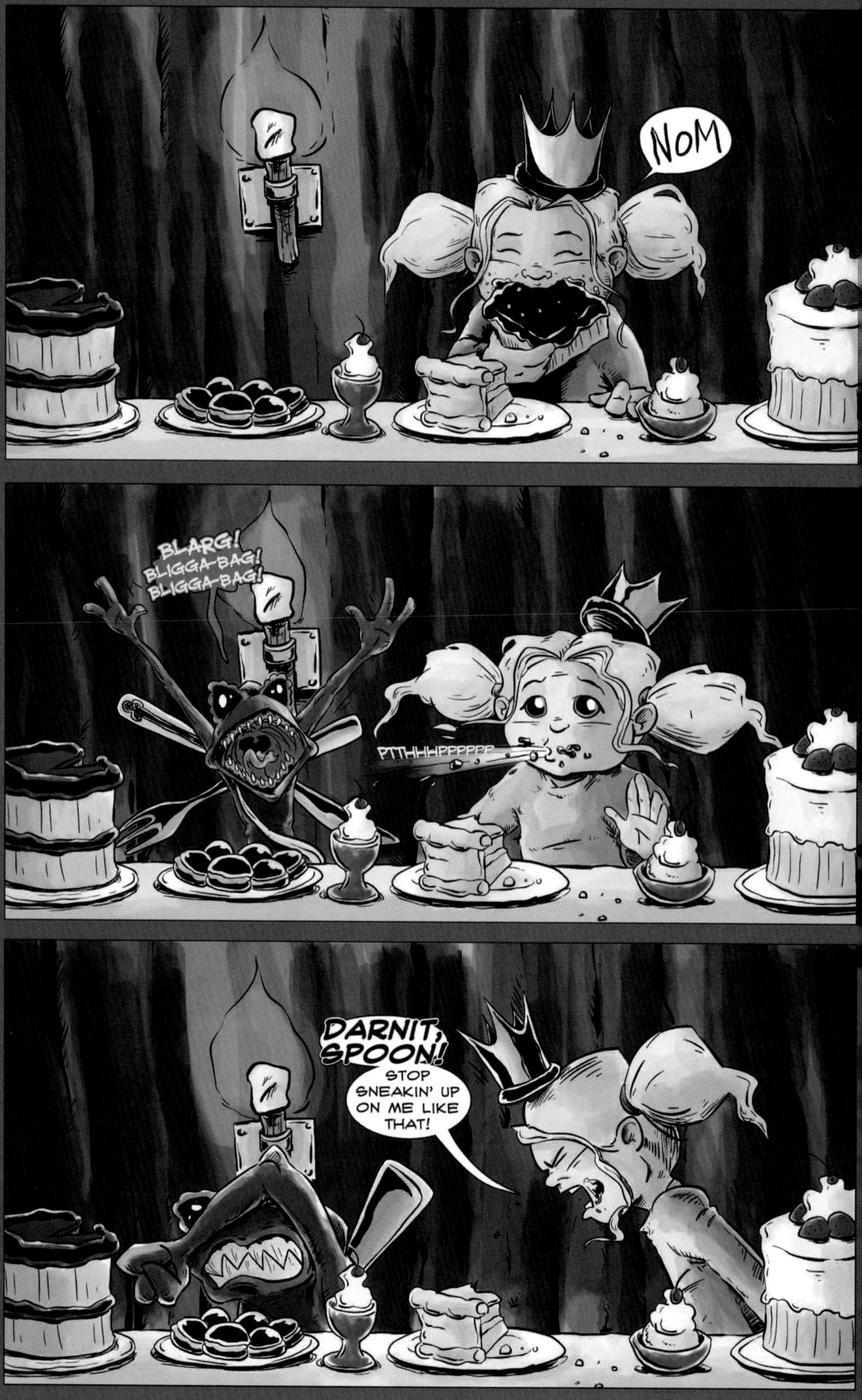
NOM
BLARG! BLIGGA-BAG! BLIGGA-BAG!
PTTHHHPPPPPP
DARNIT, SPOON!
STOP SNEAKIN' UP ON ME LIKE THAT!

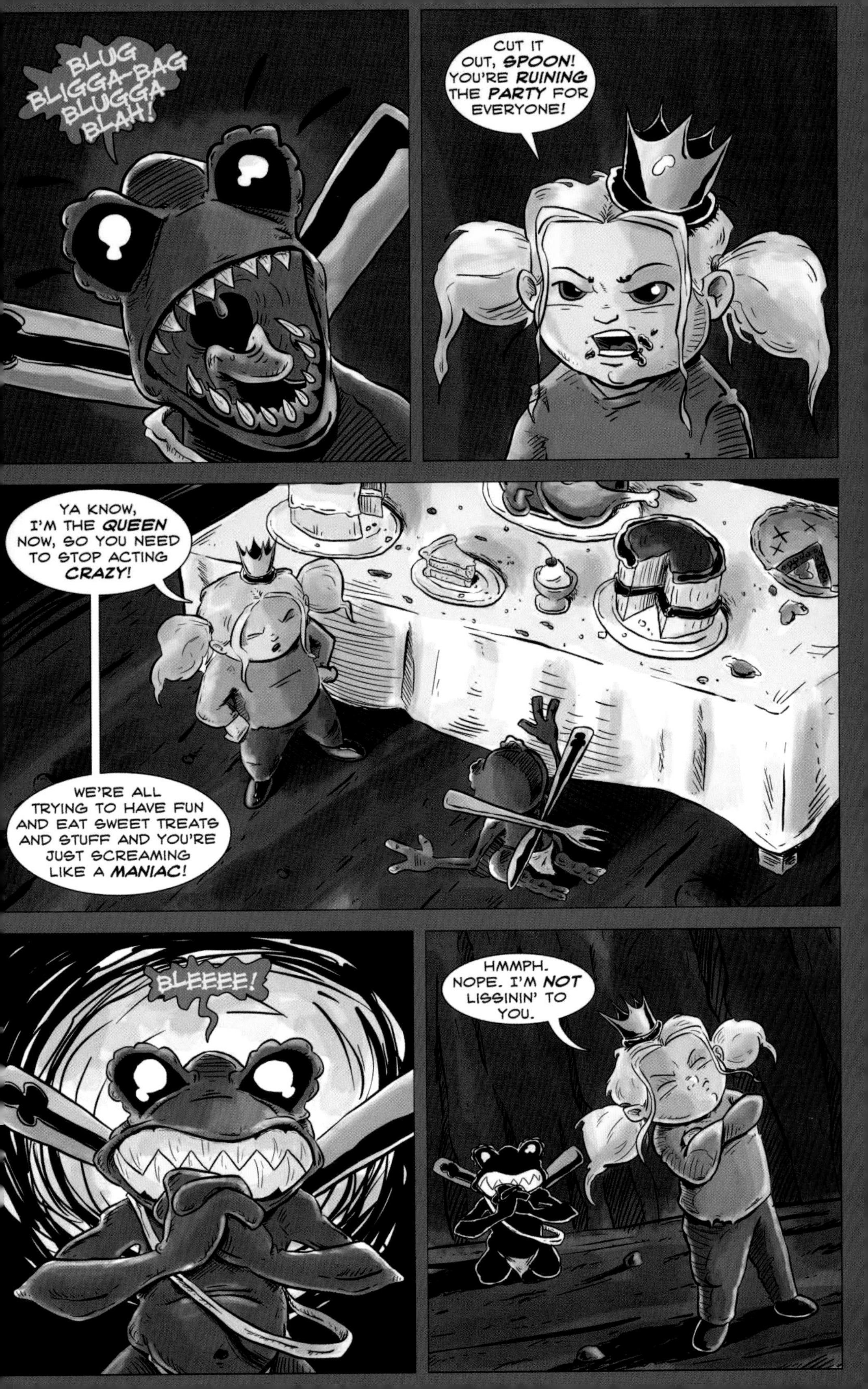
BLUG BLIGGA-BAG BLUGGA BLAH!
CUT IT OUT, SPOON! YOU'RE RUINING THE PARTY FOR EVERYONE!
YA KNOW, I'M THE QUEEN NOW, SO YOU NEED TO STOP ACTING CRAZY!
WE'RE ALL TRYING TO HAVE FUN AND EAT SWEET TREATS AND STUFF AND YOU'RE JUST SCREAMING LIKE A MANIAC!
BLEEEEE!
HMMPH. NOPE. I'M NOT LISSININ' TO YOU.

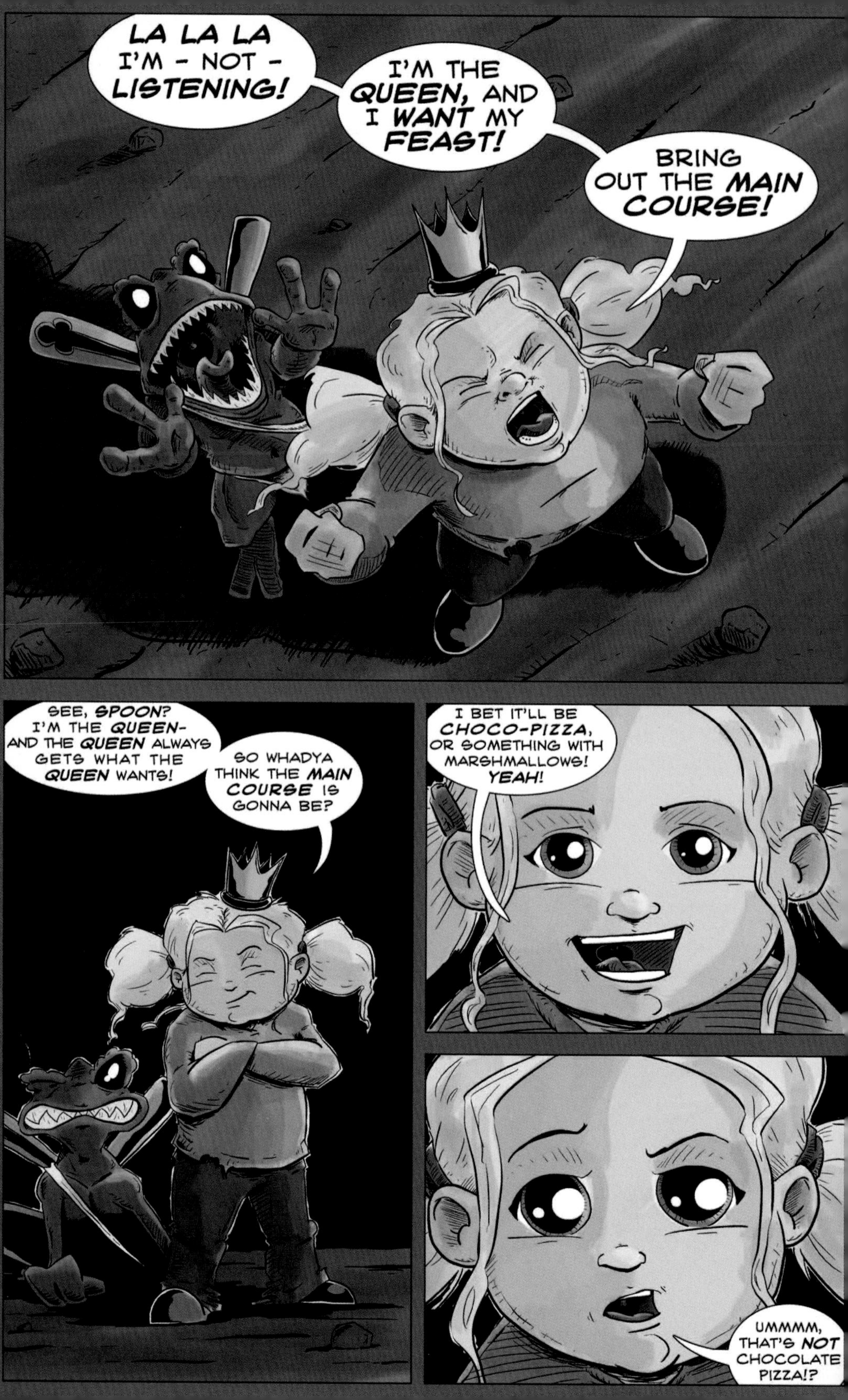
LA LA LA I'M - NOT - LISTENING!
I'M THE QUEEN, AND I WANT MY FEAST!
BRING OUT THE MAIN COURSE!
SEE, SPOON? I'M THE QUEEN- AND THE QUEEN ALWAYS GETS WHAT THE QUEEN WANTS!
SO WHADYA THINK THE MAIN COURSE IS GONNA BE?
I BET IT'LL BE CHOCO-PIZZA, OR SOMETHING WITH MARSHMALLOWS! YEAH!
UMMMM, THAT'S NOT CHOCOLATE PIZZA!?

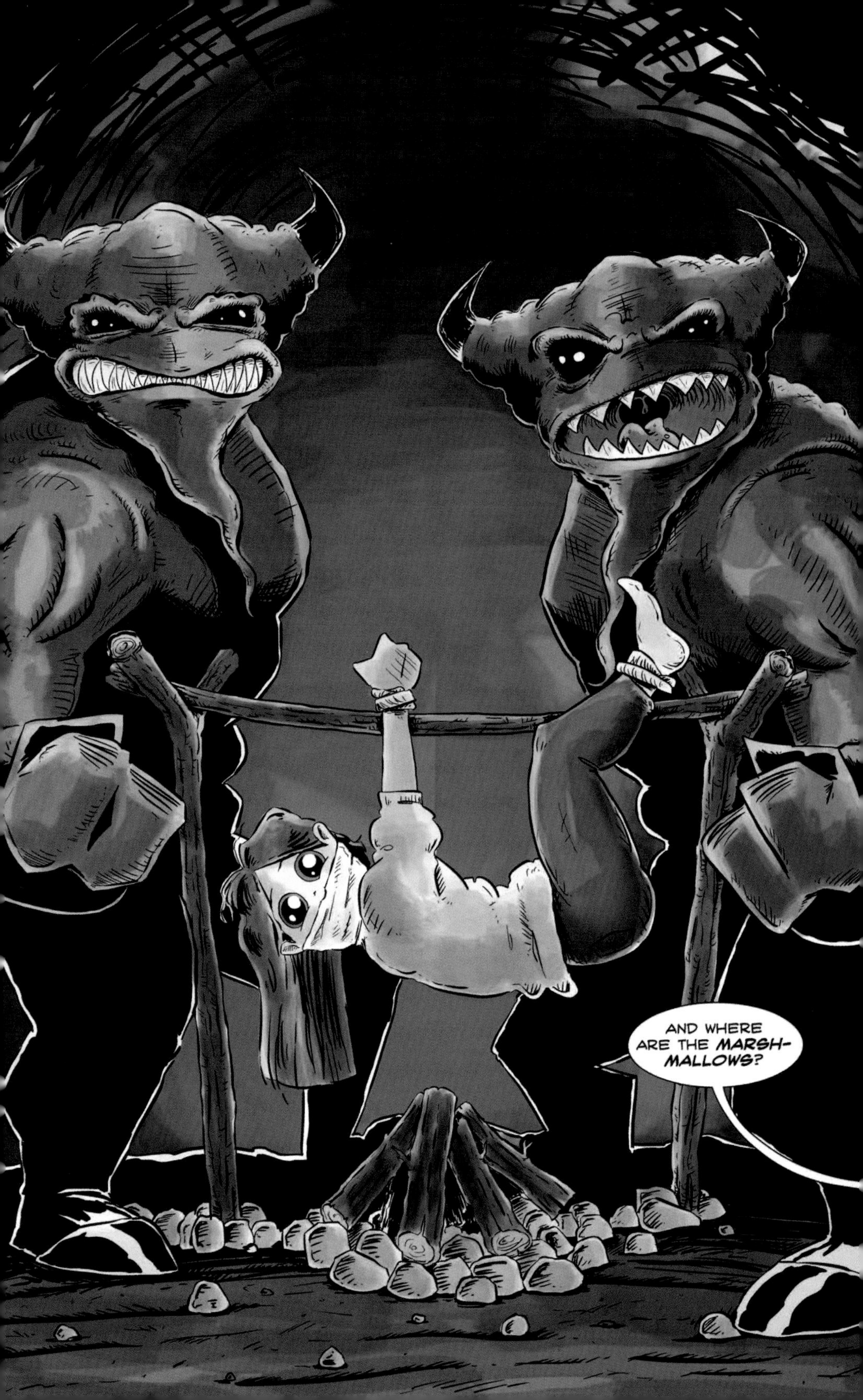
AND WHERE ARE THE MARSH-MALLOWS?

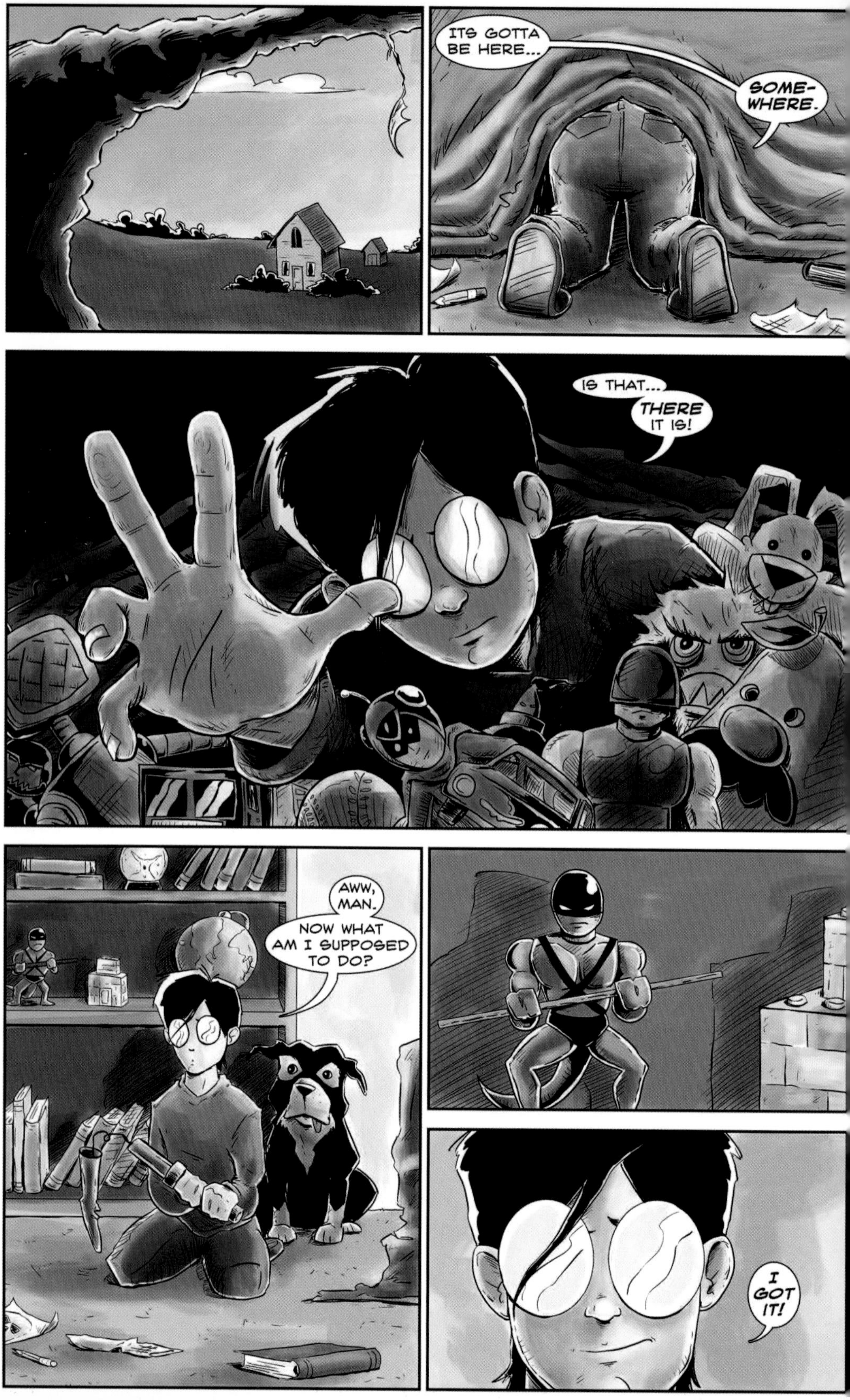
ITS GOTTA BE HERE...
SOME-WHERE.
IS THAT...
THERE IT IS!
AWW, MAN.
NOW WHAT AM I SUPPOSED TO DO?
I GOT IT!

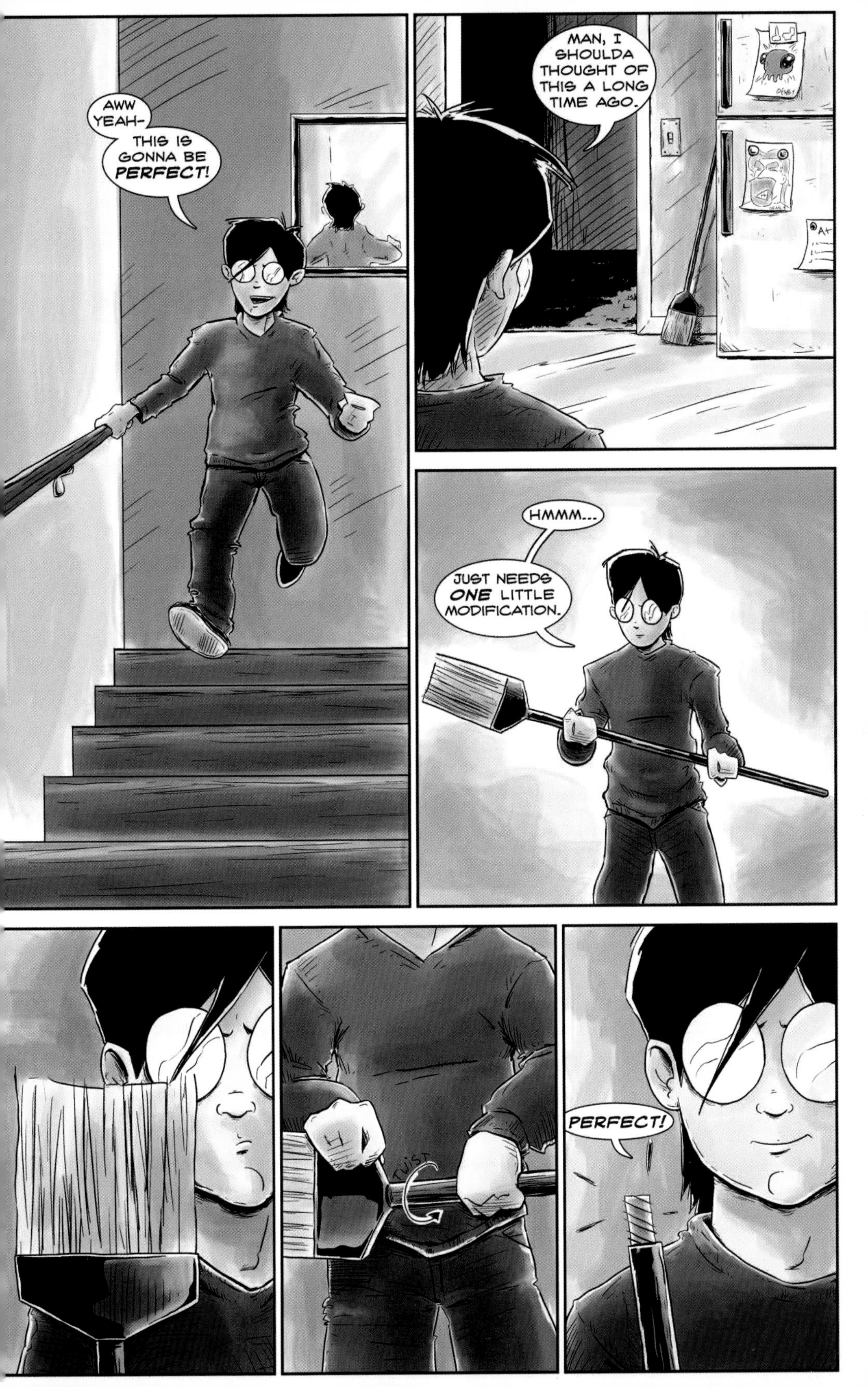
AWW YEAH-
THIS IS GONNA BE *PERFECT!*
MAN, I SHOULDA THOUGHT OF THIS A LONG TIME AGO.
HMMM...
JUST NEEDS *ONE* LITTLE MODIFICATION.
TWIST
PERFECT!

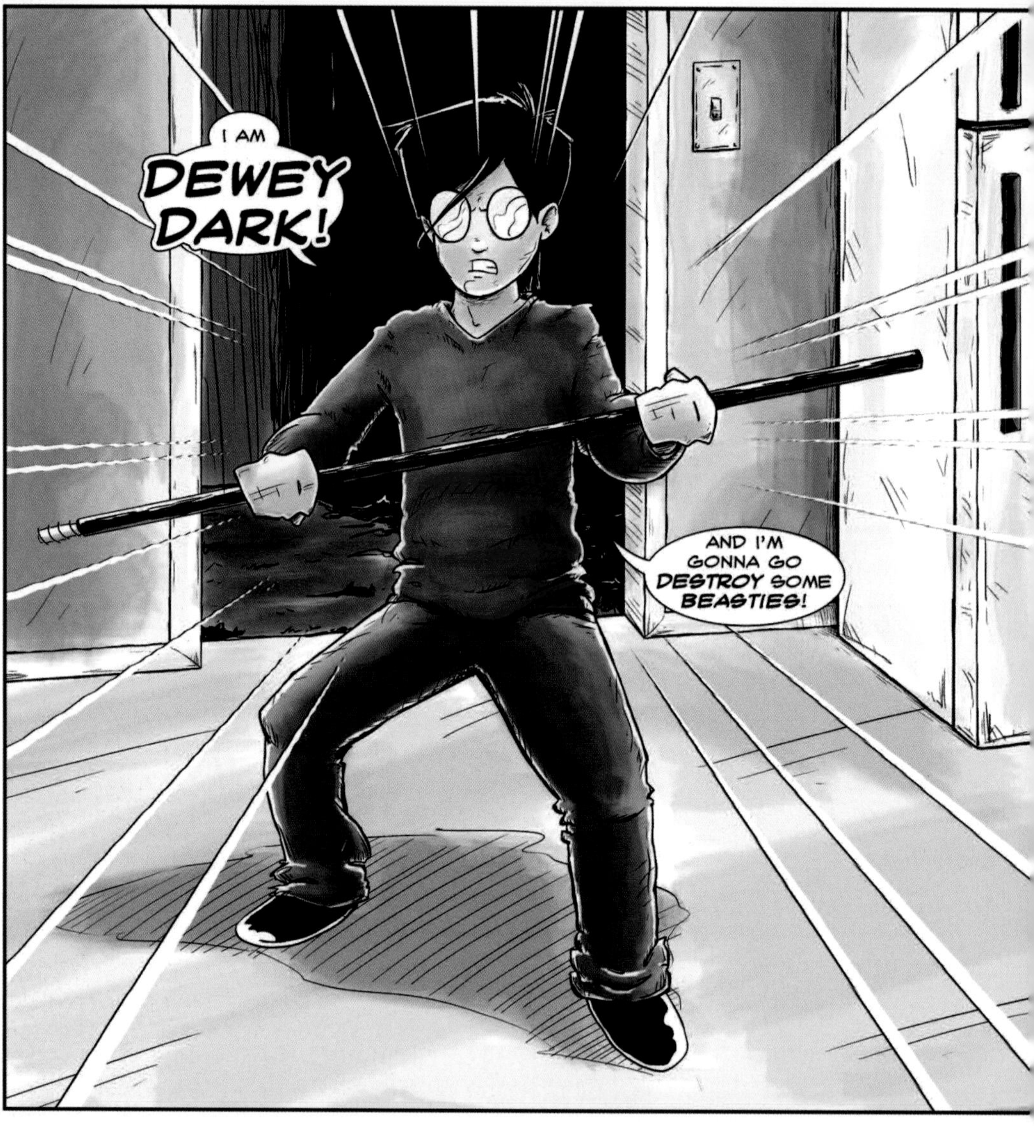
I AM DEWEY DARK!
AND I'M GONNA GO DESTROY SOME BEASTIES!

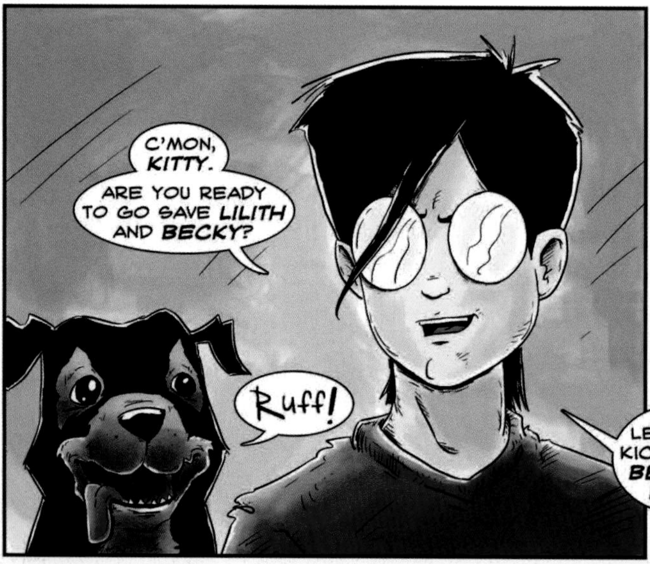
C'MON, KITTY.
ARE YOU READY TO GO SAVE LILITH AND BECKY?
Ruff!
LET'S GO KICK SOME BEASTIE BUTT!

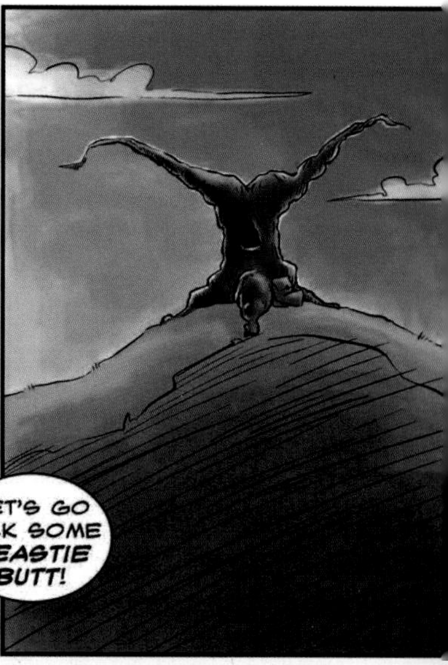

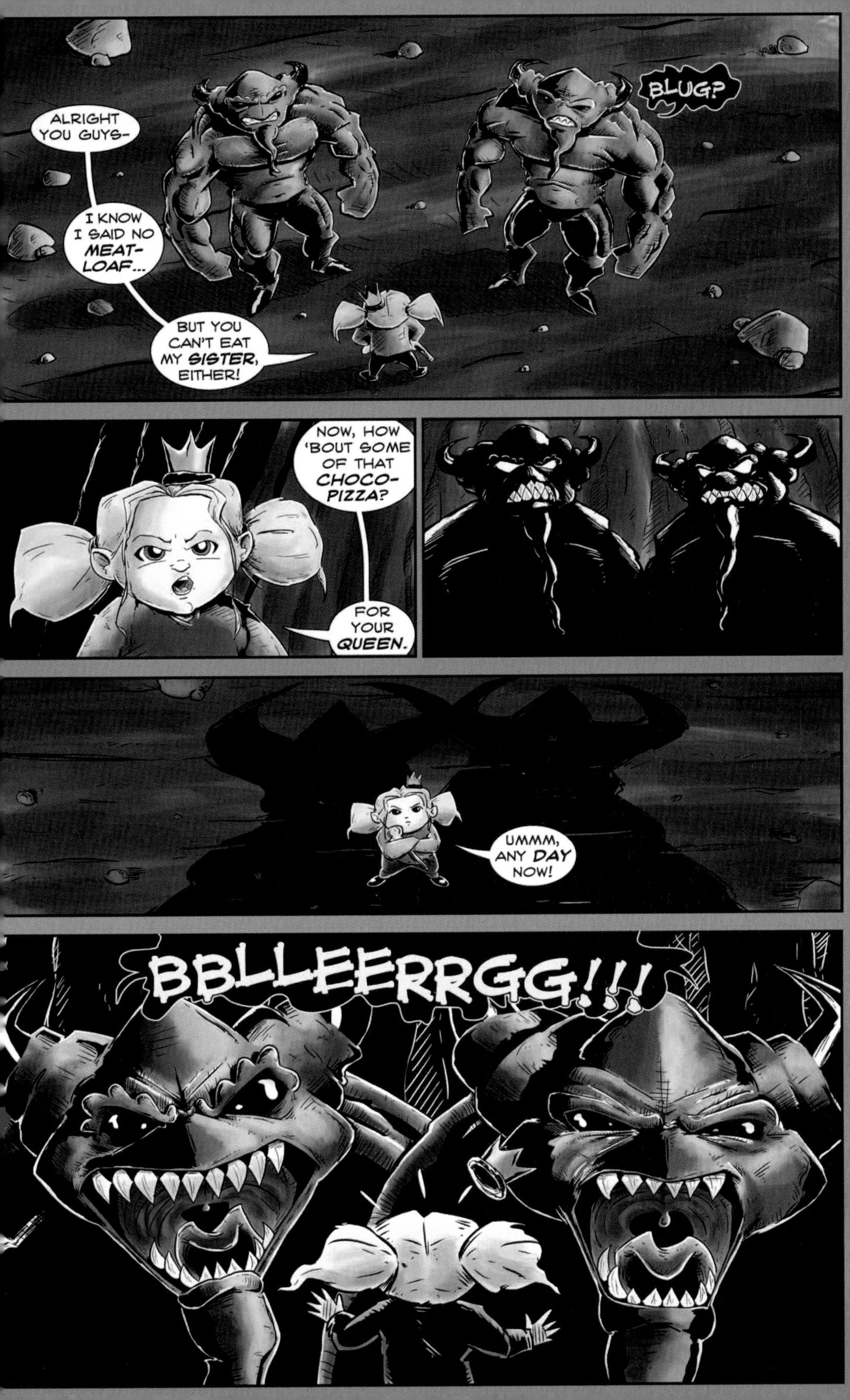

ALRIGHT YOU GUYS-
I KNOW I SAID NO MEAT-LOAF...
BUT YOU CAN'T EAT MY SISTER, EITHER!
BLUG?
NOW, HOW 'BOUT SOME OF THAT CHOCO-PIZZA?
FOR YOUR QUEEN.
UMMM, ANY DAY NOW!
BBLLEERRGG!!!

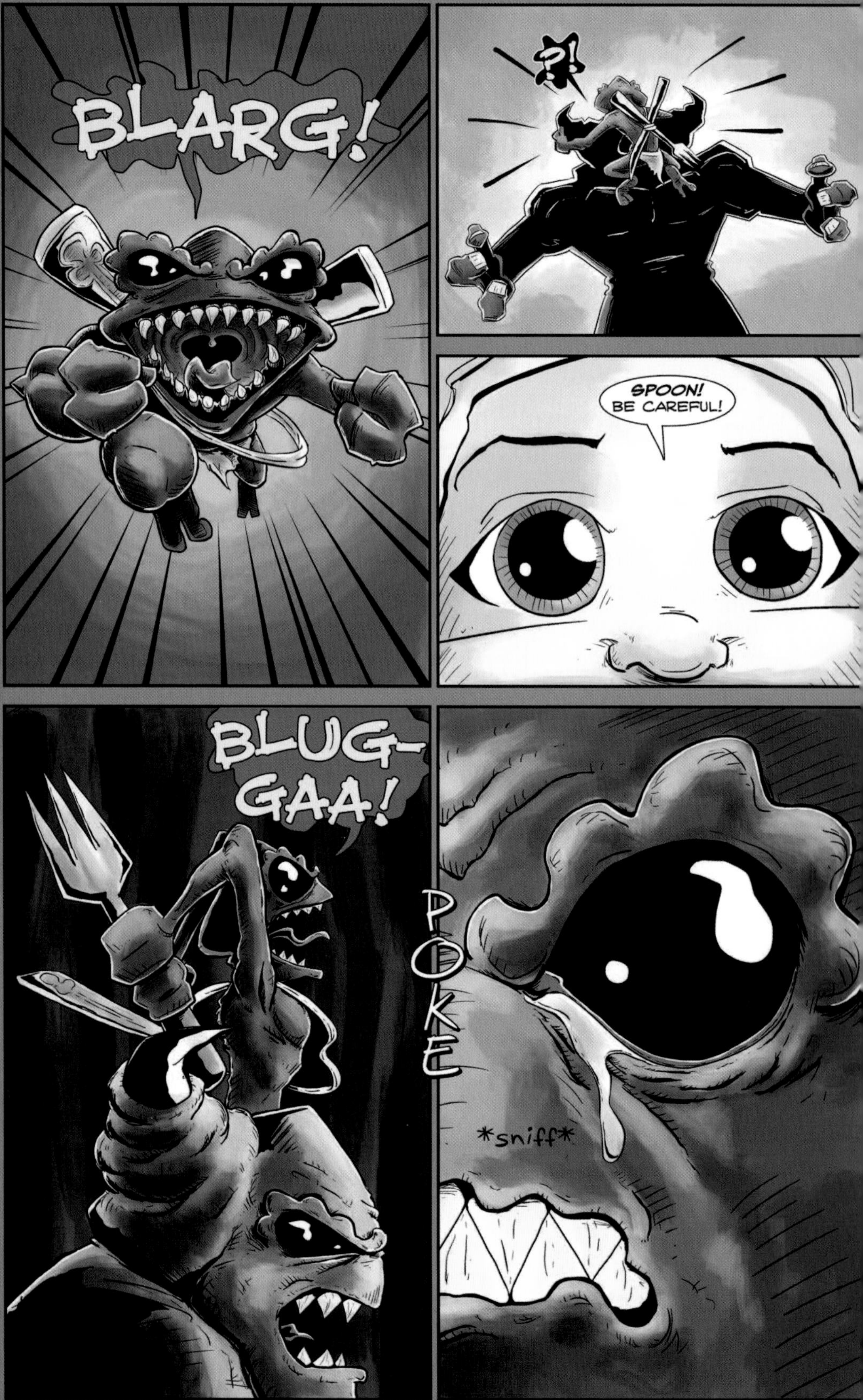
BLARG!
?!
SPOON! BE CAREFUL!
BLUG-GAA!
POKE
sniff

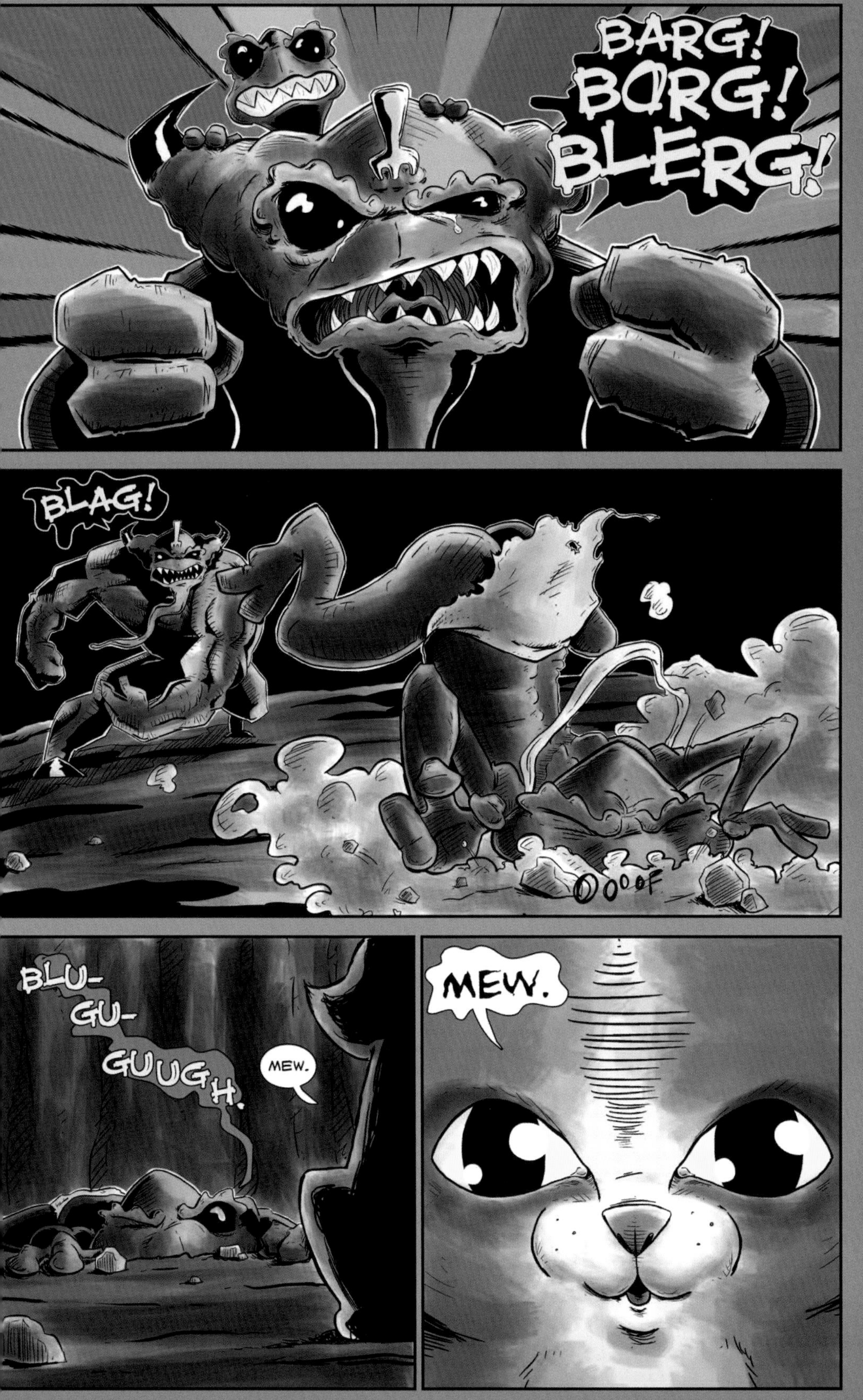
BARG!
BORG!
BLERG!
BLAG!
OOOOF
BLU-
GU-
GUUGH.
MEW.
MEW.

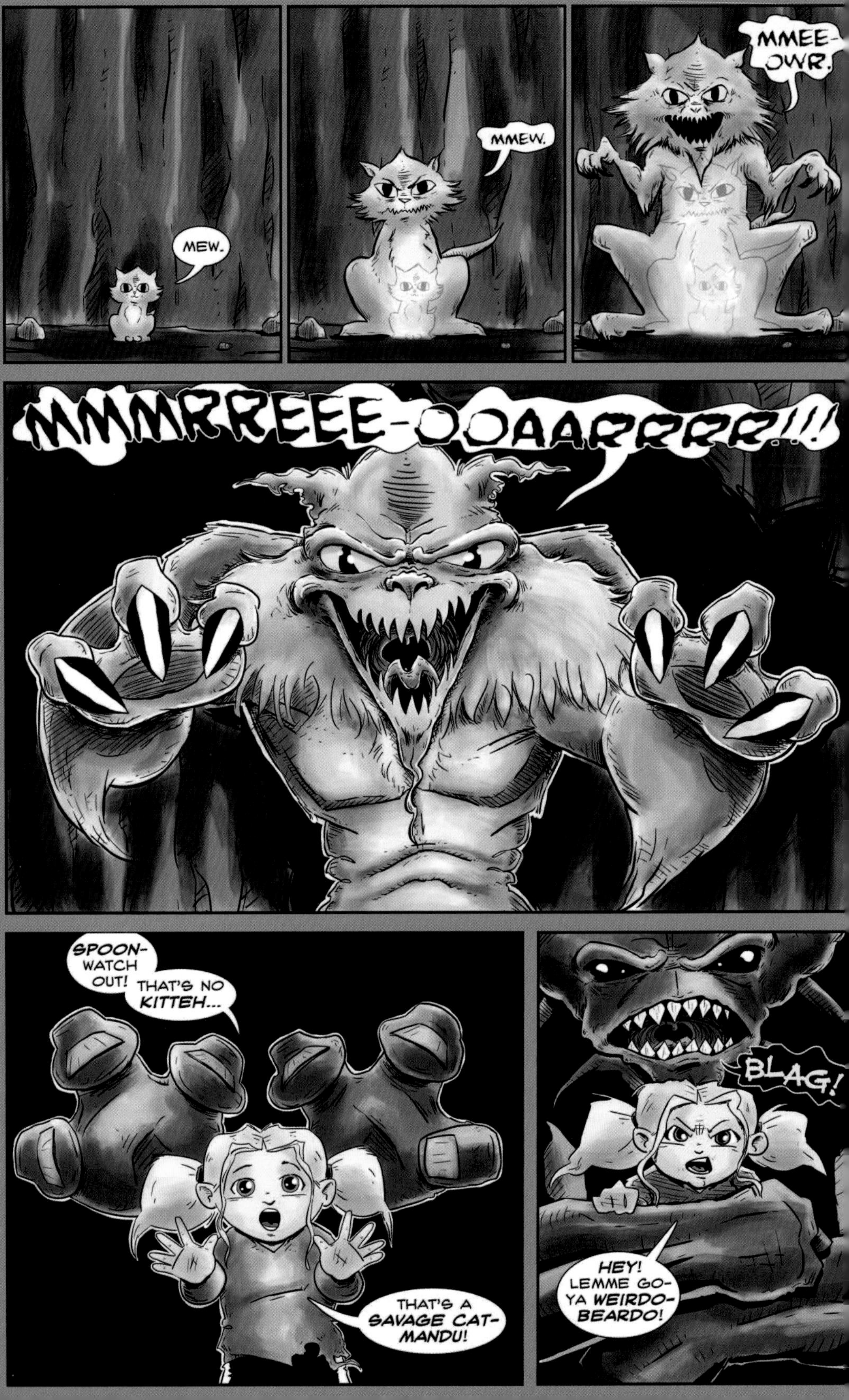
MEW.
MMEW.
MMEE-OWR.
MMMRREEE-OOAARRRR!!
SPOON- WATCH OUT! THAT'S NO KITTEH...
THAT'S A SAVAGE CAT-MANDU!
BLAG!
HEY! LEMME GO- YA WEIRDO-BEARDO!

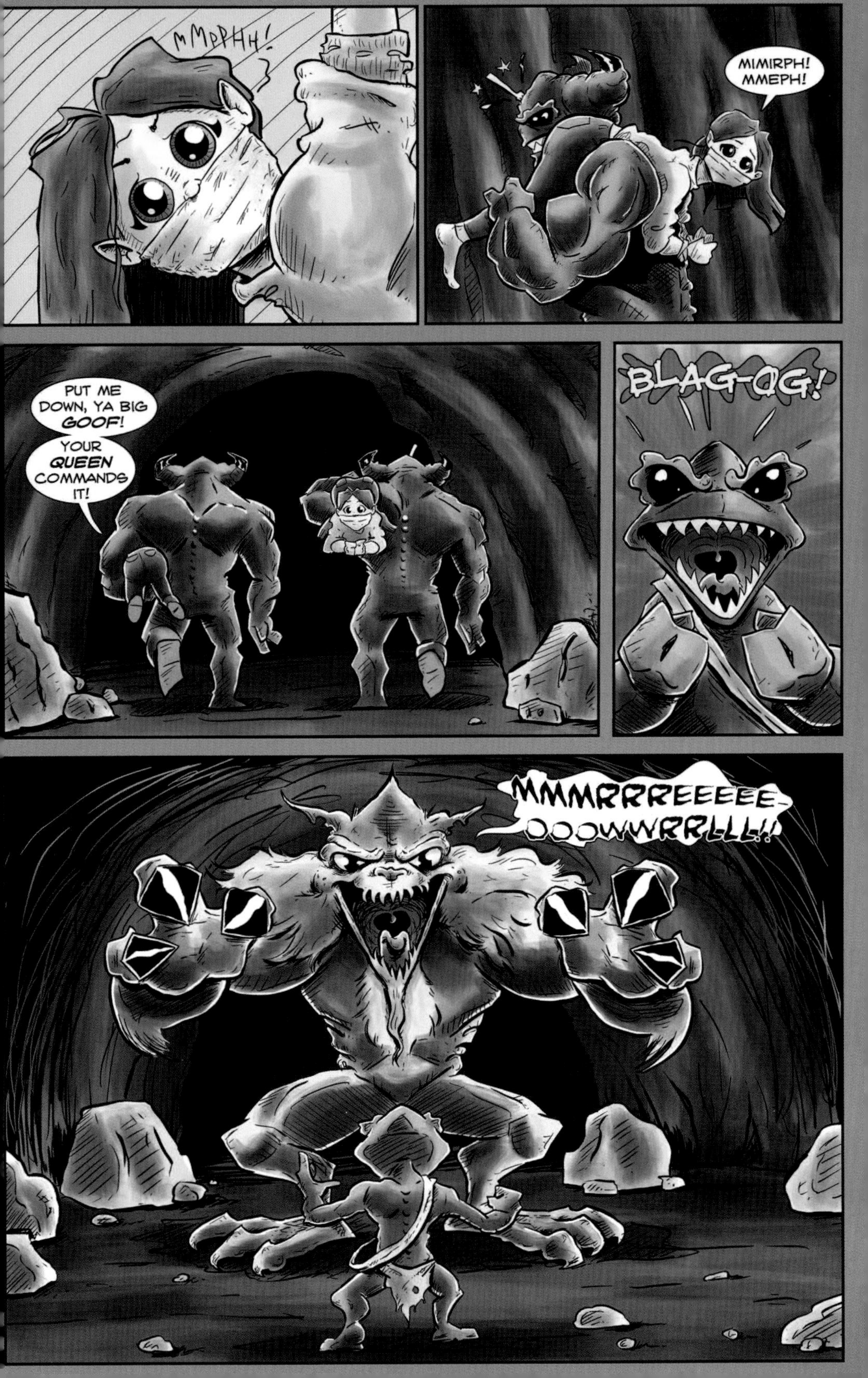
MMPPHH!
MIMIRPH! MMEPH!
PUT ME DOWN, YA BIG GOOF!
YOUR QUEEN COMMANDS IT!
BLAG-OG!
MMMRRREEEEEE-OOOWWRRLLL!!

HERE YOU GO, BOY. YOU WAIT HERE AND KEEP AN EYE ON LILITH'S BAG.

NOW WHATEVER YOU DO, DON'T LET ANY BEASTIES COME IN OR OUT OF THIS TREE, OK?

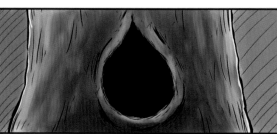

OK, DEWEY, TIME TO SAVE YOUR SISTERS.

* gulp *

SCRITCH

B-BRING IT ON B-B-BEASTIE!

I'M NOT SCARED OF YOU!

GRRRRRRR!

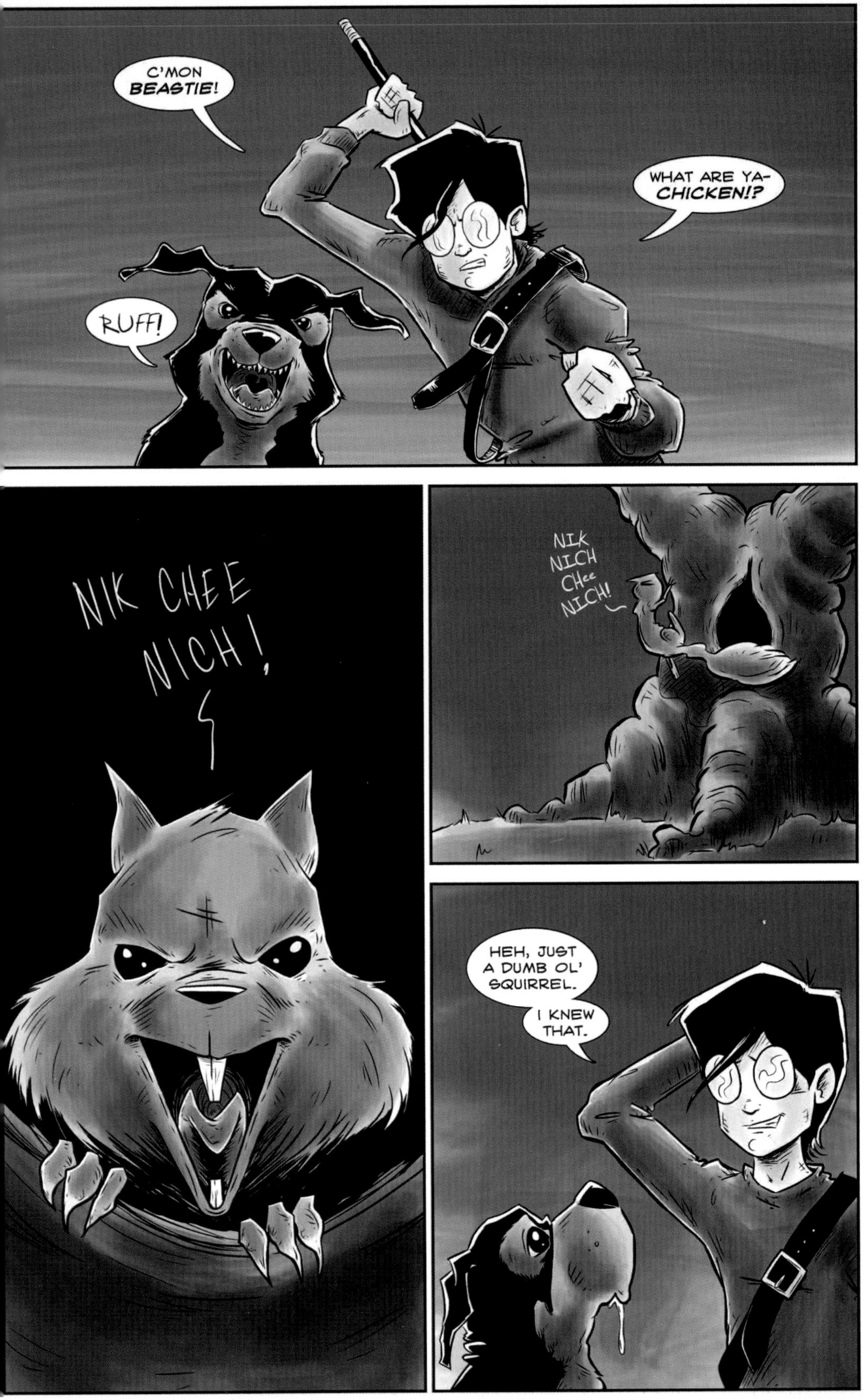
C'MON BEASTIE!
WHAT ARE YA- CHICKEN!?
RUFF!
NIK CHEE NICH!
NIK NICH CHee NICH!
HEH, JUST A DUMB OL' SQUIRREL.
I KNEW THAT.

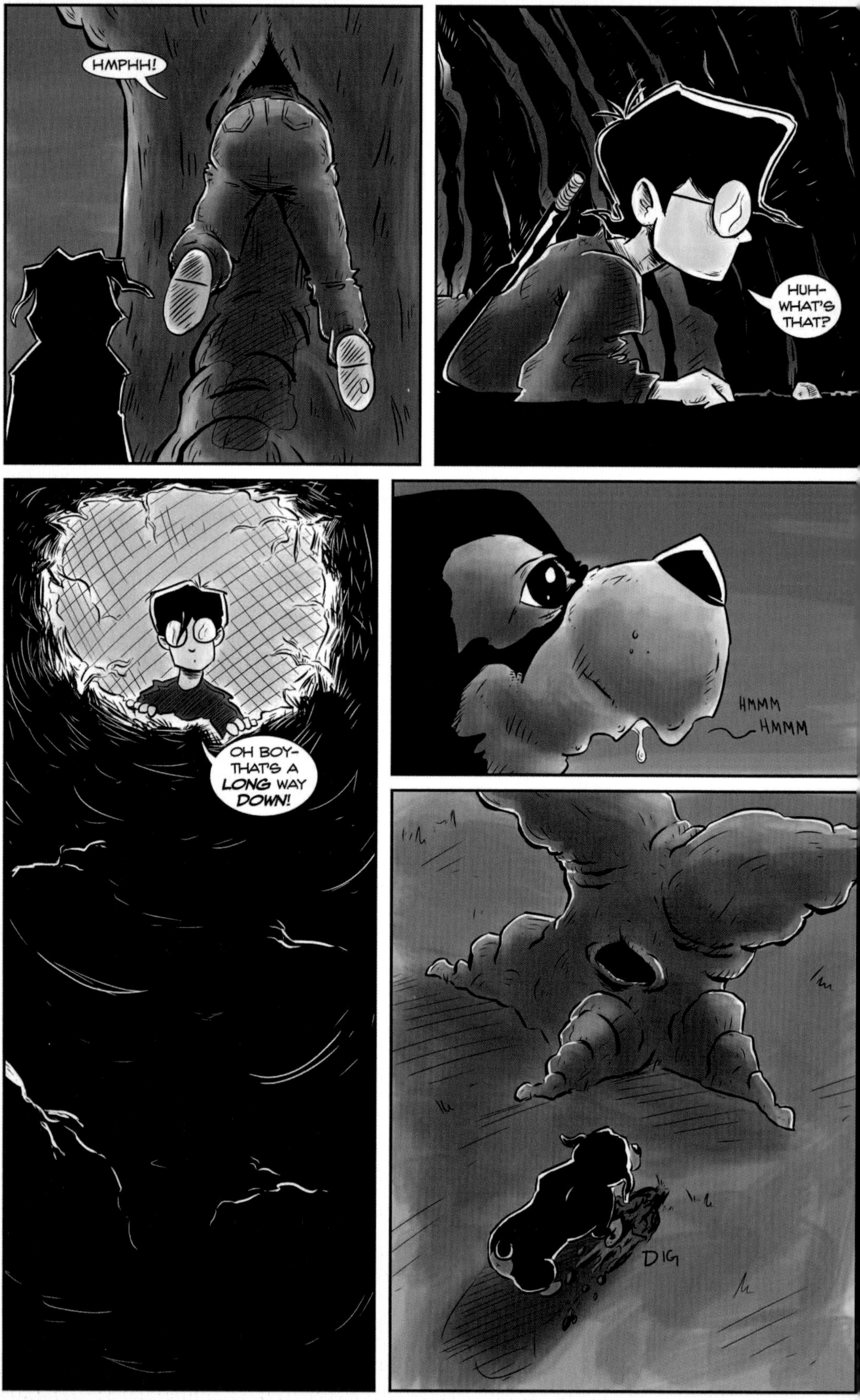
HMPHH!
HUH- WHAT'S THAT?
OH BOY- THAT'S A LONG WAY DOWN!
HMMM HMMM
DIG

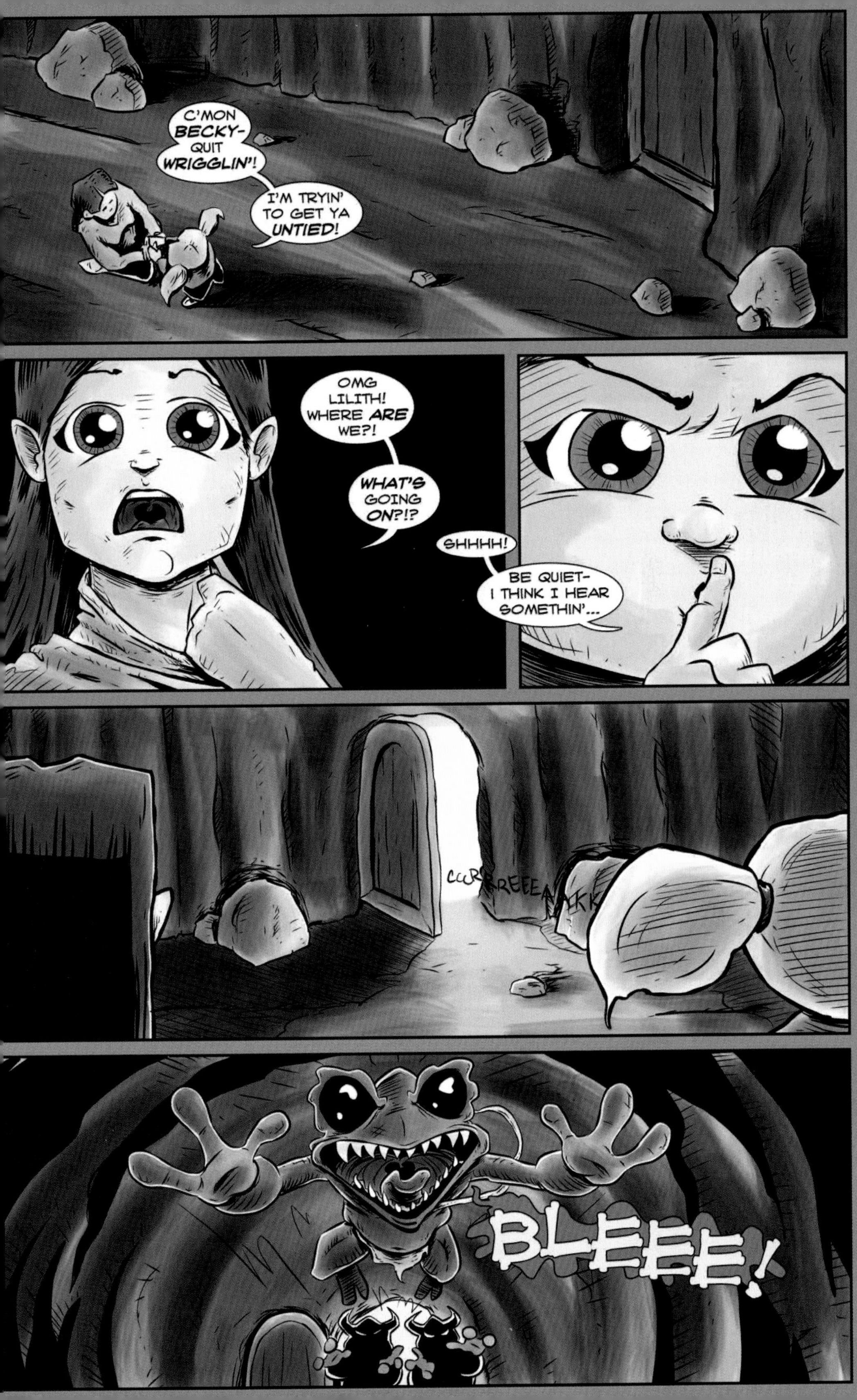
C'MON BECKY- QUIT WRIGGLIN'!
I'M TRYIN' TO GET YA UNTIED!
OMG LILITH! WHERE ARE WE?!
WHAT'S GOING ON?!?
SHHHH!
BE QUIET- I THINK I HEAR SOMETHIN'...
CCURREEEAKK
BLEEE!

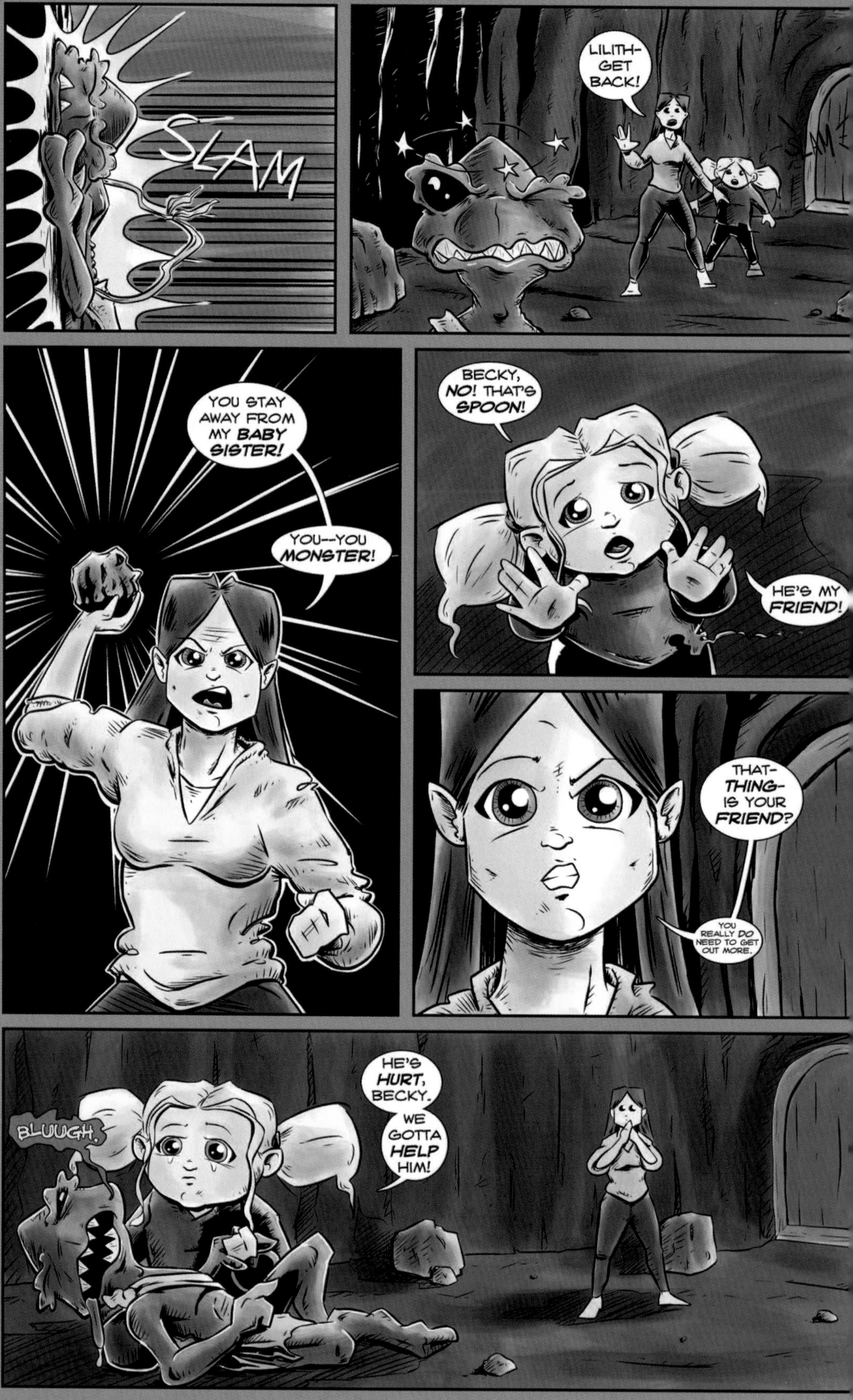
SLAM
LILITH-
GET
BACK!
SLAM
YOU STAY AWAY FROM MY BABY SISTER!
YOU--YOU MONSTER!
BECKY, NO! THAT'S SPOON!
HE'S MY FRIEND!
THAT- THING- IS YOUR FRIEND?
YOU REALLY DO NEED TO GET OUT MORE.
BLUUGH.
HE'S HURT, BECKY.
WE GOTTA HELP HIM!

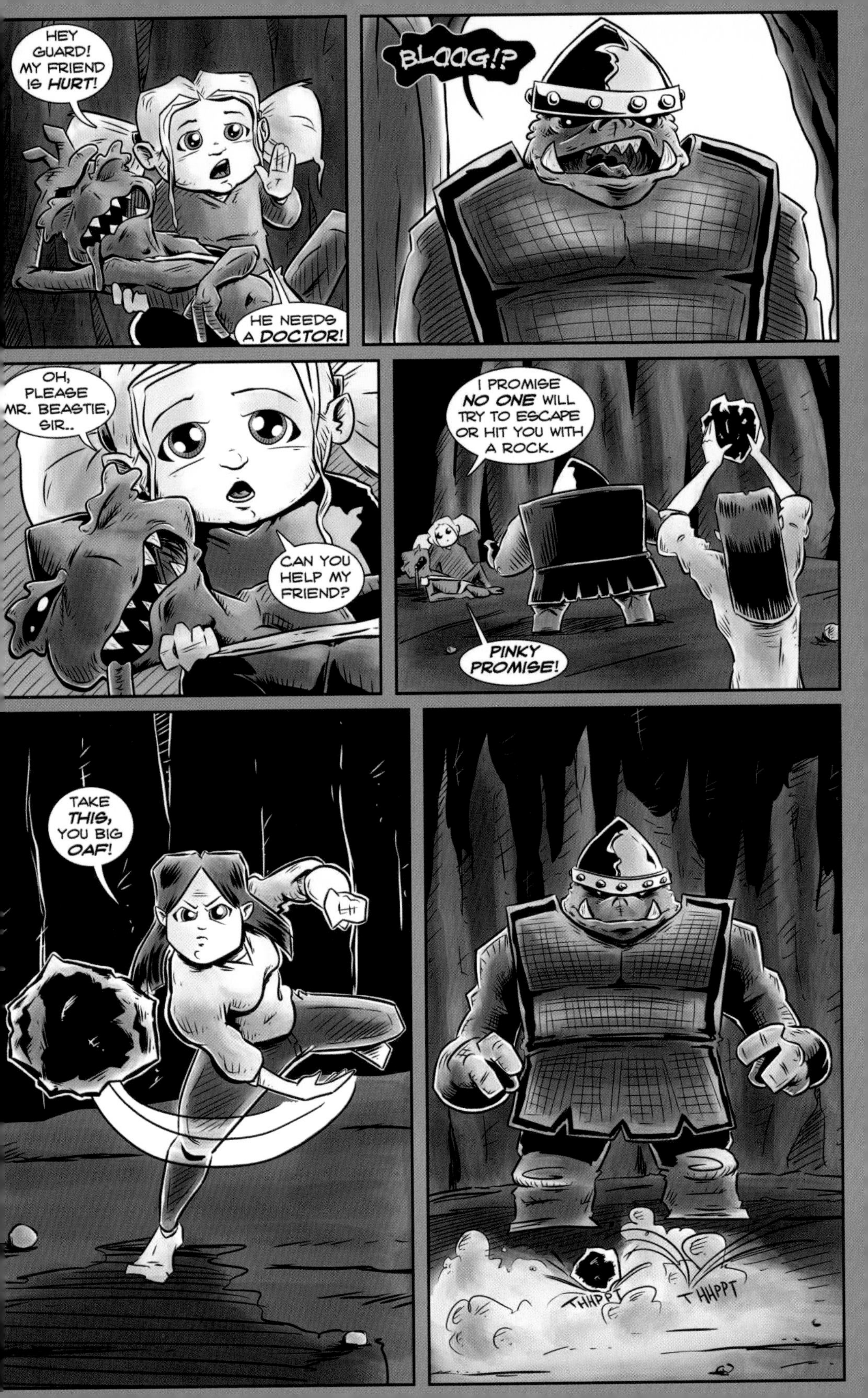
HEY GUARD! MY FRIEND IS HURT!
HE NEEDS A DOCTOR!
BLOOG!?
OH, PLEASE MR. BEASTIE, SIR..
CAN YOU HELP MY FRIEND?
I PROMISE NO ONE WILL TRY TO ESCAPE OR HIT YOU WITH A ROCK.
PINKY PROMISE!
TAKE THIS, YOU BIG OAF!
THHPPT
THHPPT

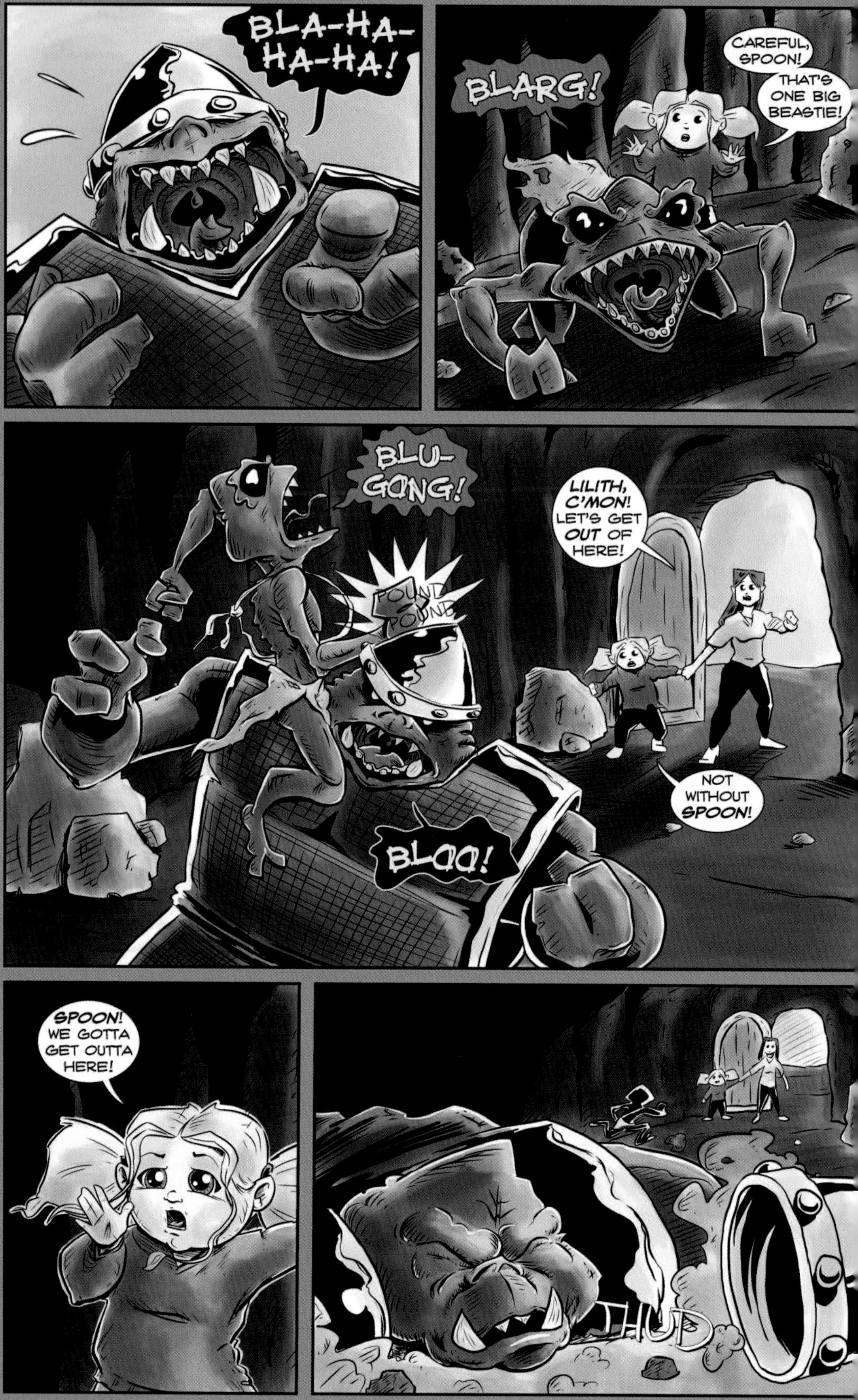
BLA-HA-HA-HA!
BLARG!
CAREFUL, SPOON!
THAT'S ONE BIG BEASTIE!
BLU-GONG!
POUND POUND
LILITH, C'MON! LET'S GET OUT OF HERE!
NOT WITHOUT SPOON!
BLOO!
SPOON! WE GOTTA GET OUTTA HERE!
THUD

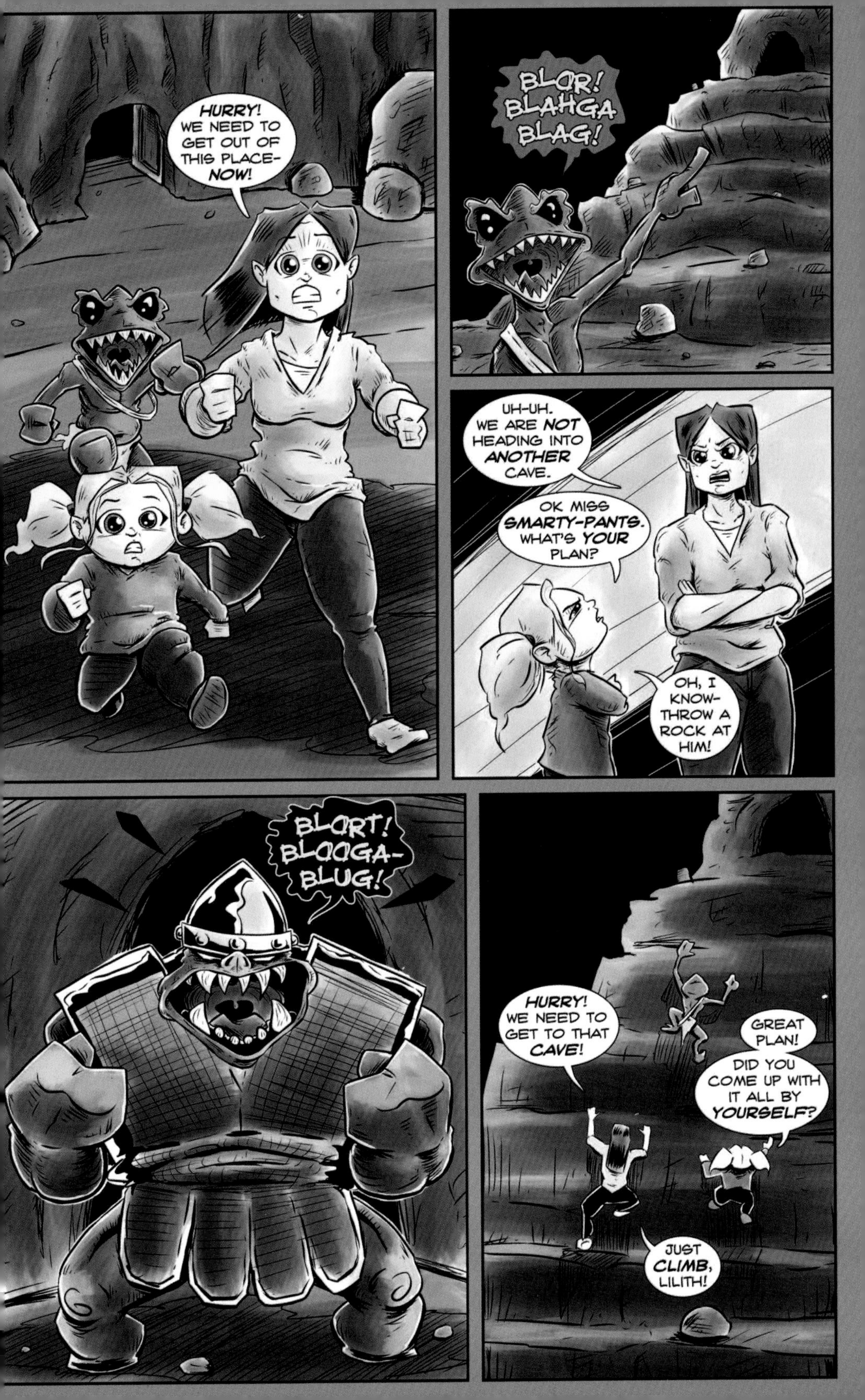
HURRY!
WE NEED TO GET OUT OF THIS PLACE- NOW!
BLOR! BLAHGA BLAG!
UH-UH. WE ARE NOT HEADING INTO ANOTHER CAVE.
OK MISS SMARTY-PANTS. WHAT'S YOUR PLAN?
OH, I KNOW- THROW A ROCK AT HIM!
BLORT! BLOOGA-BLUG!
HURRY! WE NEED TO GET TO THAT CAVE!
GREAT PLAN!
DID YOU COME UP WITH IT ALL BY YOURSELF?
JUST CLIMB, LILITH!

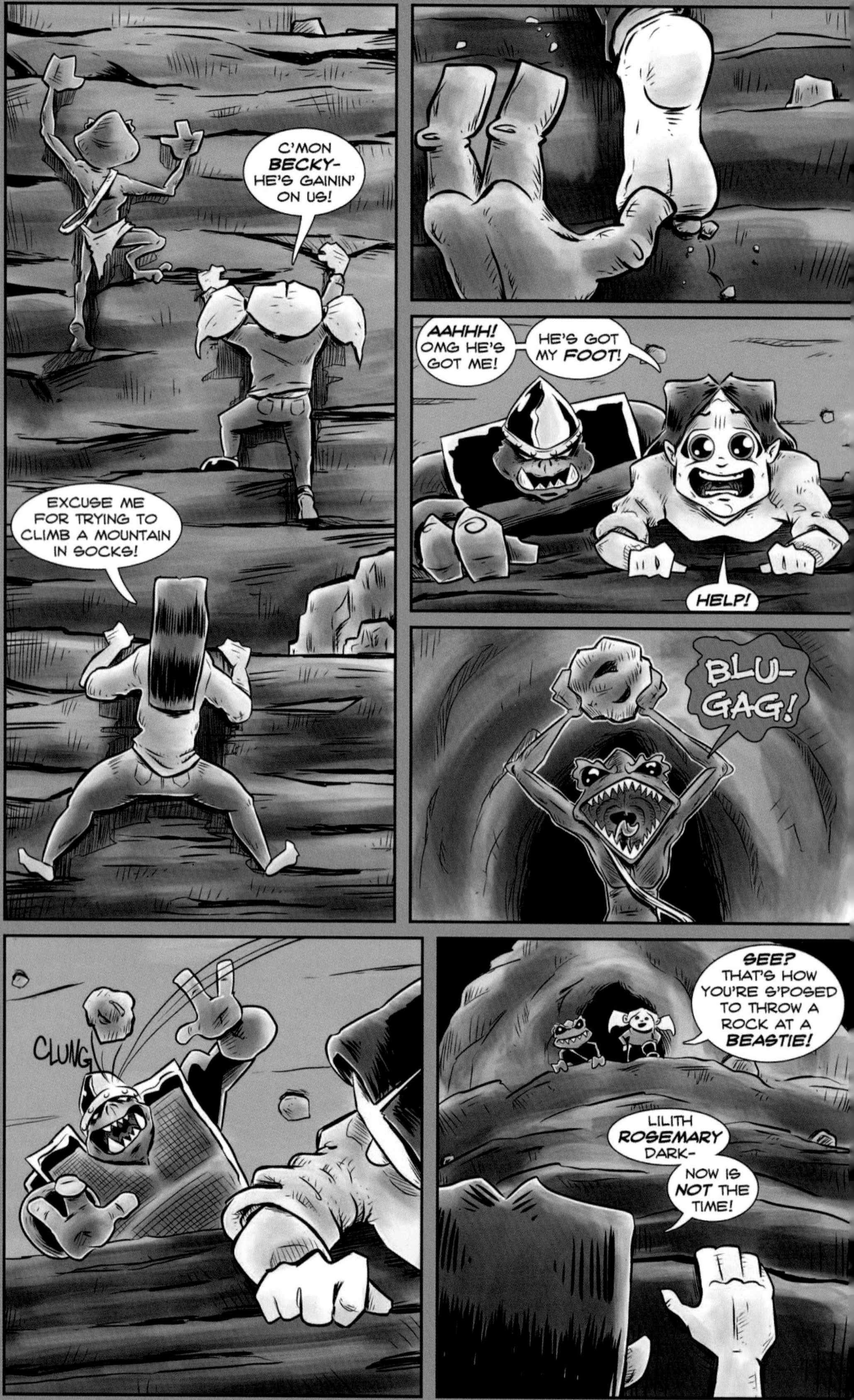
C'MON BECKY- HE'S GAININ' ON US!
EXCUSE ME FOR TRYING TO CLIMB A MOUNTAIN IN SOCKS!
AAHHH! OMG HE'S GOT ME!
HE'S GOT MY FOOT!
HELP!
BLU-GAG!
CLUNG
SEE? THAT'S HOW YOU'RE S'POSED TO THROW A ROCK AT A BEASTIE!
LILITH ROSEMARY DARK-
NOW IS NOT THE TIME!

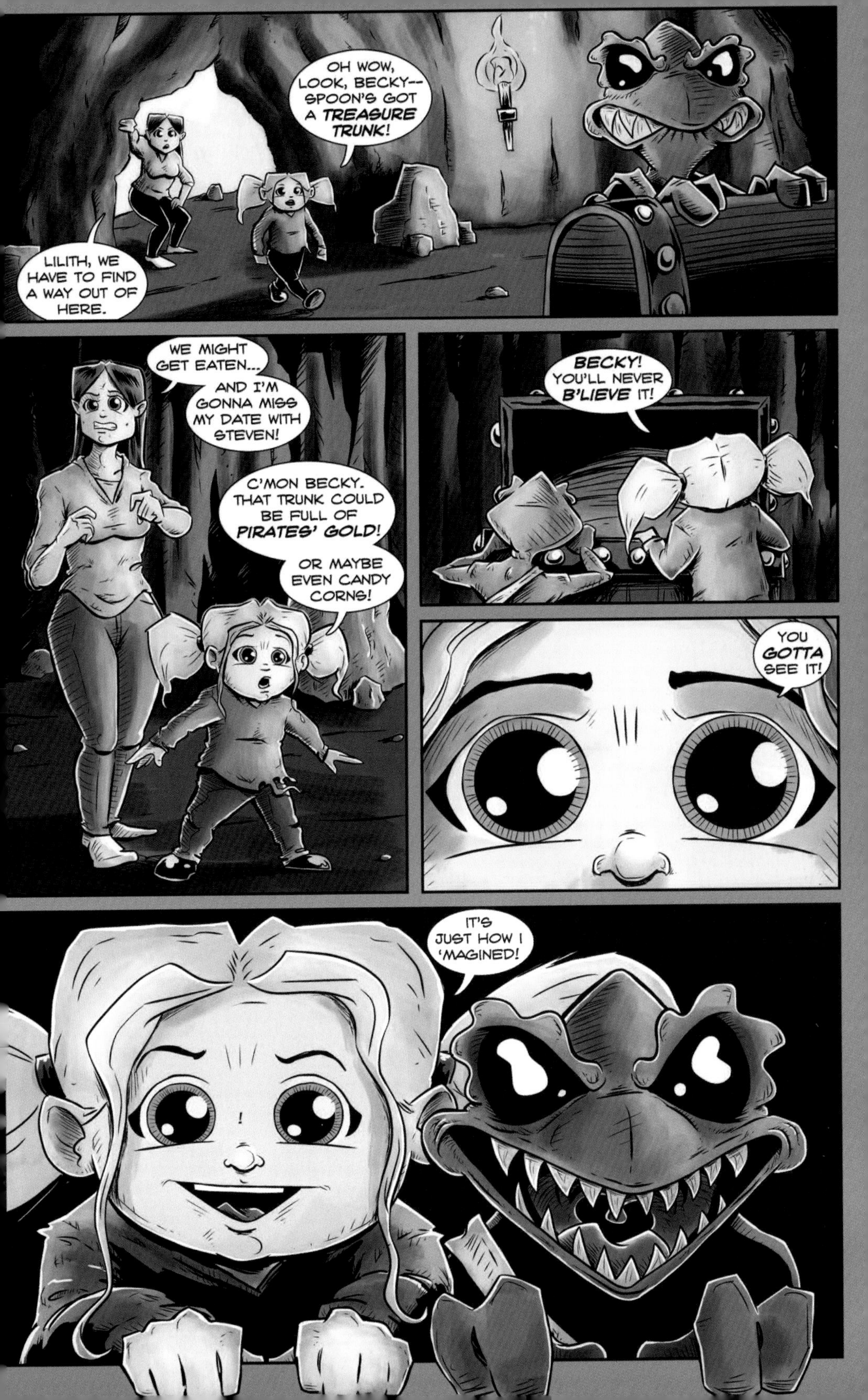

LILITH, WE HAVE TO FIND A WAY OUT OF HERE.
OH WOW, LOOK, BECKY-- SPOON'S GOT A TREASURE TRUNK!
WE MIGHT GET EATEN...
AND I'M GONNA MISS MY DATE WITH STEVEN!
C'MON BECKY. THAT TRUNK COULD BE FULL OF PIRATES' GOLD!
OR MAYBE EVEN CANDY CORNS!
BECKY! YOU'LL NEVER B'LIEVE IT!
YOU GOTTA SEE IT!
IT'S JUST HOW I 'MAGINED!

WHAT IS IT, LILITH?
WHAT'S IN THE TRUNK?
UHH, WHA-?
UMMM...
LILITH- I DON'T THINK WE SHOULD...
LOOK AT IT, BECKY. IT'S SO...
AWESOME!
BLAG!
C'MON, BECKY. IT'S TIME FOR US TO GET OUT OF THIS DUMB OL' TREE.

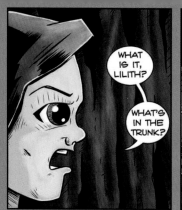

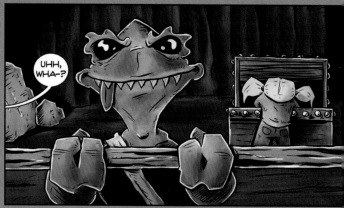

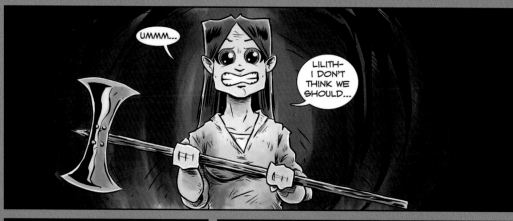

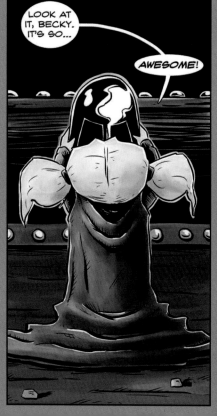

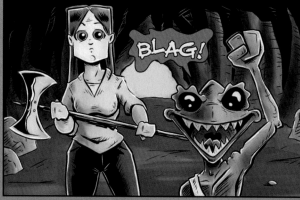

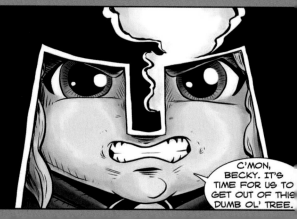

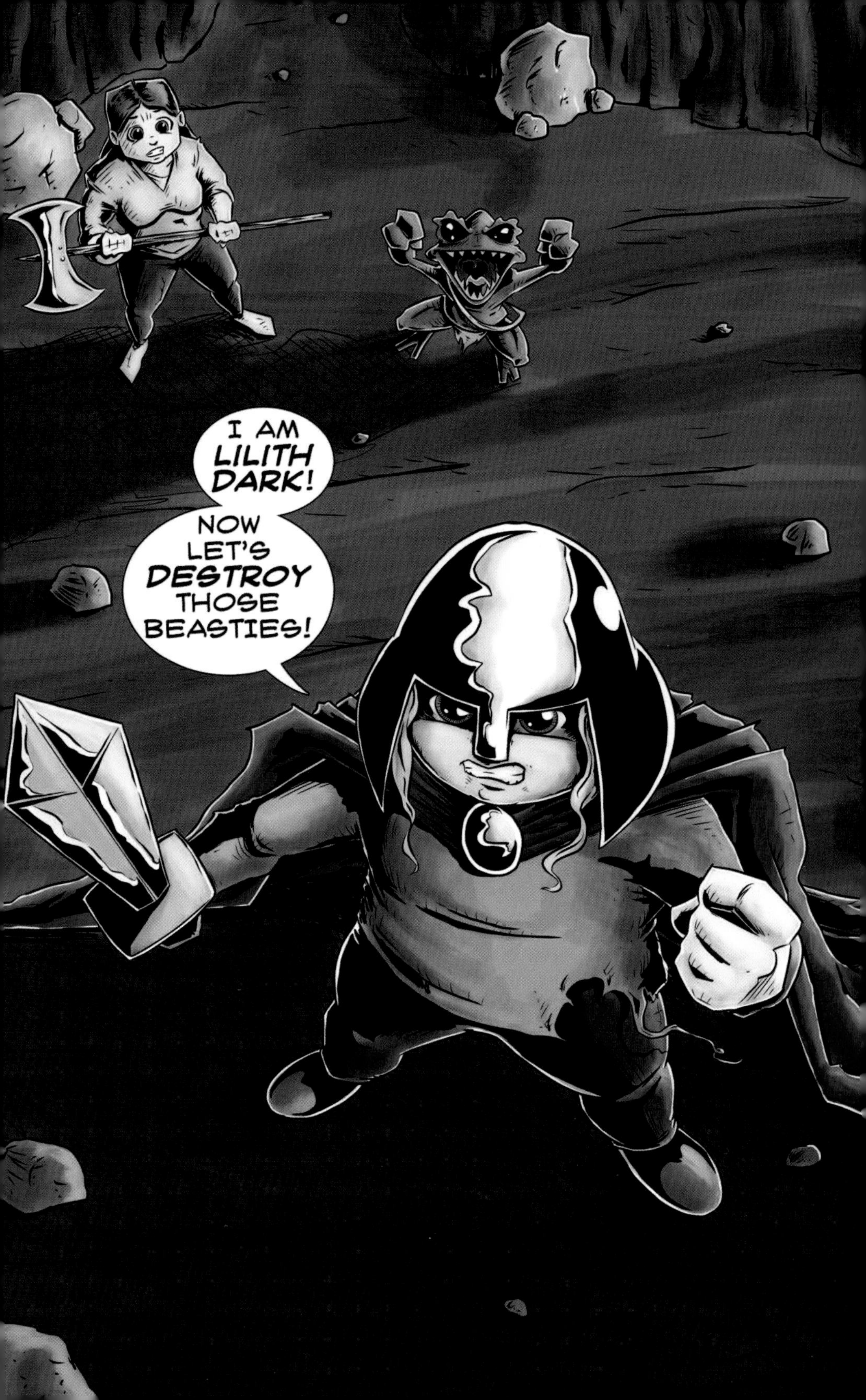

I AM LILITH DARK!
NOW LET'S DESTROY THOSE BEASTIES!

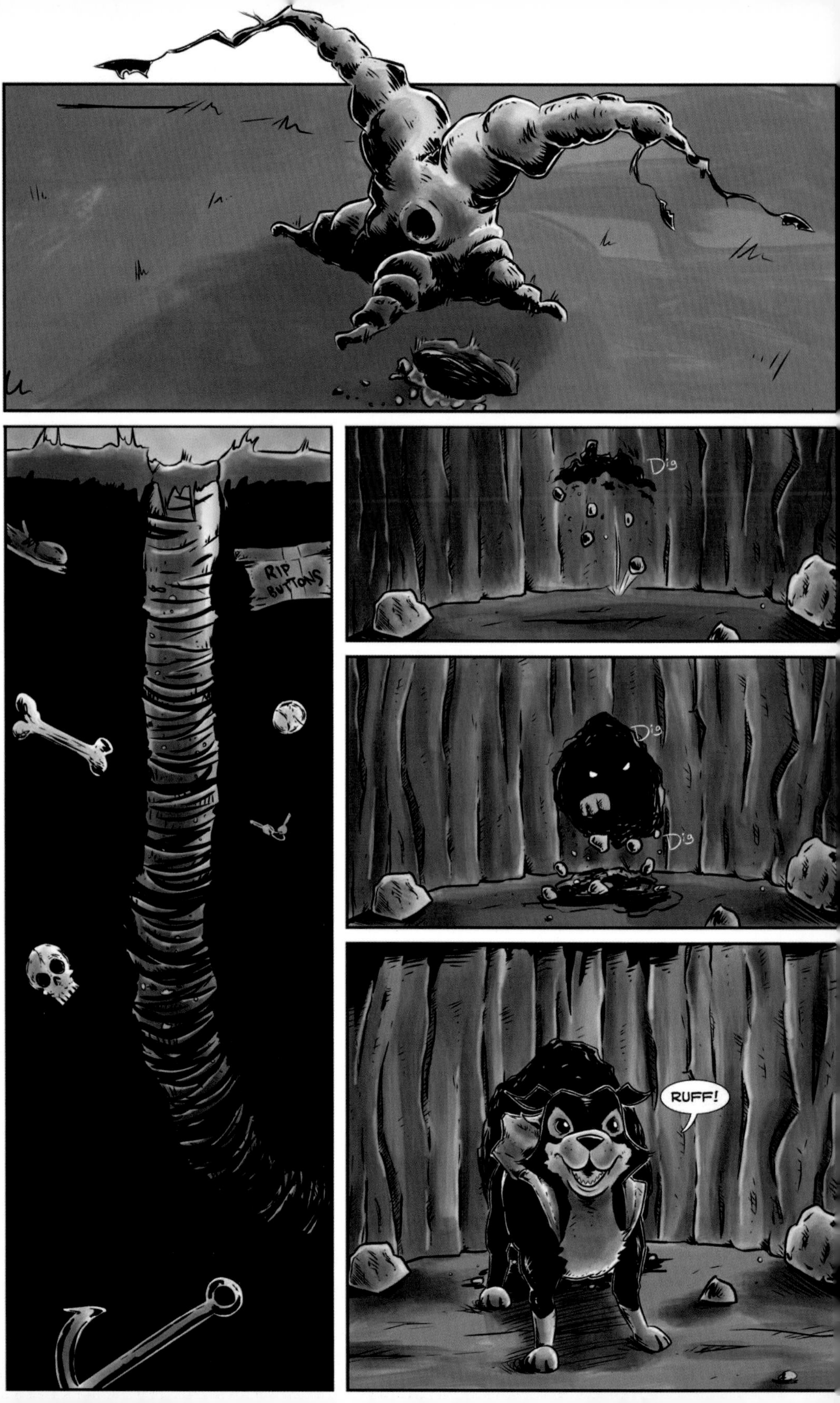
RIP
BUTTONS
Dig
Dig
Dig
RUFF!

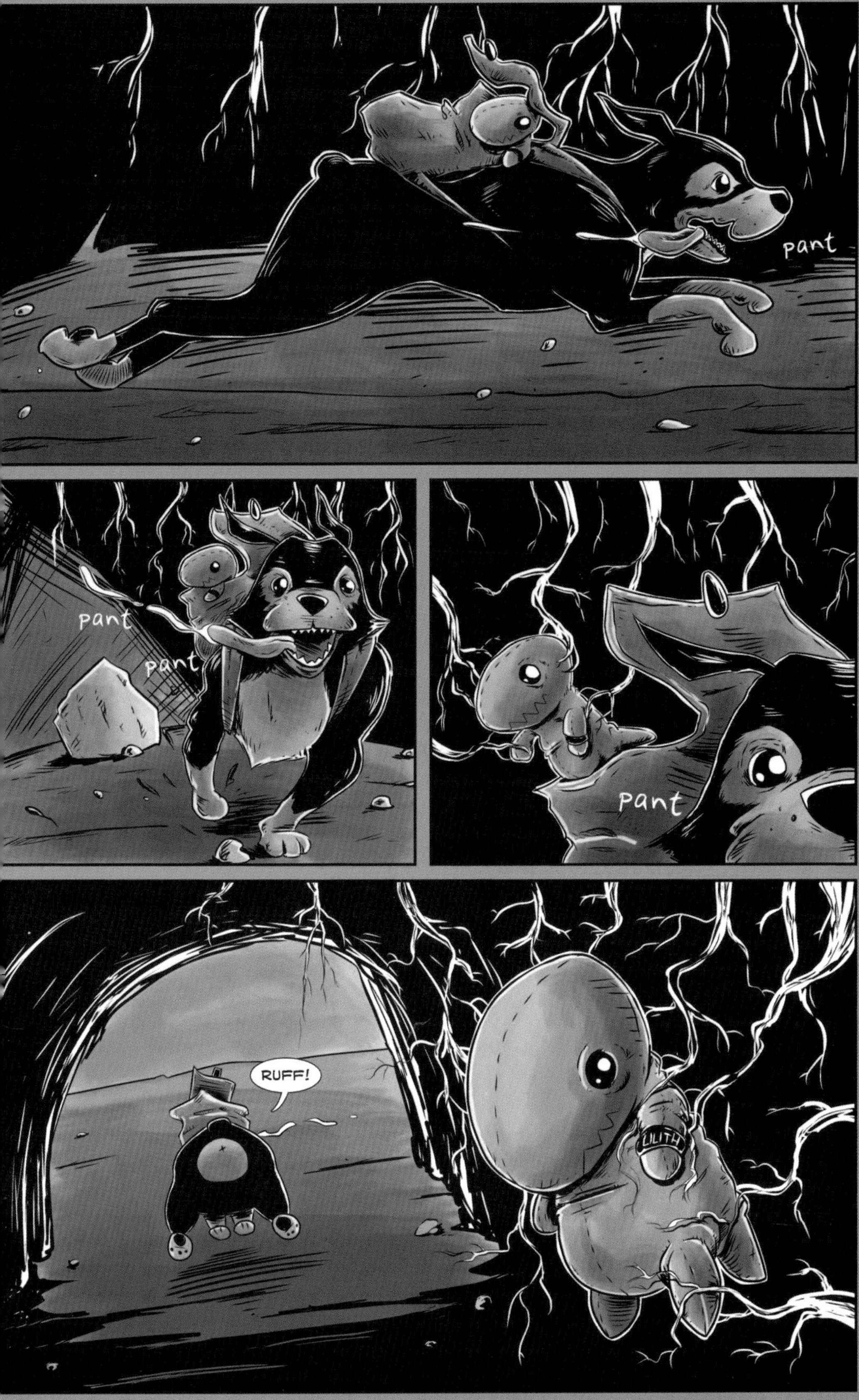
pant
pant
pant
pant
RUFF!
LILITH

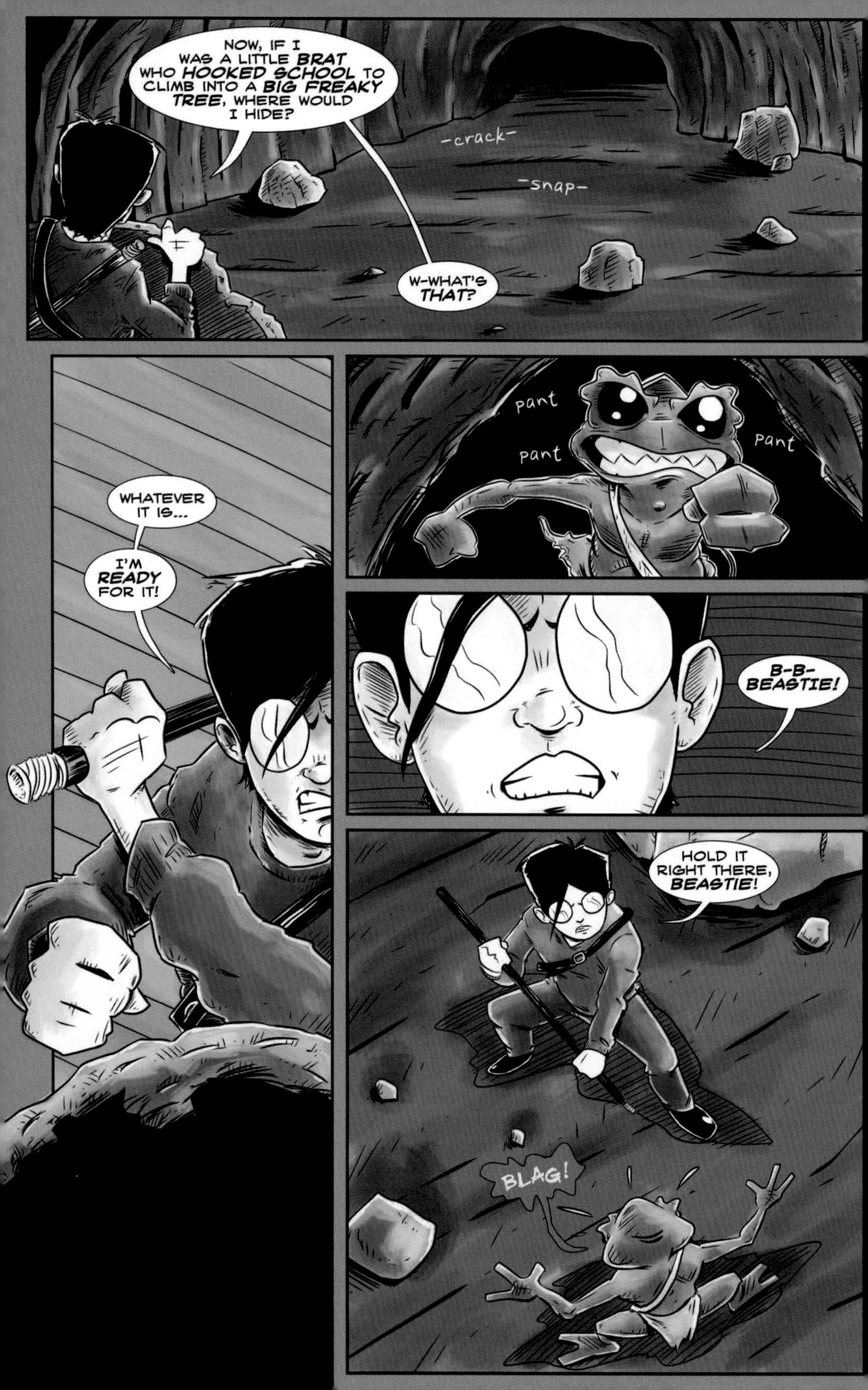
NOW, IF I WAS A LITTLE BRAT WHO HOOKED SCHOOL TO CLIMB INTO A BIG FREAKY TREE, WHERE WOULD I HIDE?
-crack-
-snap-
W-WHAT'S THAT?
WHATEVER IT IS...
I'M READY FOR IT!
pant
pant
pant
B-B-BEASTIE!
HOLD IT RIGHT THERE, BEASTIE!
BLAG!

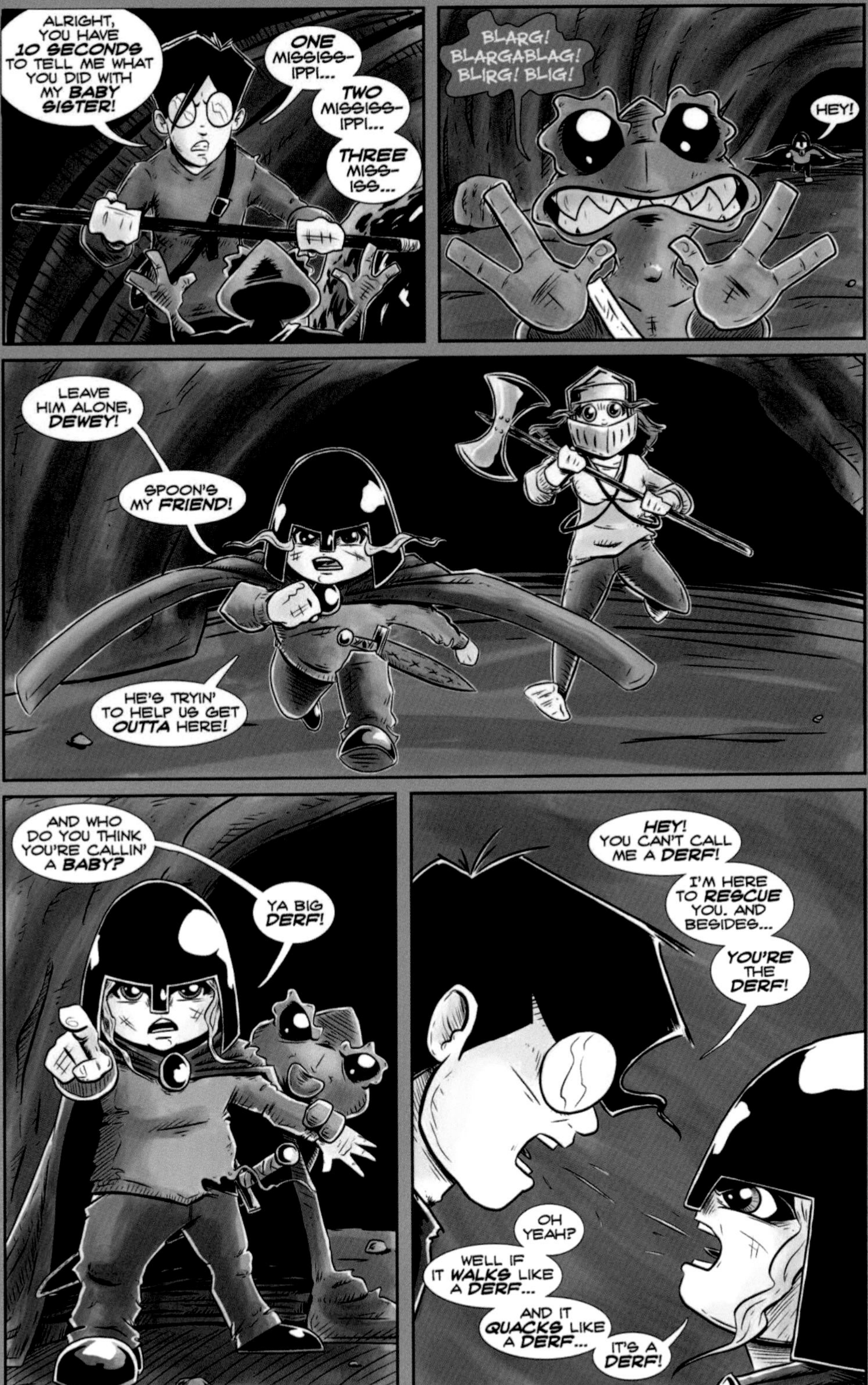
ALRIGHT, YOU HAVE 10 SECONDS TO TELL ME WHAT YOU DID WITH MY BABY SISTER!
ONE MISSISS-IPPI...
TWO MISSISS-IPPI...
THREE MISS-ISS...
BLARG! BLARGABLAG! BLIRG! BLIG!
HEY!
LEAVE HIM ALONE, DEWEY!
SPOON'S MY FRIEND!
HE'S TRYIN' TO HELP US GET OUTTA HERE!
AND WHO DO YOU THINK YOU'RE CALLIN' A BABY?
YA BIG DERF!
HEY! YOU CAN'T CALL ME A DERF!
I'M HERE TO RESCUE YOU. AND BESIDES...
YOU'RE THE DERF!
OH YEAH?
WELL IF IT WALKS LIKE A DERF...
AND IT QUACKS LIKE A DERF...
IT'S A DERF!

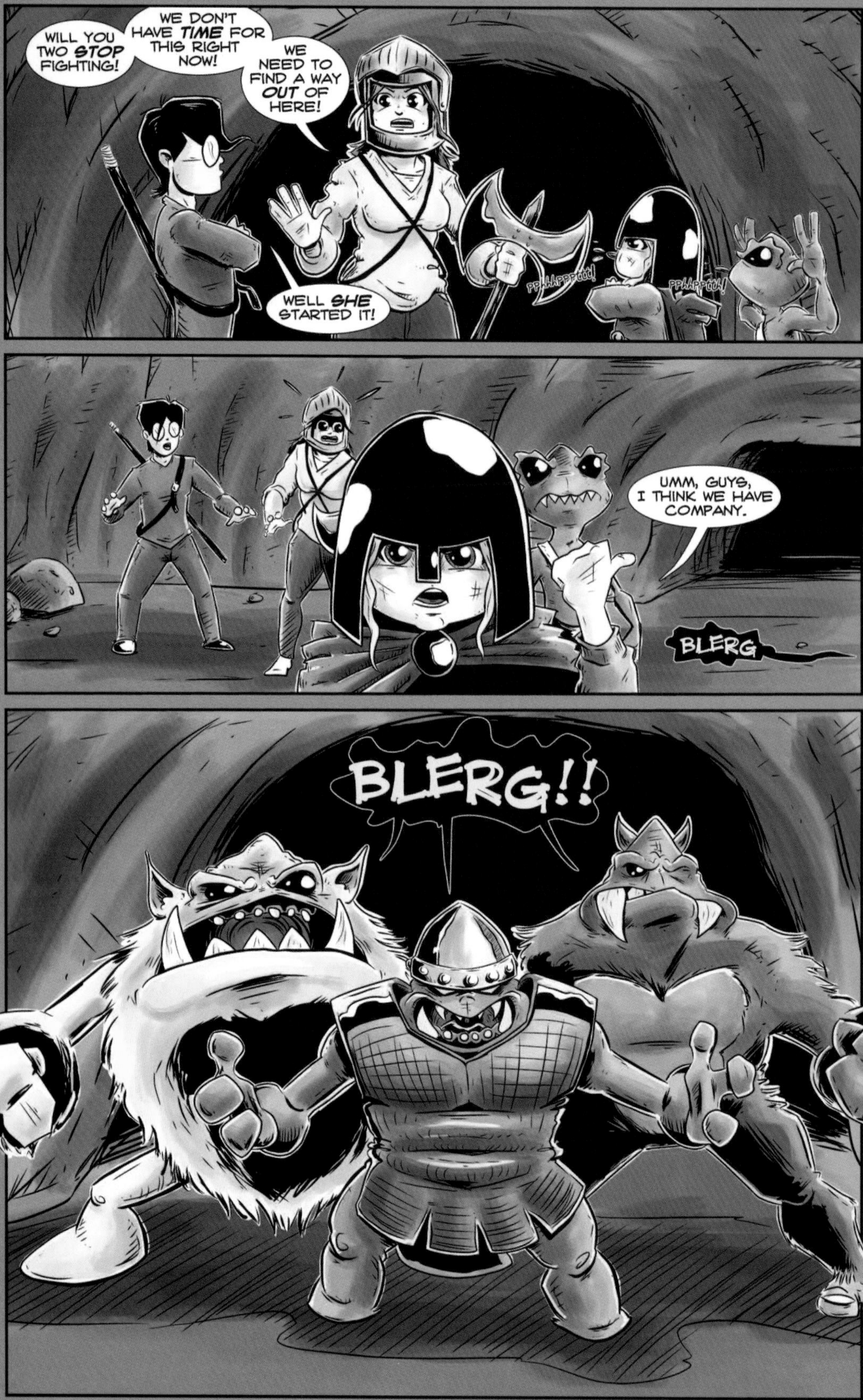

WILL YOU TWO STOP FIGHTING!
WE DON'T HAVE TIME FOR THIS RIGHT NOW!
WE NEED TO FIND A WAY OUT OF HERE!
WELL SHE STARTED IT!
PPhhhPPPttt!
PPhhPPtth!
UMM, GUYS, I THINK WE HAVE COMPANY.
BLERG
BLERG!!

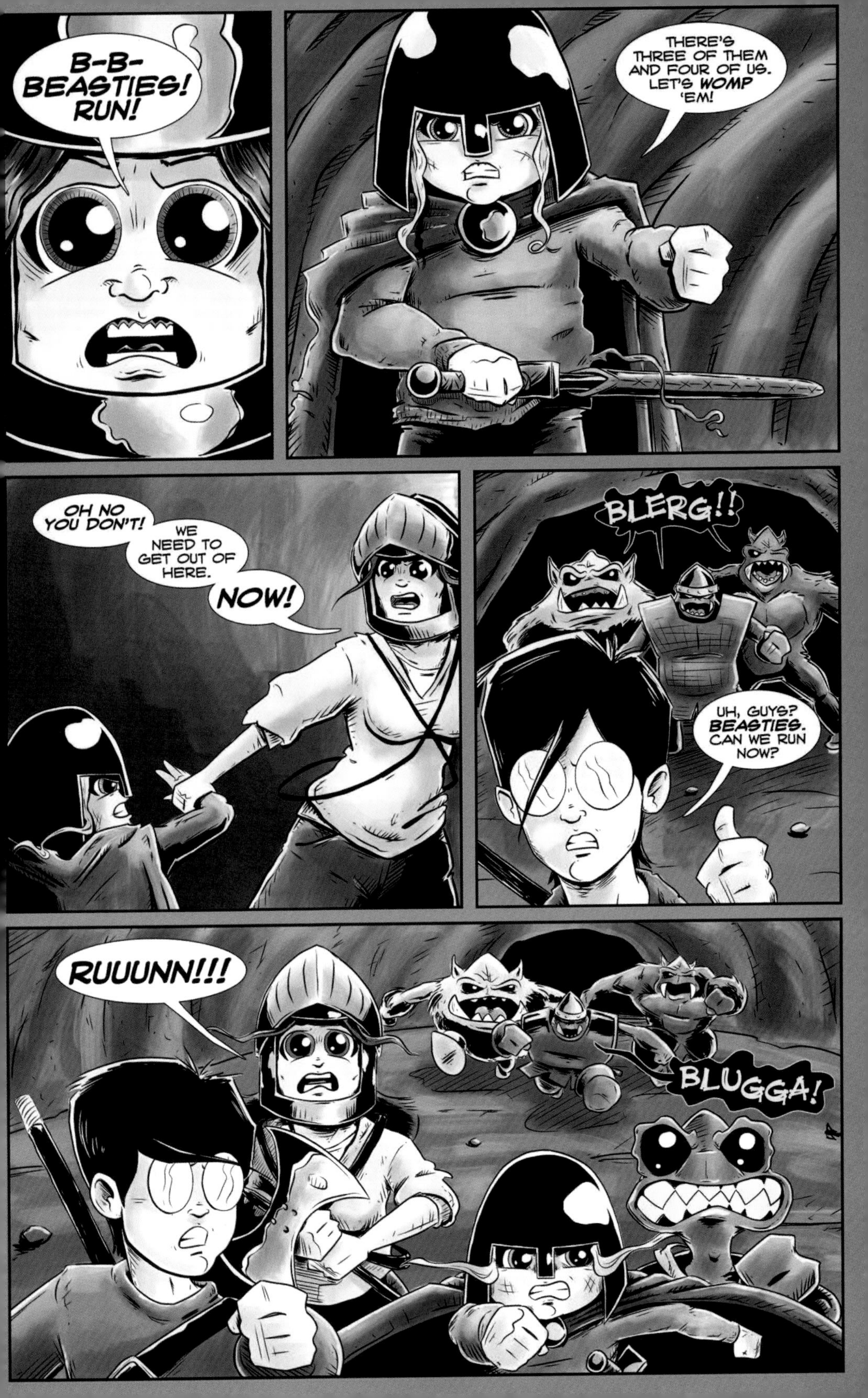
B-B-BEASTIES! RUN!
THERE'S THREE OF THEM AND FOUR OF US. LET'S WOMP 'EM!
OH NO YOU DON'T!
WE NEED TO GET OUT OF HERE.
NOW!
BLERG!!
UH, GUYS? BEASTIES. CAN WE RUN NOW?
RUUUNN!!!
BLUGGA!

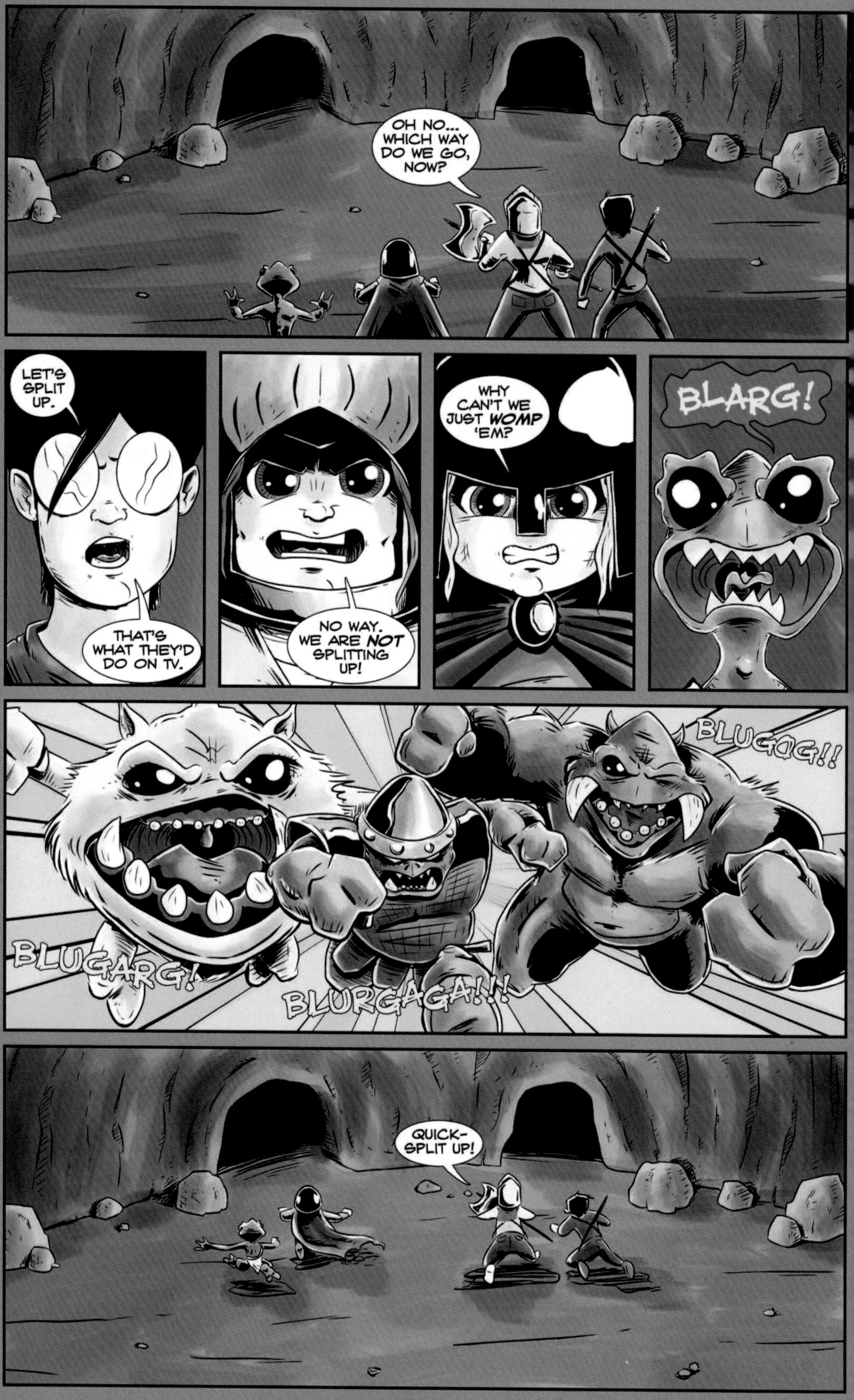
OH NO... WHICH WAY DO WE GO, NOW?
LET'S SPLIT UP.
THAT'S WHAT THEY'D DO ON TV.
NO WAY. WE ARE **NOT** SPLITTING UP!
WHY CAN'T WE JUST **WOMP** 'EM?
BLARG!
BLUGOG!!
BLUGARG!
BLURGAGA!!!
QUICK- SPLIT UP!

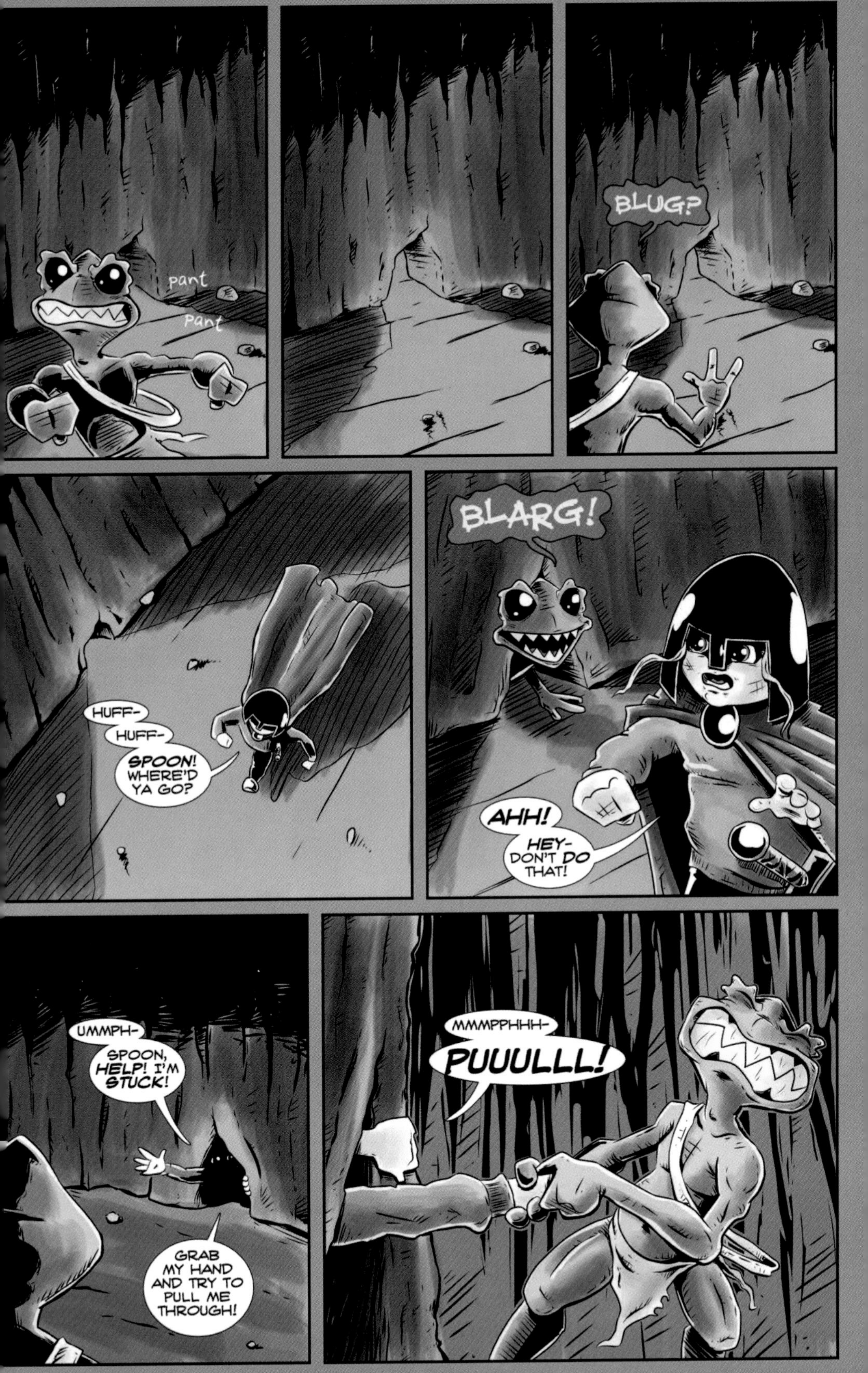
pant
pant
BLUG?
HUFF-
HUFF-
SPOON! WHERE'D YA GO?
BLARG!
AHH!
HEY- DON'T DO THAT!
UMMPH-
SPOON, HELP! I'M STUCK!
GRAB MY HAND AND TRY TO PULL ME THROUGH!
MMMPPHHH-
PUUULLL!

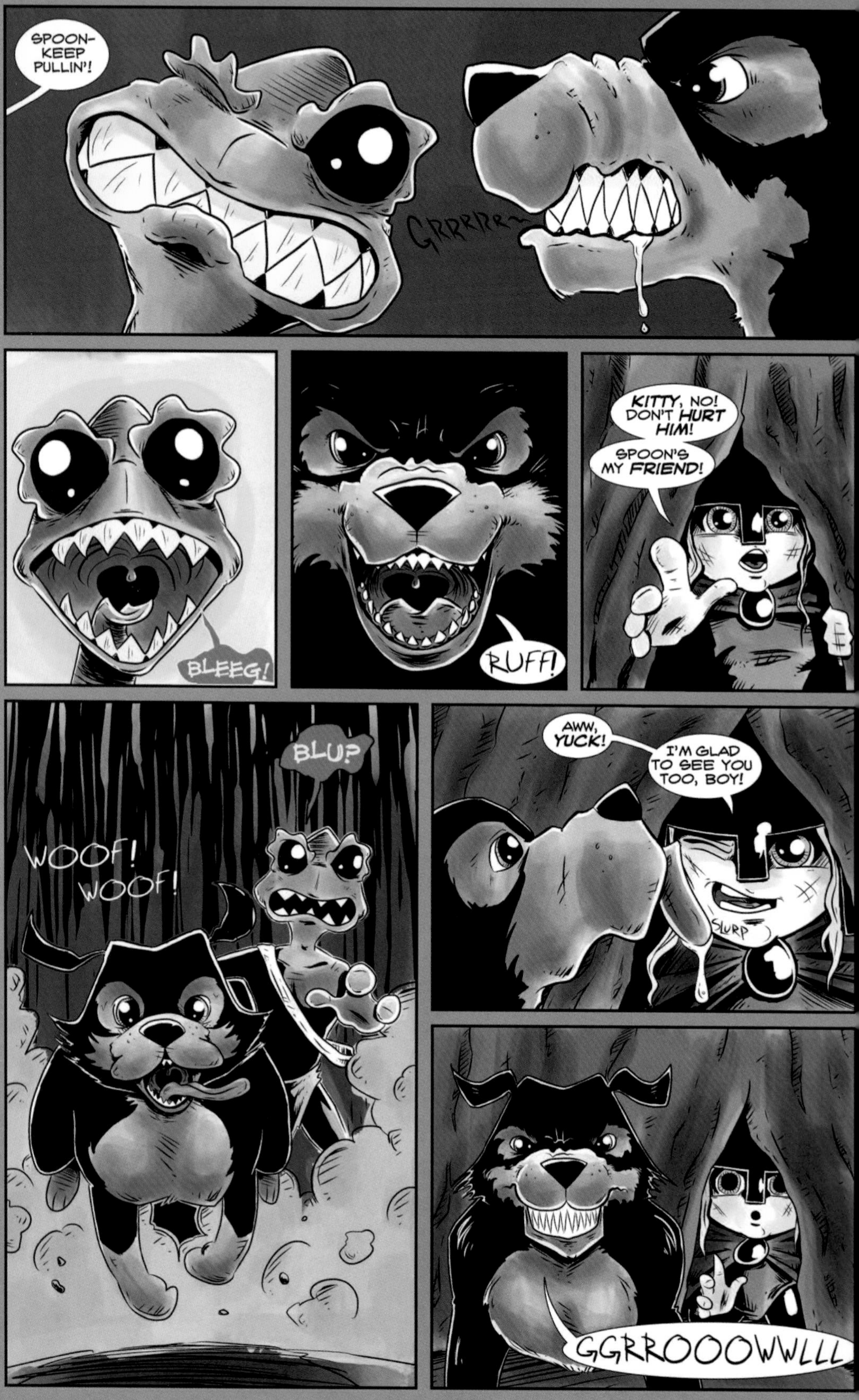

SPOON-KEEP PULLIN'!
GRRRRR~
BLEEG!
RUFF!
KITTY, NO! DON'T HURT HIM!
SPOON'S MY FRIEND!
BLU?
WOOF! WOOF!
AWW, YUCK!
I'M GLAD TO SEE YOU TOO, BOY!
SLURP
GGRROOOWLLL

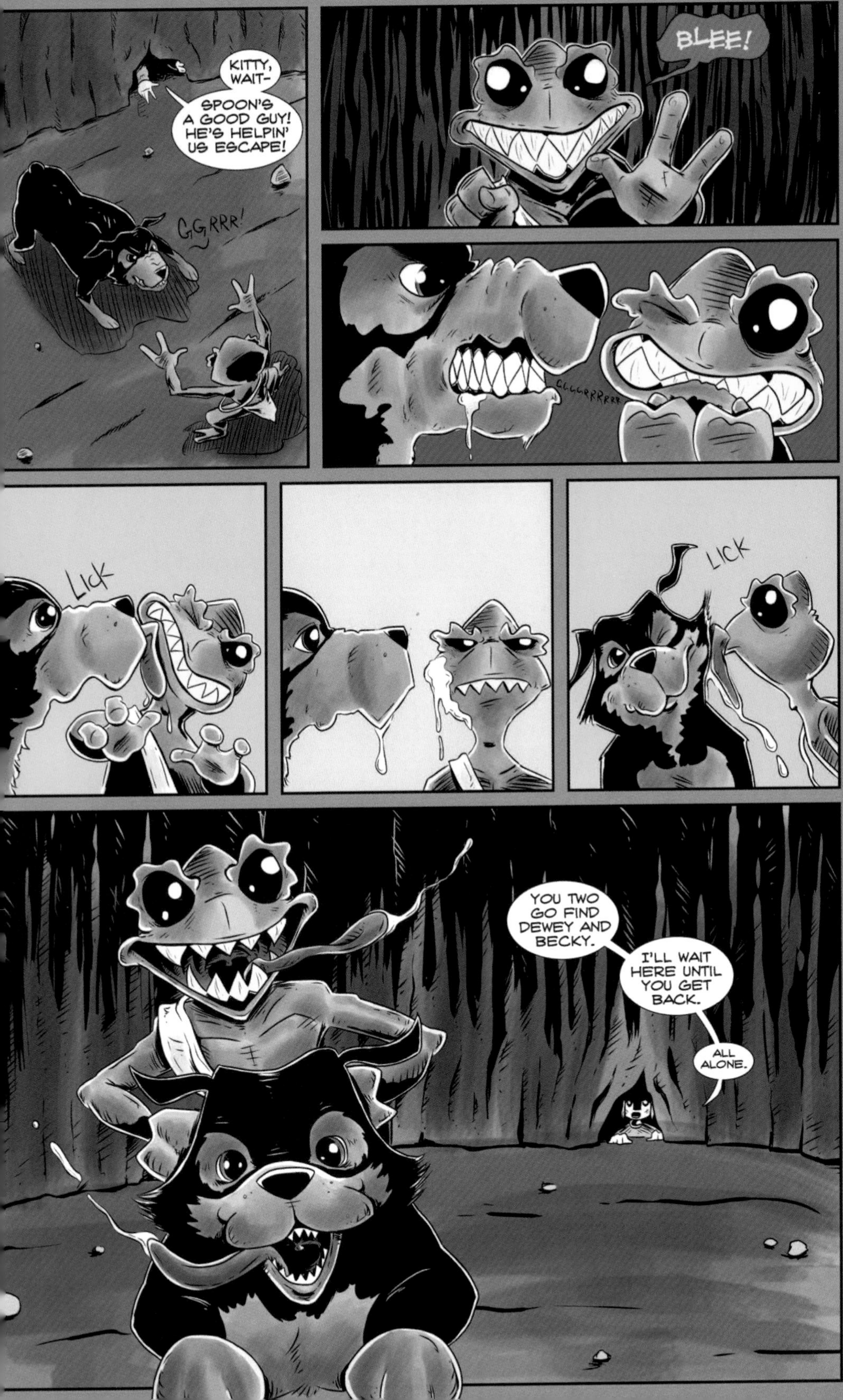
KITTY, WAIT–
SPOON'S A GOOD GUY! HE'S HELPIN' US ESCAPE!
GGRRR!
BLEE!
GGGGRRRRRR
LICK
LICK
YOU TWO GO FIND DEWEY AND BECKY.
I'LL WAIT HERE UNTIL YOU GET BACK.
ALL ALONE.

I SURE HOPE THEY FIND DEWEY AND BECKY QUICK.
SNAP
W-WHO'S THERE?
SHINK
C'MON OUT, YA FRAIDY CAT!
I'M IN THE MOOD FOR A WOMPIN'!
BLOG!
ALLOW ME TO INTRODUCE MYSELF, BEASTIE.
I AM LILITH DARK...
...SLAYER OF BEASTIES AND DESTROYER OF WICKED CREATURES!
...
...AND I'M NOT ASCARED OF YOU.

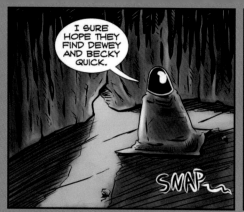

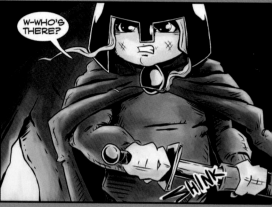

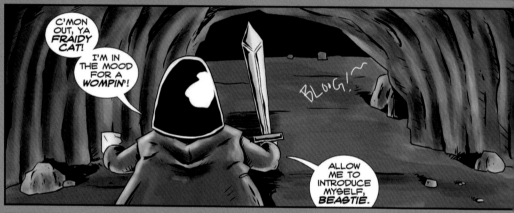

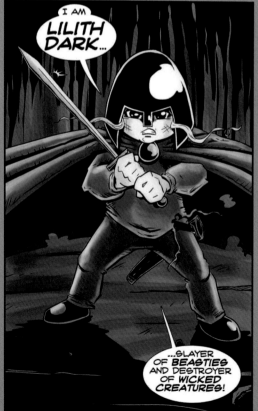

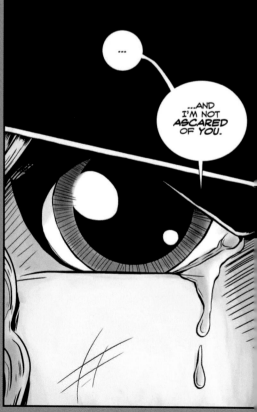

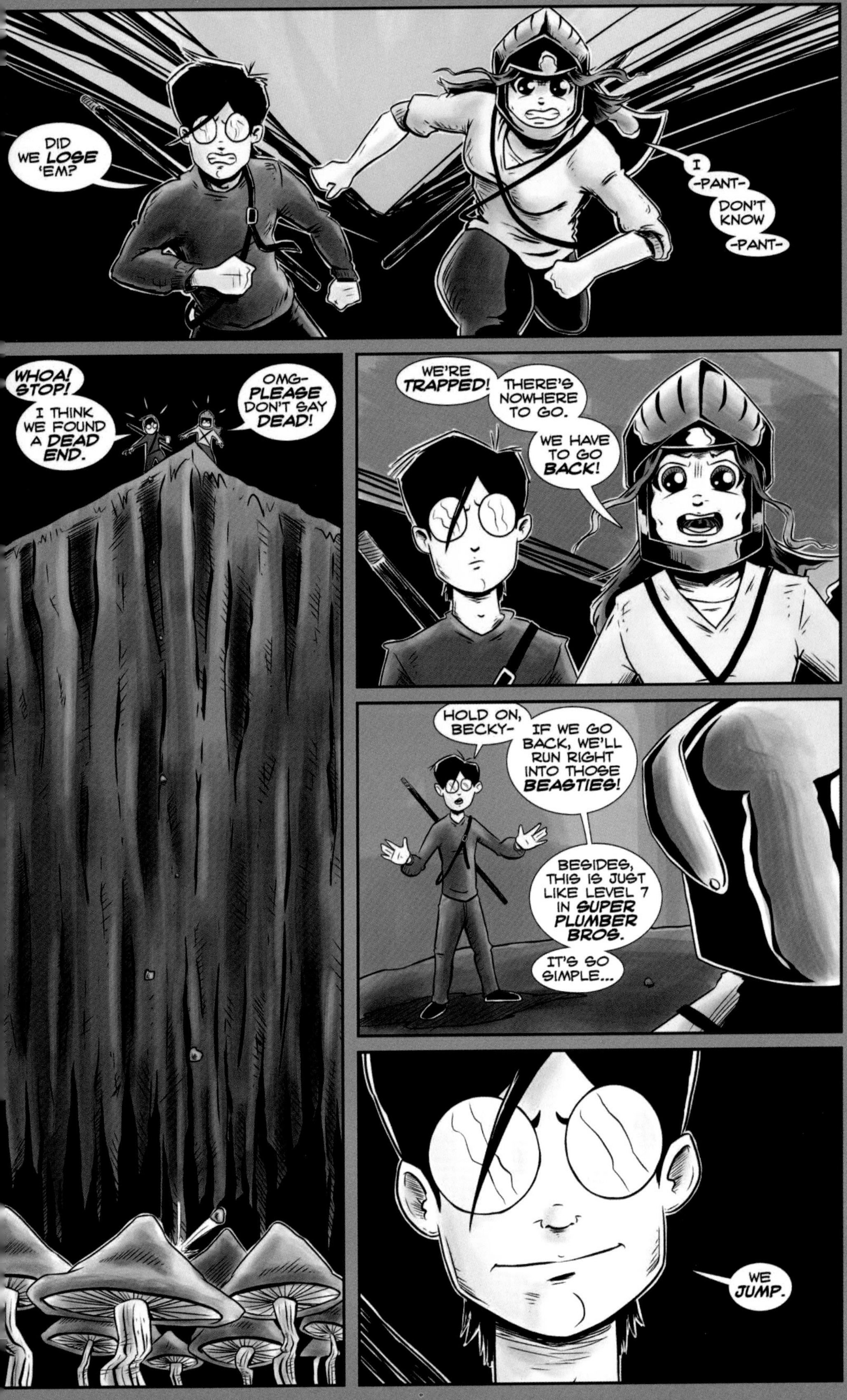
DID WE LOSE 'EM?
I -PANT- DON'T KNOW -PANT-
WHOA! STOP!
I THINK WE FOUND A DEAD END.
OMG- PLEASE DON'T SAY DEAD!
WE'RE TRAPPED!
THERE'S NOWHERE TO GO.
WE HAVE TO GO BACK!
HOLD ON, BECKY-
IF WE GO BACK, WE'LL RUN RIGHT INTO THOSE BEASTIES!
BESIDES, THIS IS JUST LIKE LEVEL 7 IN SUPER PLUMBER BROS.
IT'S SO SIMPLE...
WE JUMP.

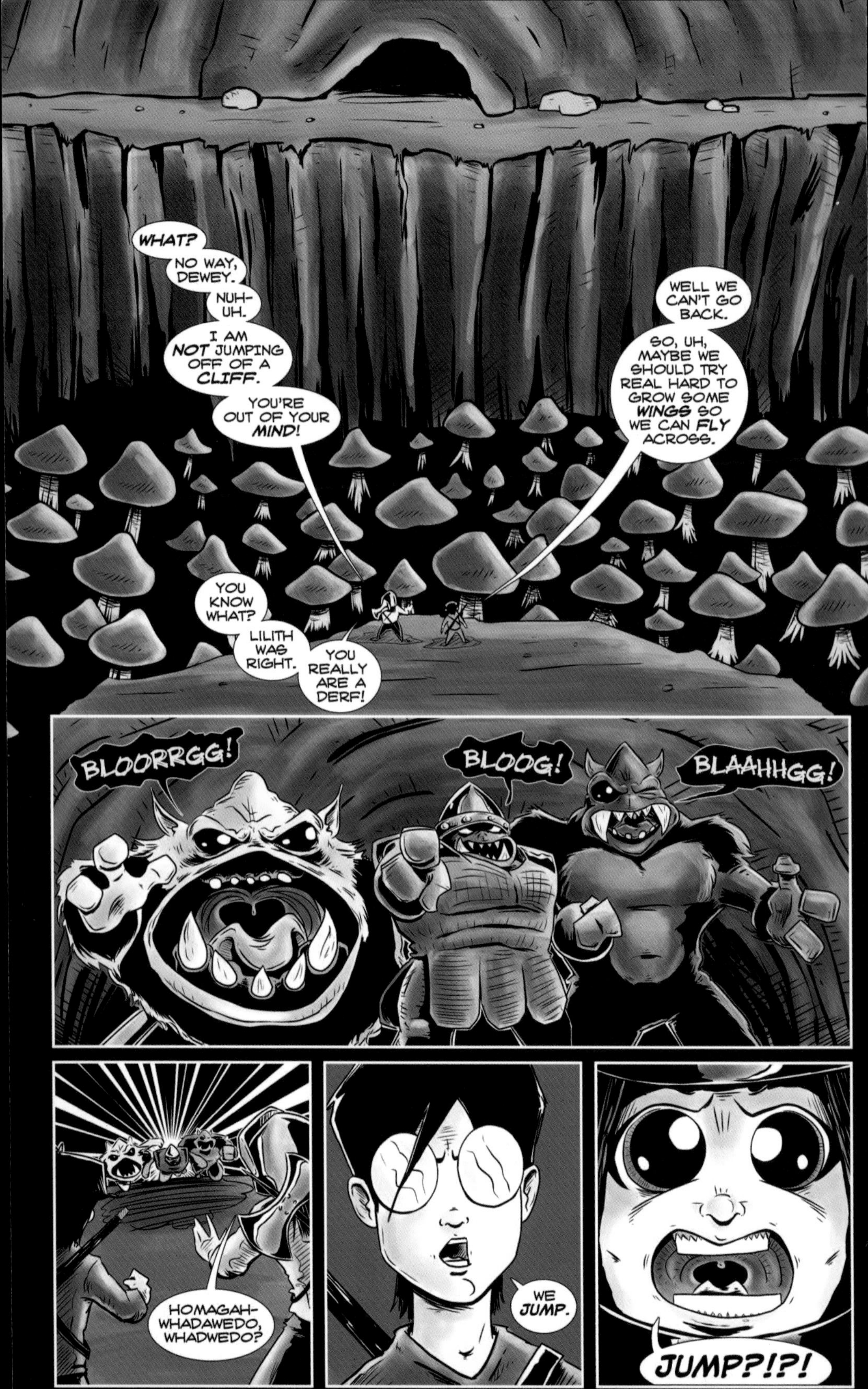

WHAT?
NO WAY, DEWEY.
NUH-UH.
I AM NOT JUMPING OFF OF A CLIFF.
YOU'RE OUT OF YOUR MIND!
WELL WE CAN'T GO BACK.
SO, UH, MAYBE WE SHOULD TRY REAL HARD TO GROW SOME WINGS SO WE CAN FLY ACROSS.
YOU KNOW WHAT?
LILITH WAS RIGHT.
YOU REALLY ARE A DERF!
BLOORRGG!
BLOOG!
BLAAHHGG!
HOMAGAH-WHADAWEDO, WHADWEDO?
WE JUMP.
JUMP?!?!

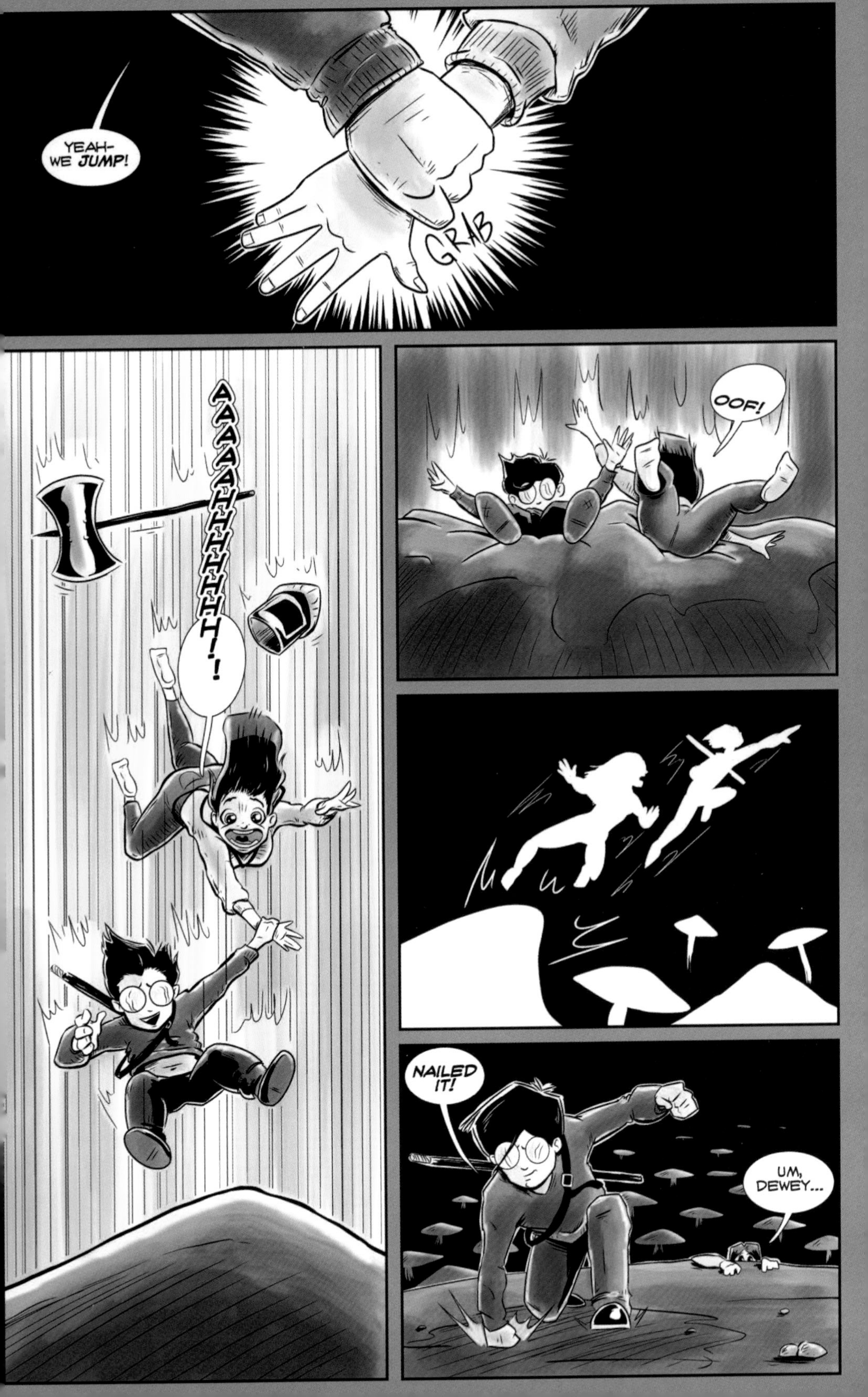
YEAH-
WE JUMP!
GRAB
AAAAAHHHHHHHH!!
OOF!
NAILED IT!
UM, DEWEY...

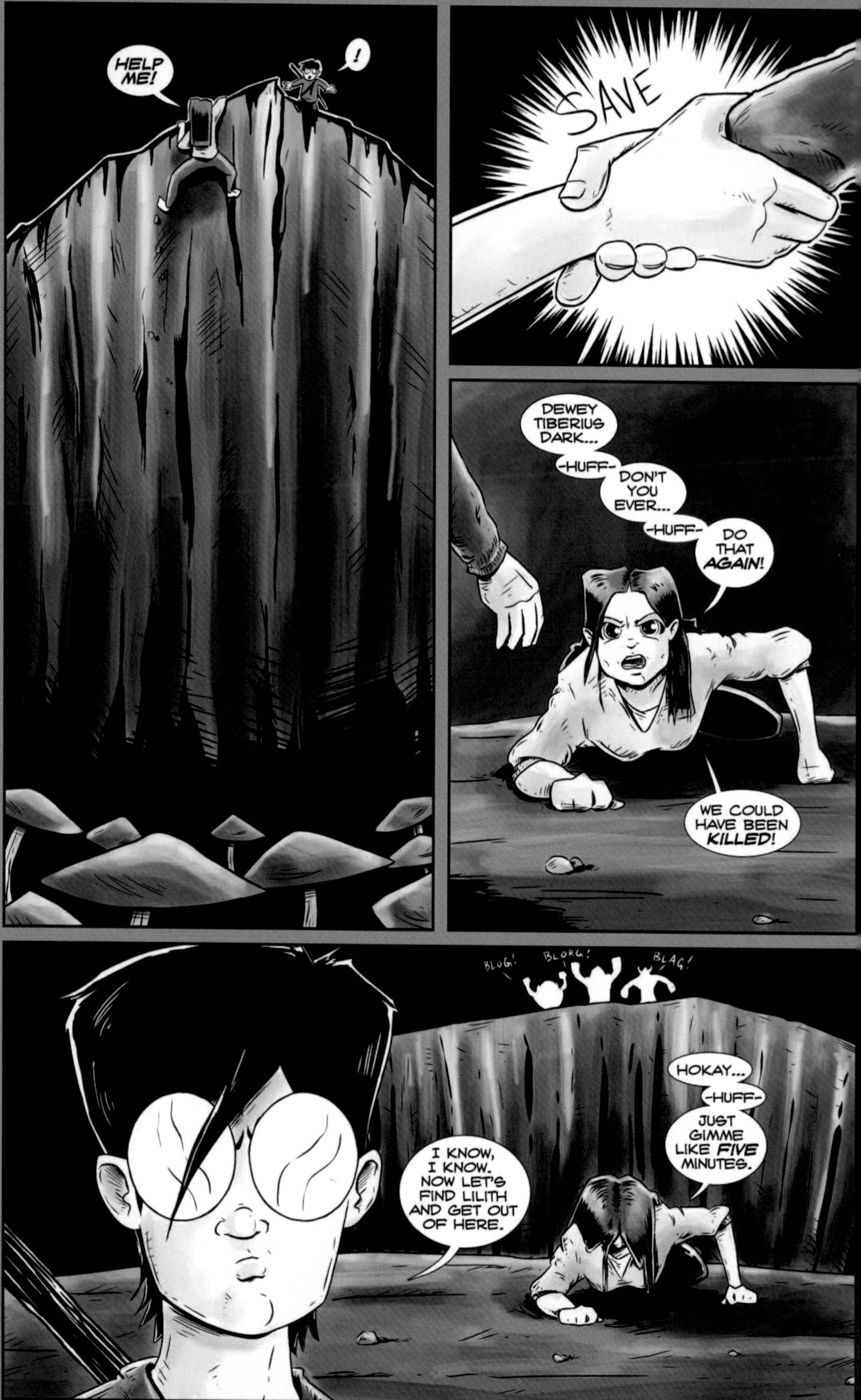
HELP ME!
!
SAVE
DEWEY TIBERIUS DARK...
-HUFF-
DON'T YOU EVER...
-HUFF-
DO THAT AGAIN!
WE COULD HAVE BEEN KILLED!
BLOG!
BLORG!
BLAG!
HOKAY...
-HUFF-
JUST GIMME LIKE FIVE MINUTES.
I KNOW, I KNOW. NOW LET'S FIND LILITH AND GET OUT OF HERE.

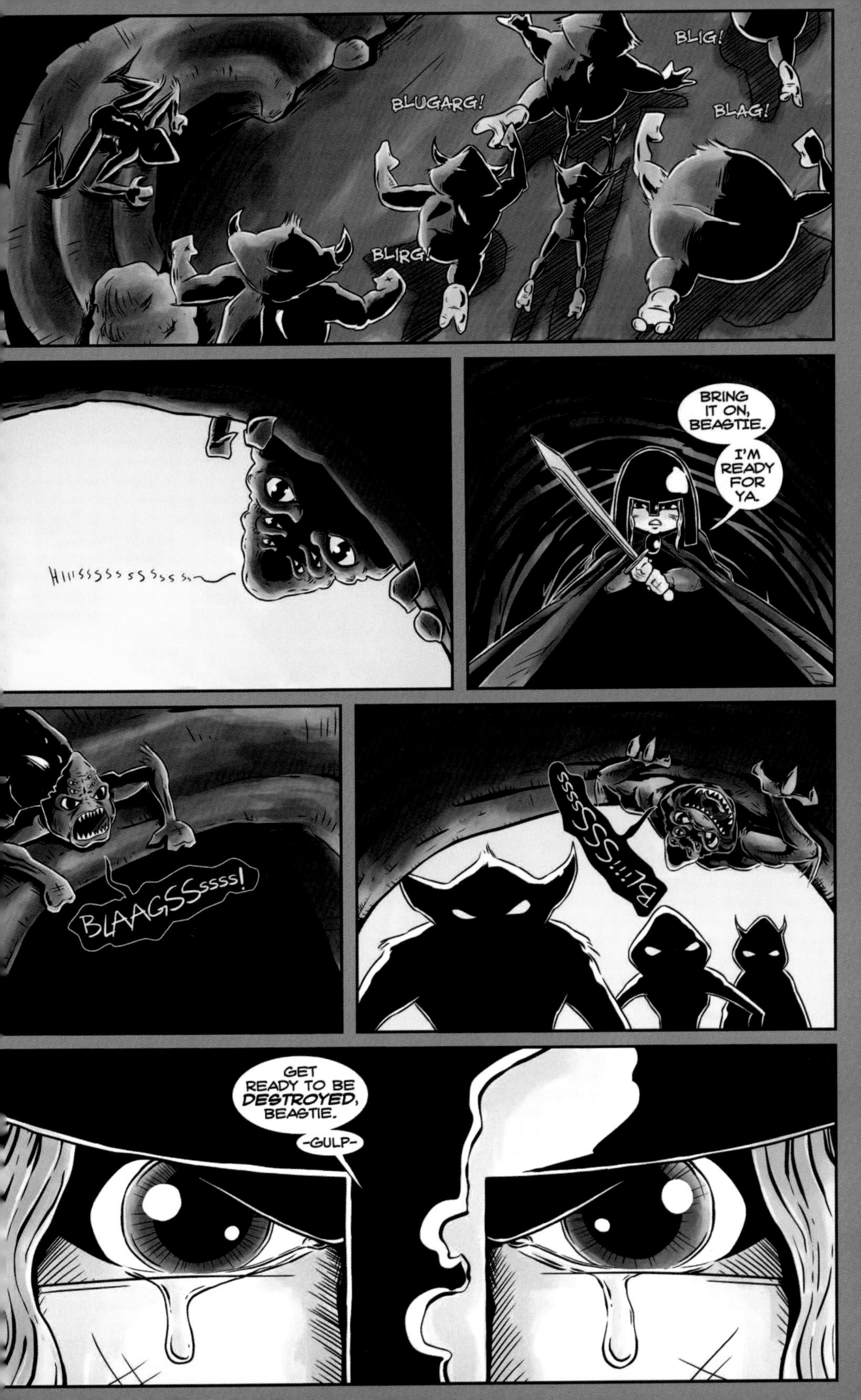
BLIG!
BLUGARG!
BLAG!
BLIRG!
HIIISSSSSSSSSSS
BRING IT ON, BEASTIE.
I'M READY FOR YA.
BLAAGSSssss!
BLIIISSSsssss
GET READY TO BE *DESTROYED*, BEASTIE.
-GULP-

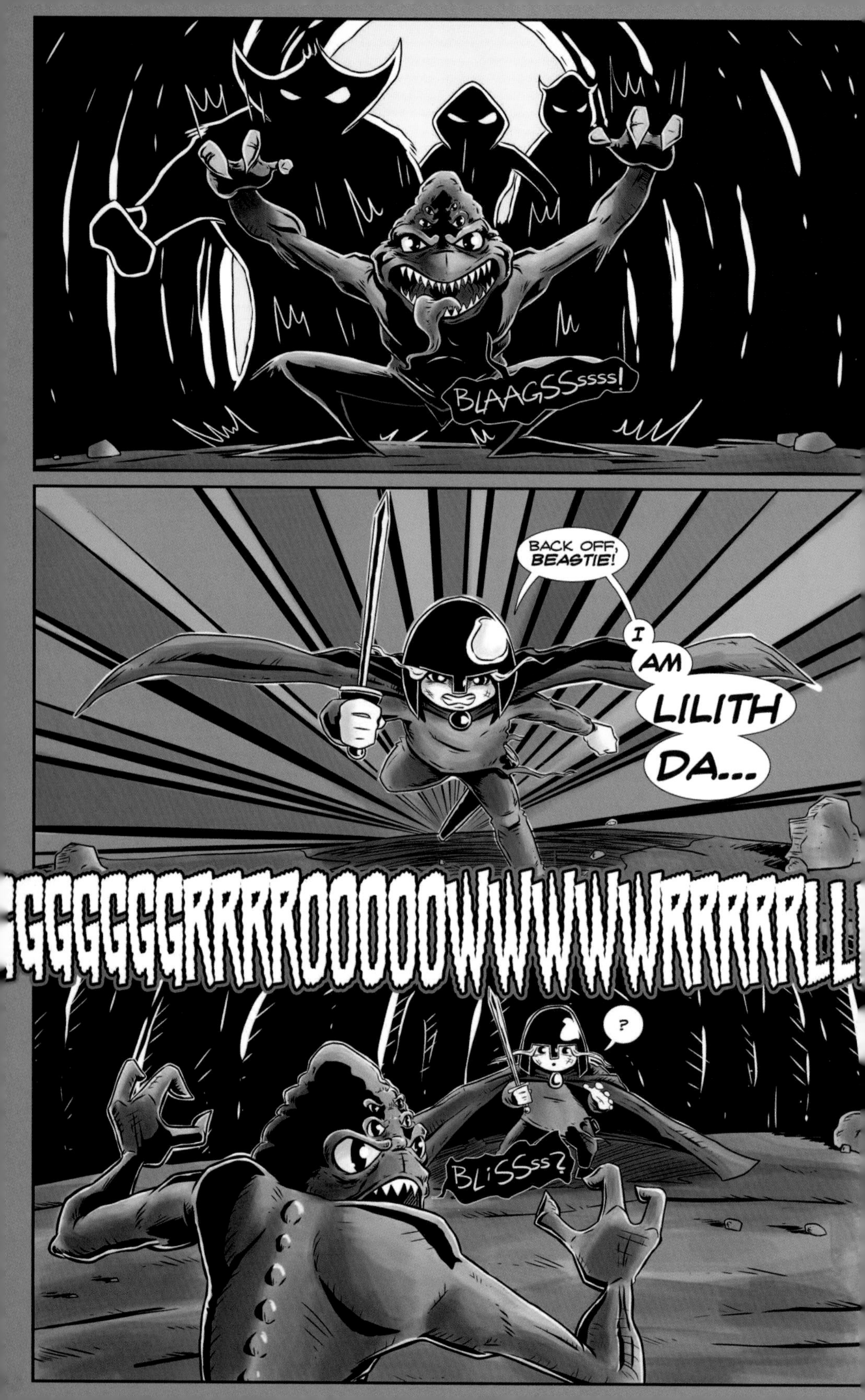
BLAAGSSssss!
BACK OFF, BEASTIE!
I AM LILITH DA...
GGGGGGRRRROOOOOOWWWWWWRRRRRLL
?
BLISSss?

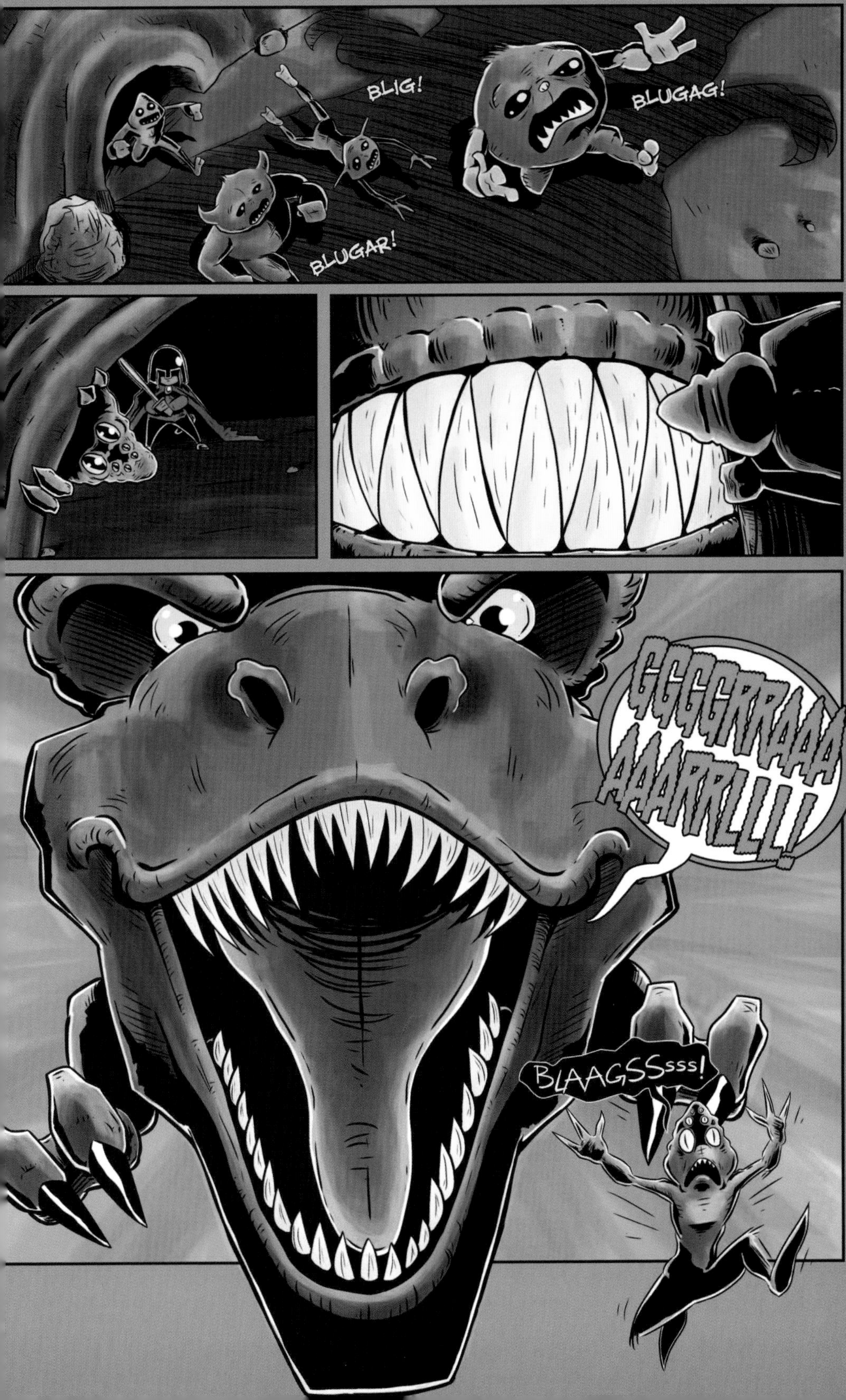
BLIG!
BLUGAG!
BLUGAR!
GGGGRRAAAAAARRLLL!!
BLAAGSSsss!

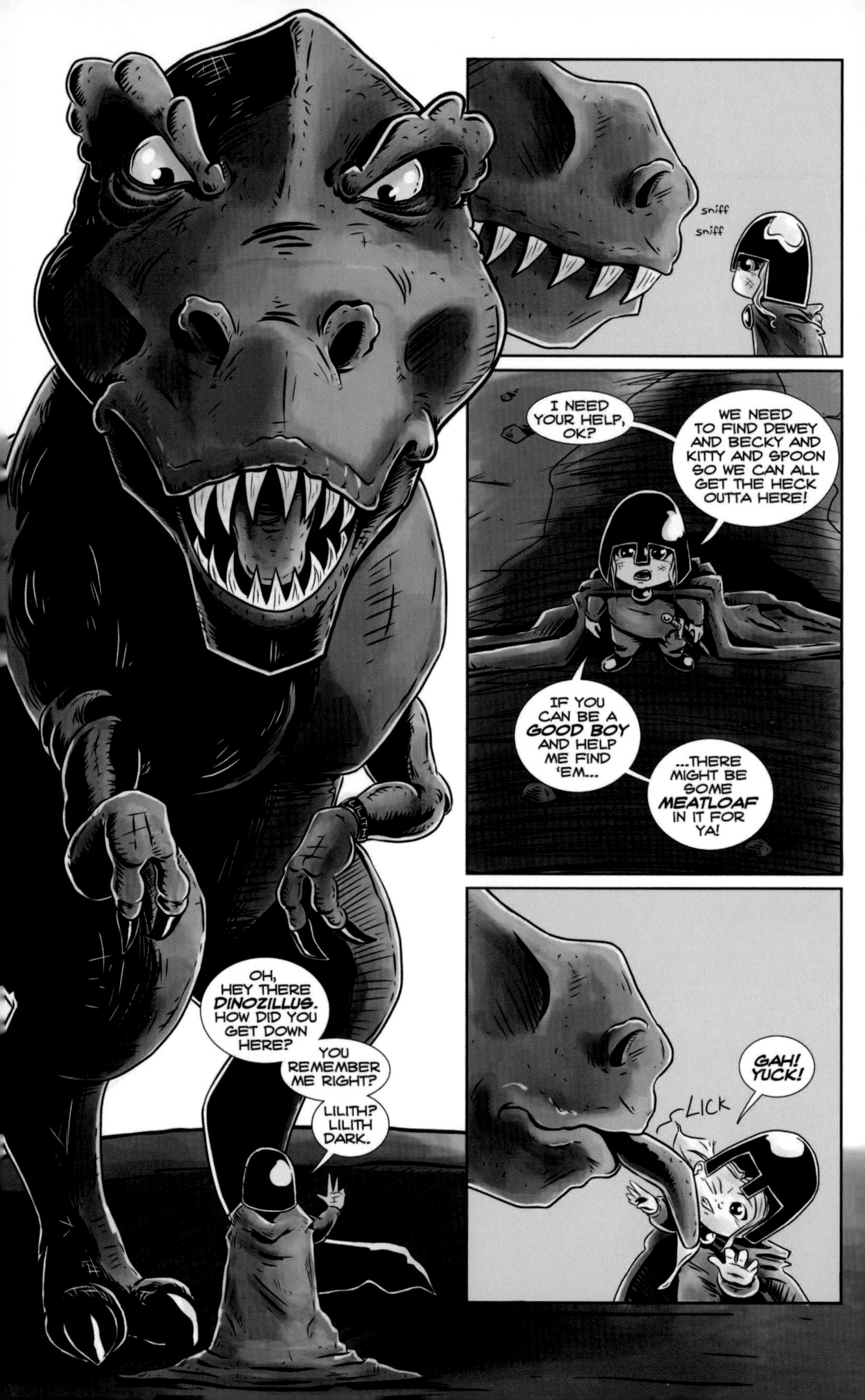

OH, HEY THERE **DINOZILLUS**. HOW DID YOU GET DOWN HERE?
YOU REMEMBER ME RIGHT?
LILITH? LILITH DARK.
sniff
sniff
I NEED YOUR HELP, OK?
WE NEED TO FIND DEWEY AND BECKY AND KITTY AND SPOON SO WE CAN ALL GET THE HECK OUTTA HERE!
IF YOU CAN BE A **GOOD BOY** AND HELP ME FIND 'EM...
...THERE MIGHT BE SOME **MEATLOAF** IN IT FOR YA!
LICK
GAH! YUCK!

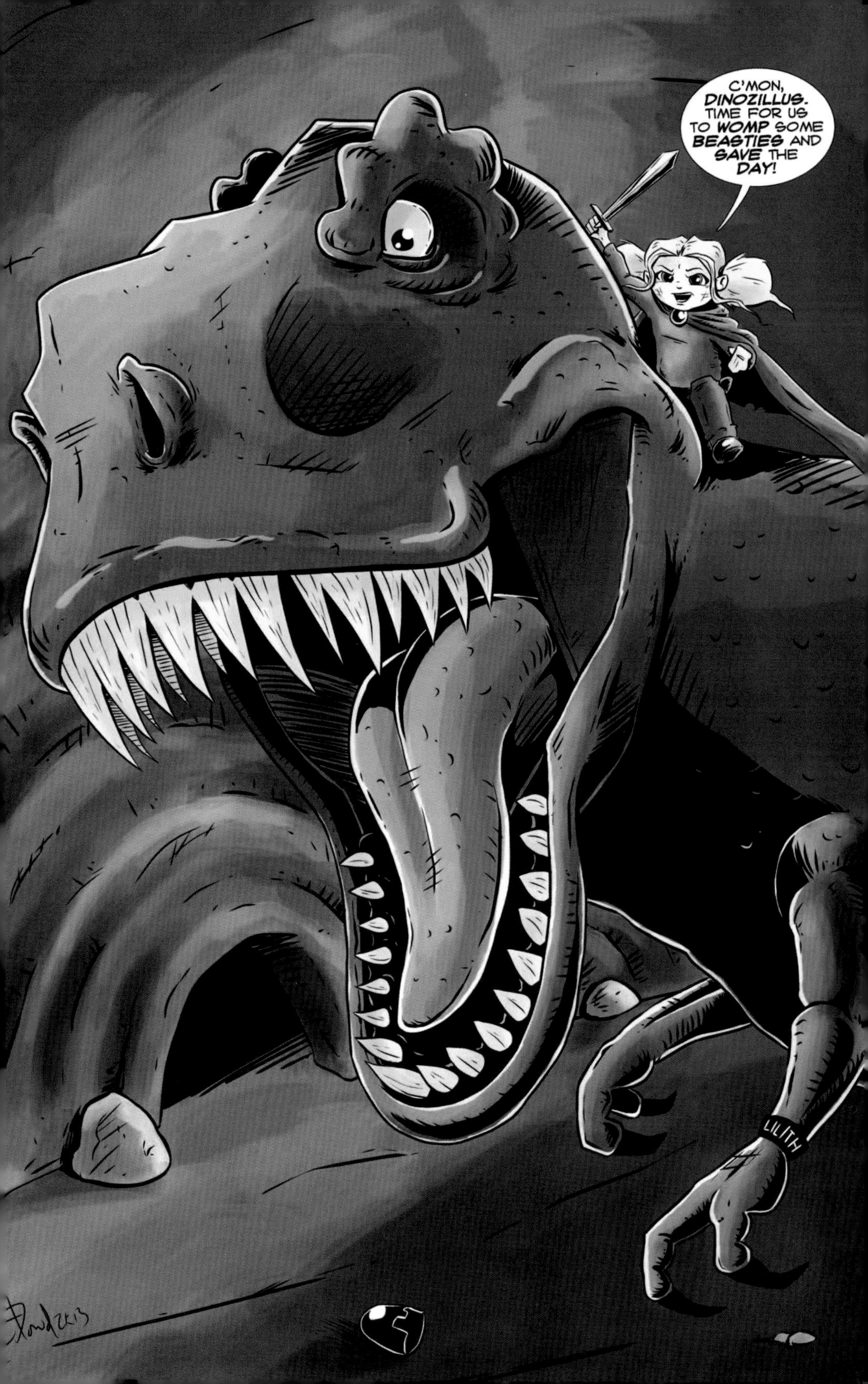
C'MON, DINOZILLUS. TIME FOR US TO WOMP SOME BEASTIES AND SAVE THE DAY!
LILITH

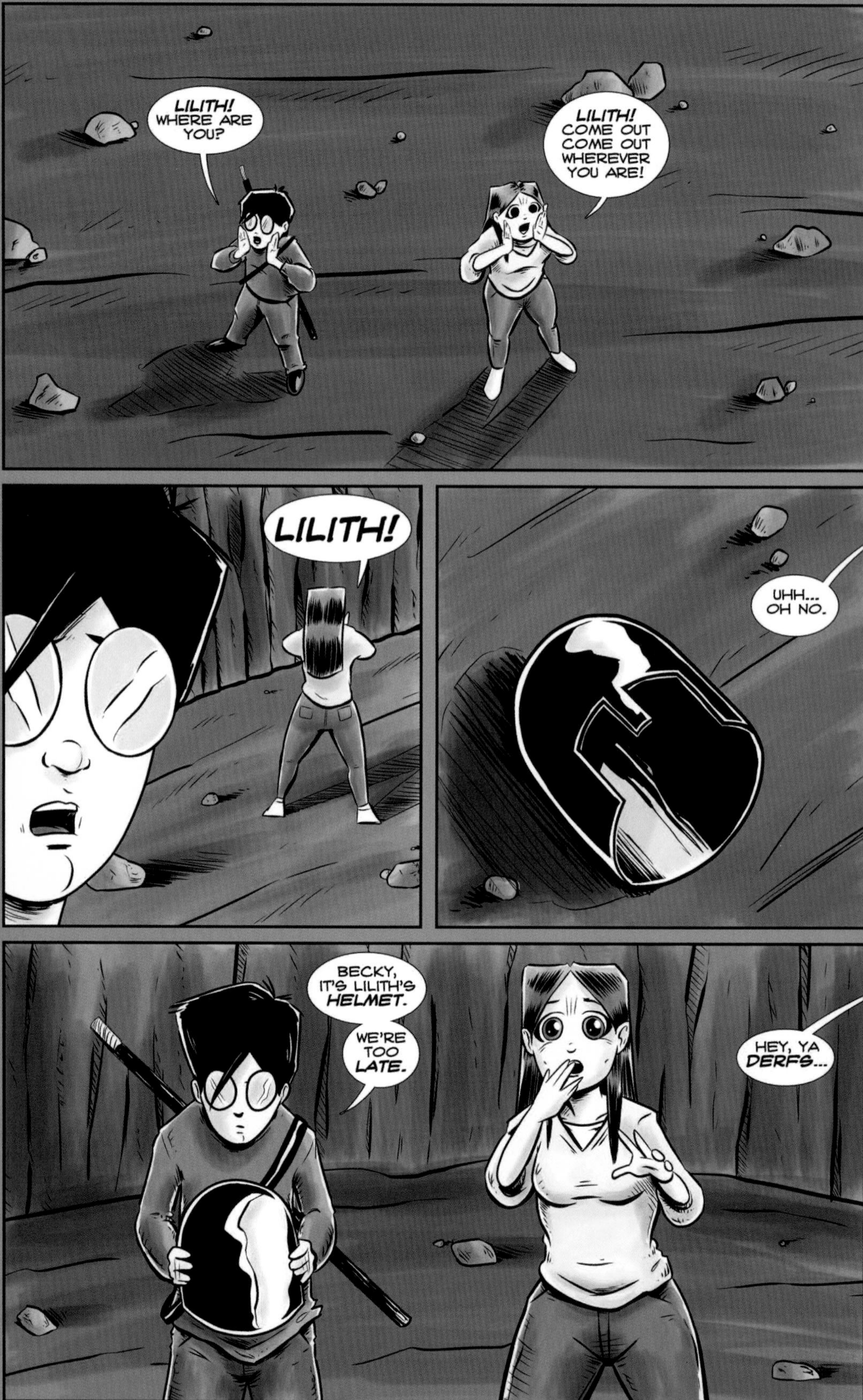
LILITH! WHERE ARE YOU?
LILITH! COME OUT COME OUT WHEREVER YOU ARE!
LILITH!
UHH... OH NO.
BECKY, IT'S LILITH'S HELMET.
WE'RE TOO LATE.
HEY, YA DERFS...

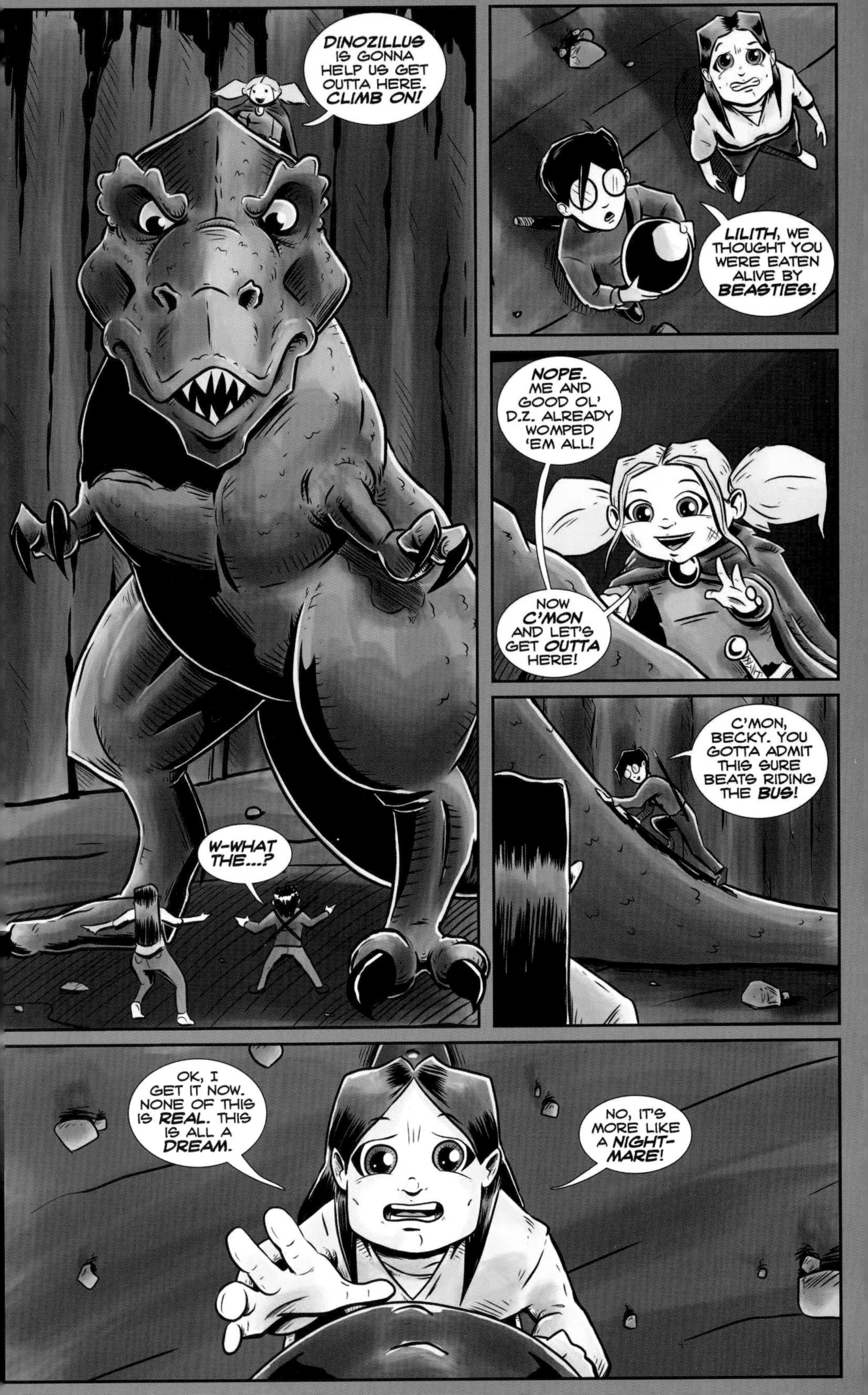
DINOZILLUS IS GONNA HELP US GET OUTTA HERE. CLIMB ON!
W-WHAT THE...?
LILITH, WE THOUGHT YOU WERE EATEN ALIVE BY BEASTIES!
NOPE. ME AND GOOD OL' D.Z. ALREADY WOMPED 'EM ALL!
NOW C'MON AND LET'S GET OUTTA HERE!
C'MON, BECKY. YOU GOTTA ADMIT THIS SURE BEATS RIDING THE BUS!
OK, I GET IT NOW. NONE OF THIS IS REAL. THIS IS ALL A DREAM.
NO, IT'S MORE LIKE A NIGHT-MARE!

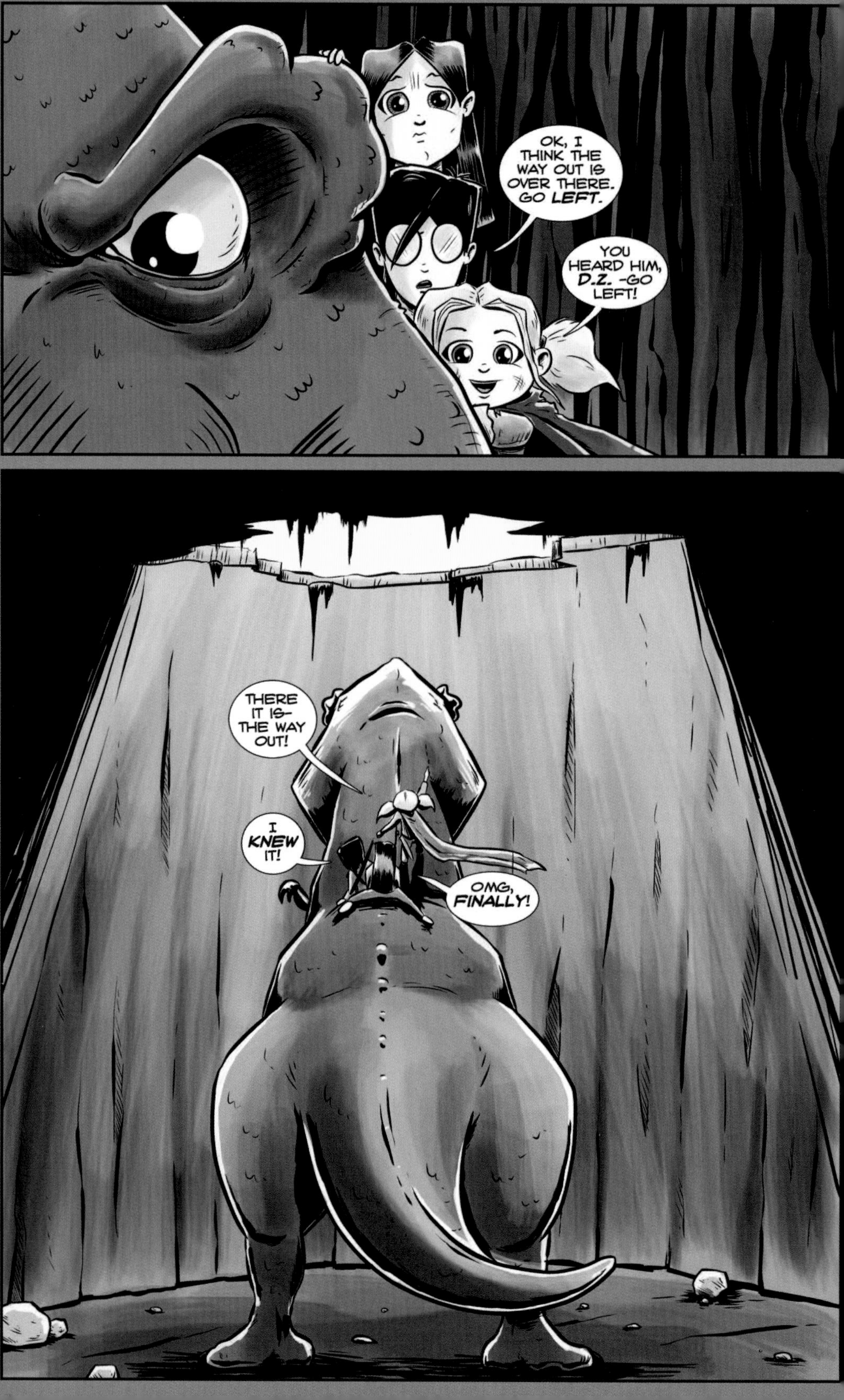
OK, I THINK THE WAY OUT IS OVER THERE. GO LEFT.
YOU HEARD HIM, D.Z. -GO LEFT!
THERE IT IS-THE WAY OUT!
I KNEW IT!
OMG, FINALLY!

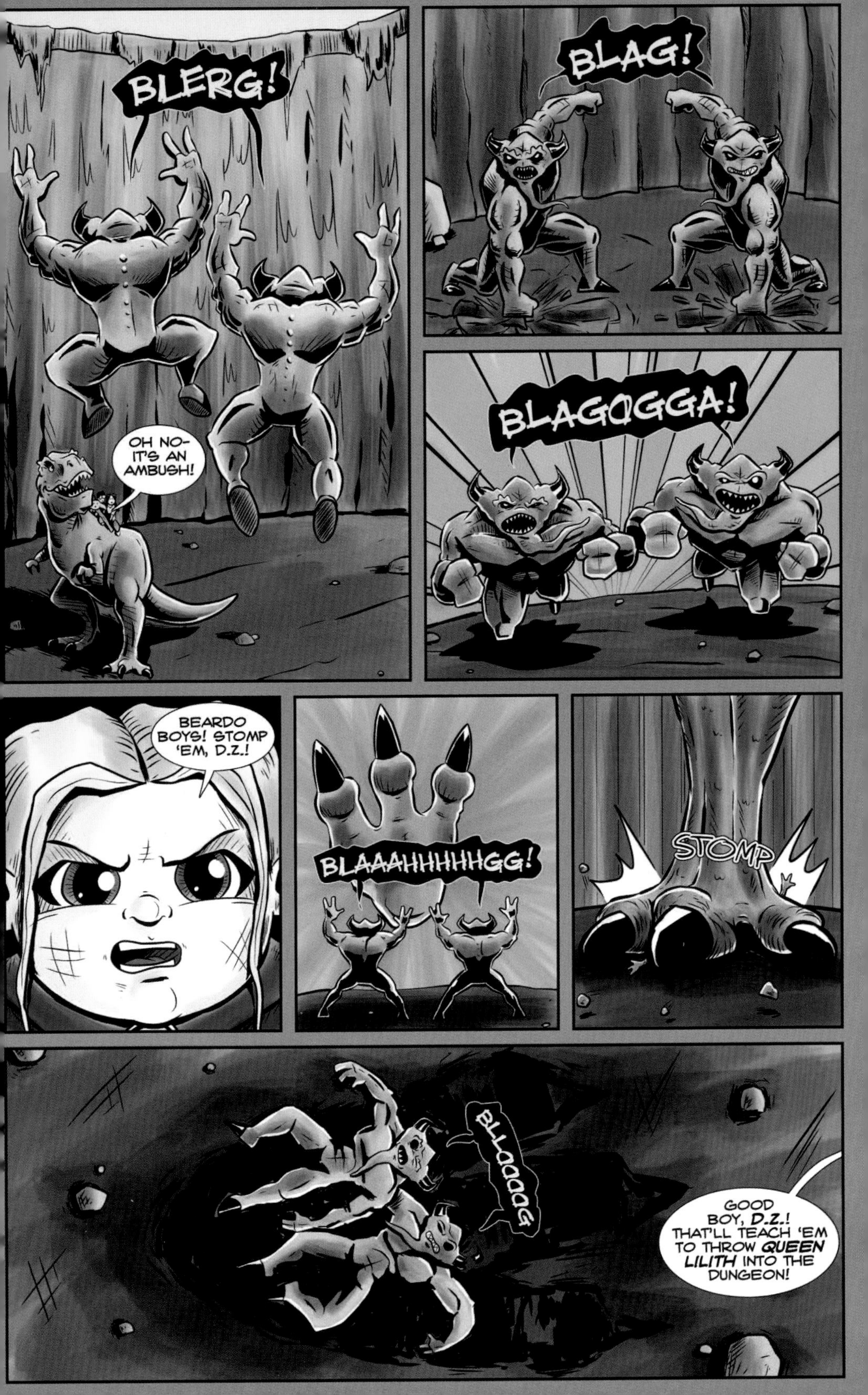
BLERG!
BLAG!
OH NO-
IT'S AN
AMBUSH!
BLAGOGGA!
BEARDO
BOYS! STOMP
'EM, D.Z.!
BLAAAHHHHHGG!
STOMP
BLLAAAAG
GOOD
BOY, D.Z.!
THAT'LL TEACH 'EM
TO THROW QUEEN
LILITH INTO THE
DUNGEON!

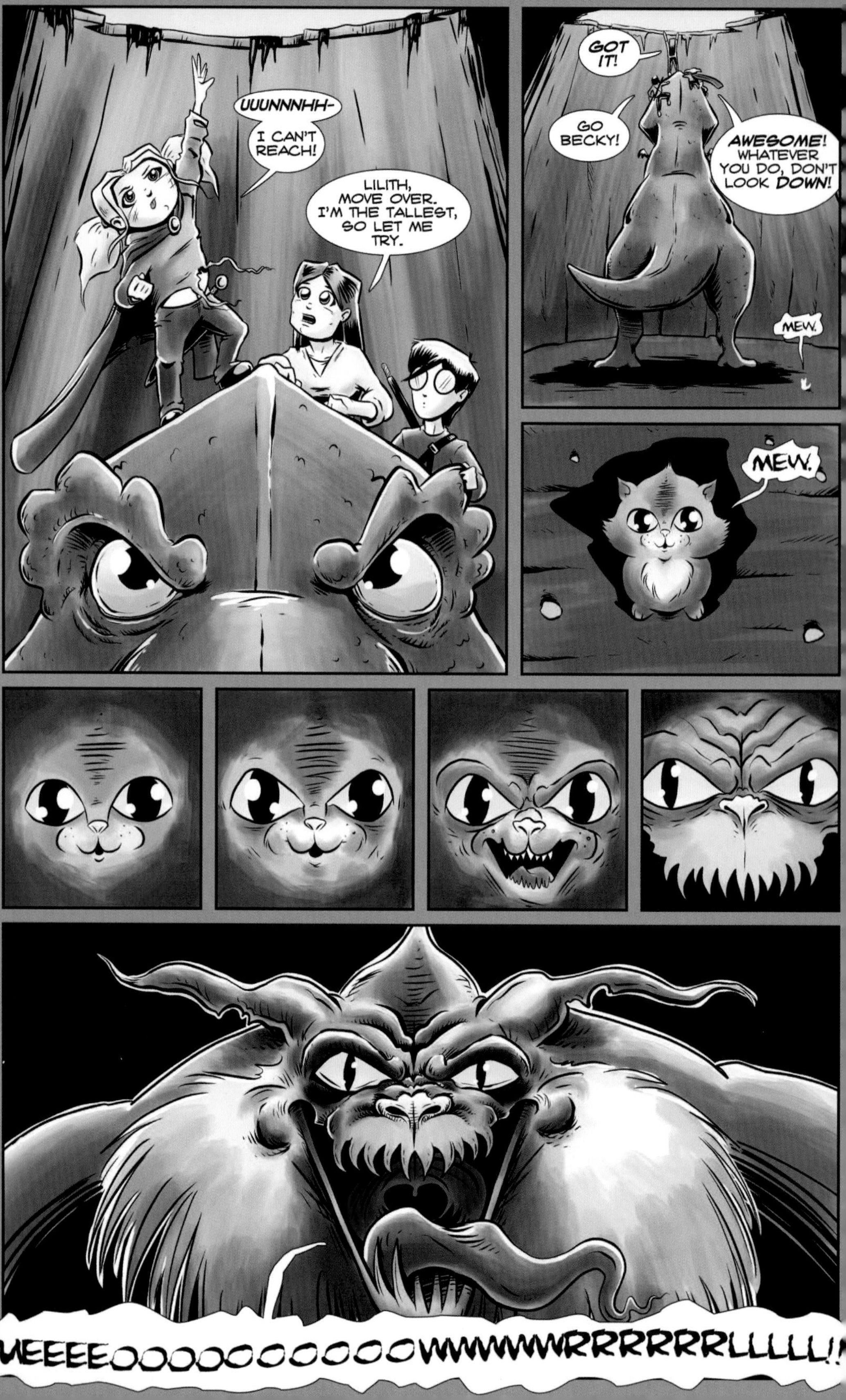
UUUNNNHH-
I CAN'T REACH!
LILITH, MOVE OVER. I'M THE TALLEST, SO LET ME TRY.
GOT IT!
GO BECKY!
AWESOME! WHATEVER YOU DO, DON'T LOOK DOWN!
MEW.
MEW.
MEEEEOOOOOOOOOOOOWWWWWRRRRRRLLLLL!!

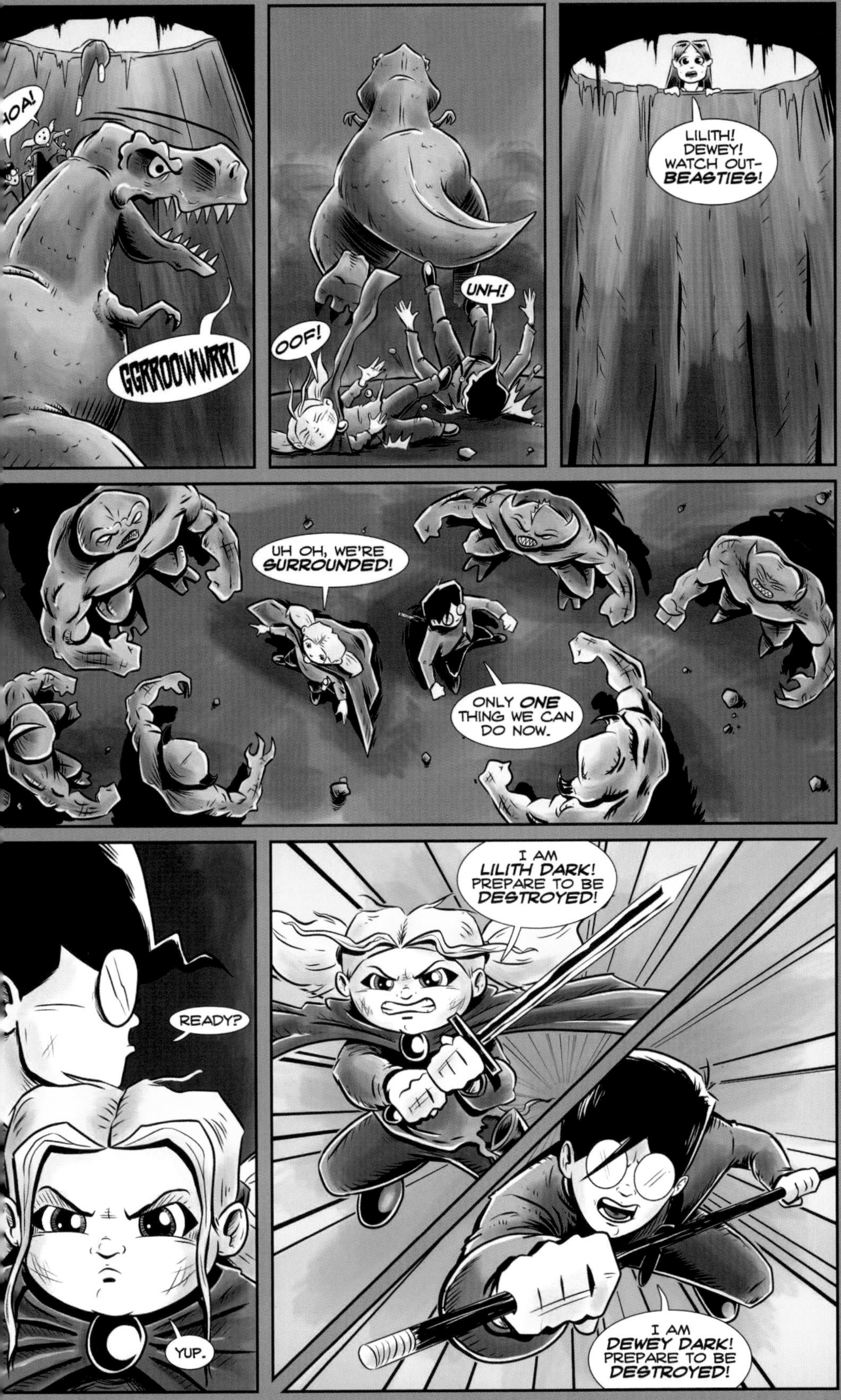
HOA!
GGRROOWWRR!
OOF!
UNH!
LILITH! DEWEY! WATCH OUT- BEASTIES!
UH OH, WE'RE SURROUNDED!
ONLY ONE THING WE CAN DO NOW.
READY?
YUP.
I AM LILITH DARK! PREPARE TO BE DESTROYED!
I AM DEWEY DARK! PREPARE TO BE DESTROYED!

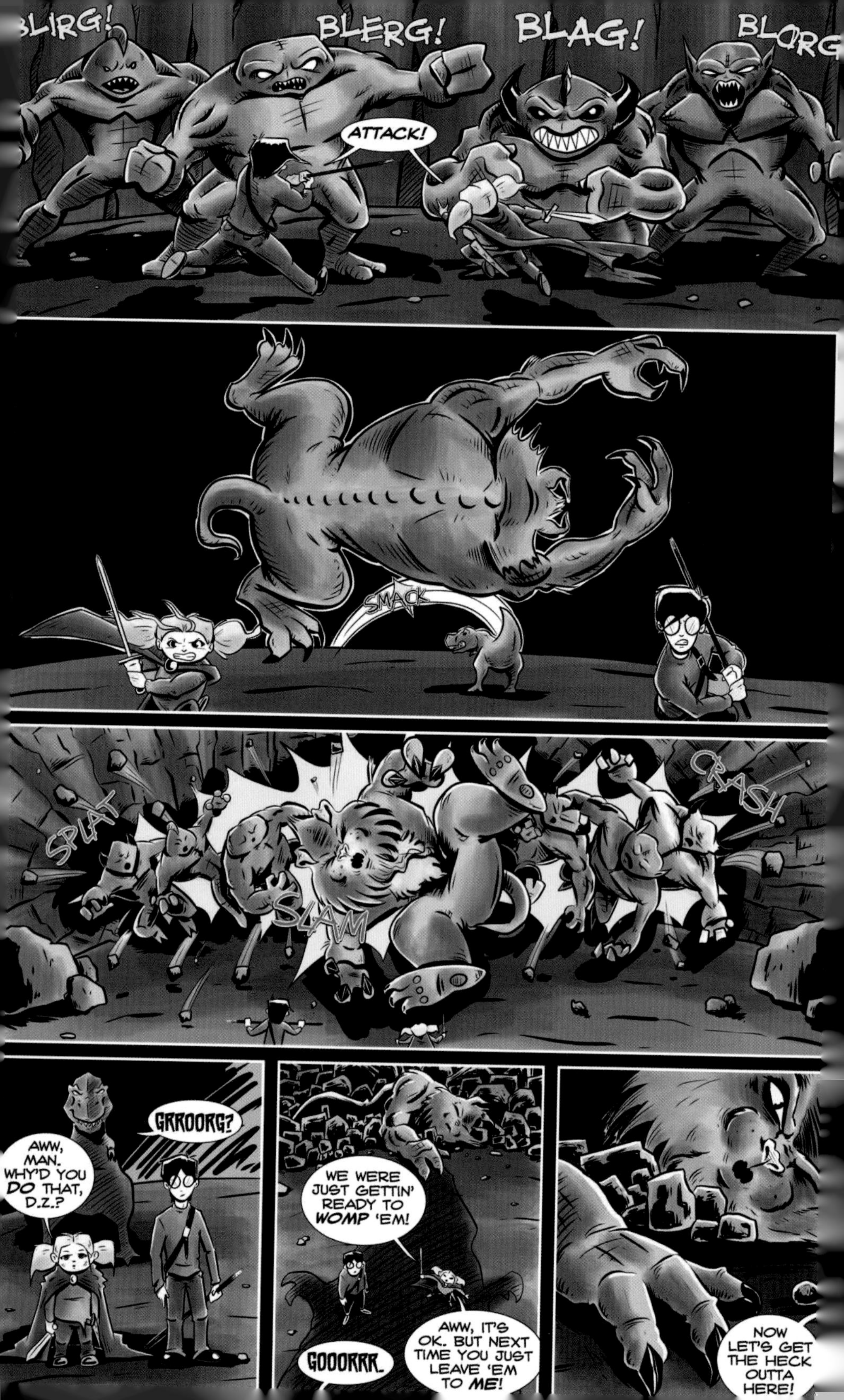
BLIRG!
BLERG!
BLAG!
BLORG
ATTACK!
SMACK
SPLAT
CRASH
SLAM
AWW, MAN. WHY'D YOU DO THAT, D.Z.?
GRROORG?
WE WERE JUST GETTIN' READY TO WOMP 'EM!
GOOORRR
AWW, IT'S OK. BUT NEXT TIME YOU JUST LEAVE 'EM TO ME!
NOW LET'S GET THE HECK OUTTA HERE!

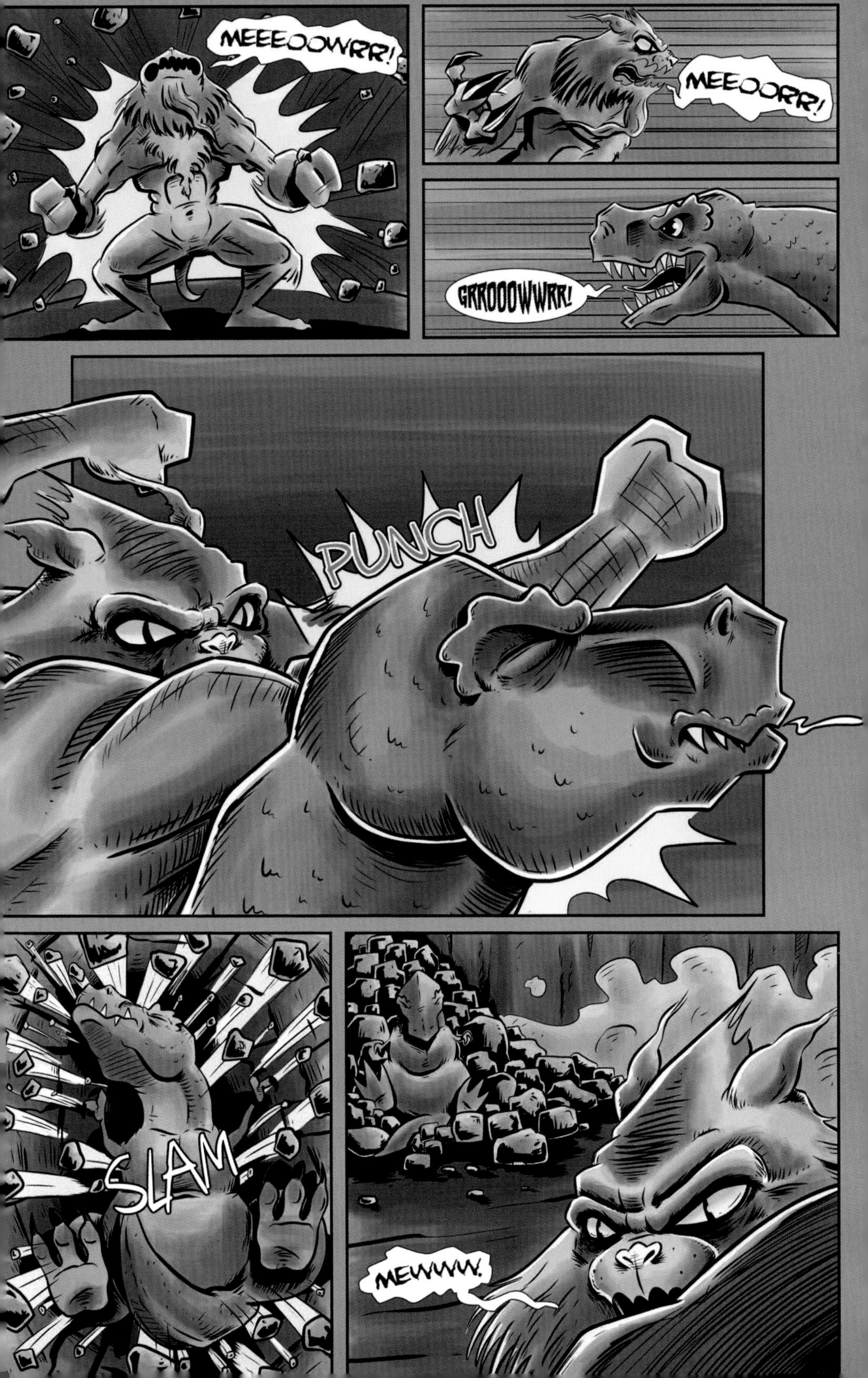
MEEEOOWRR!
MEEOORR!
GRROOOWWRR!
PUNCH
SLAM
MEWWW.

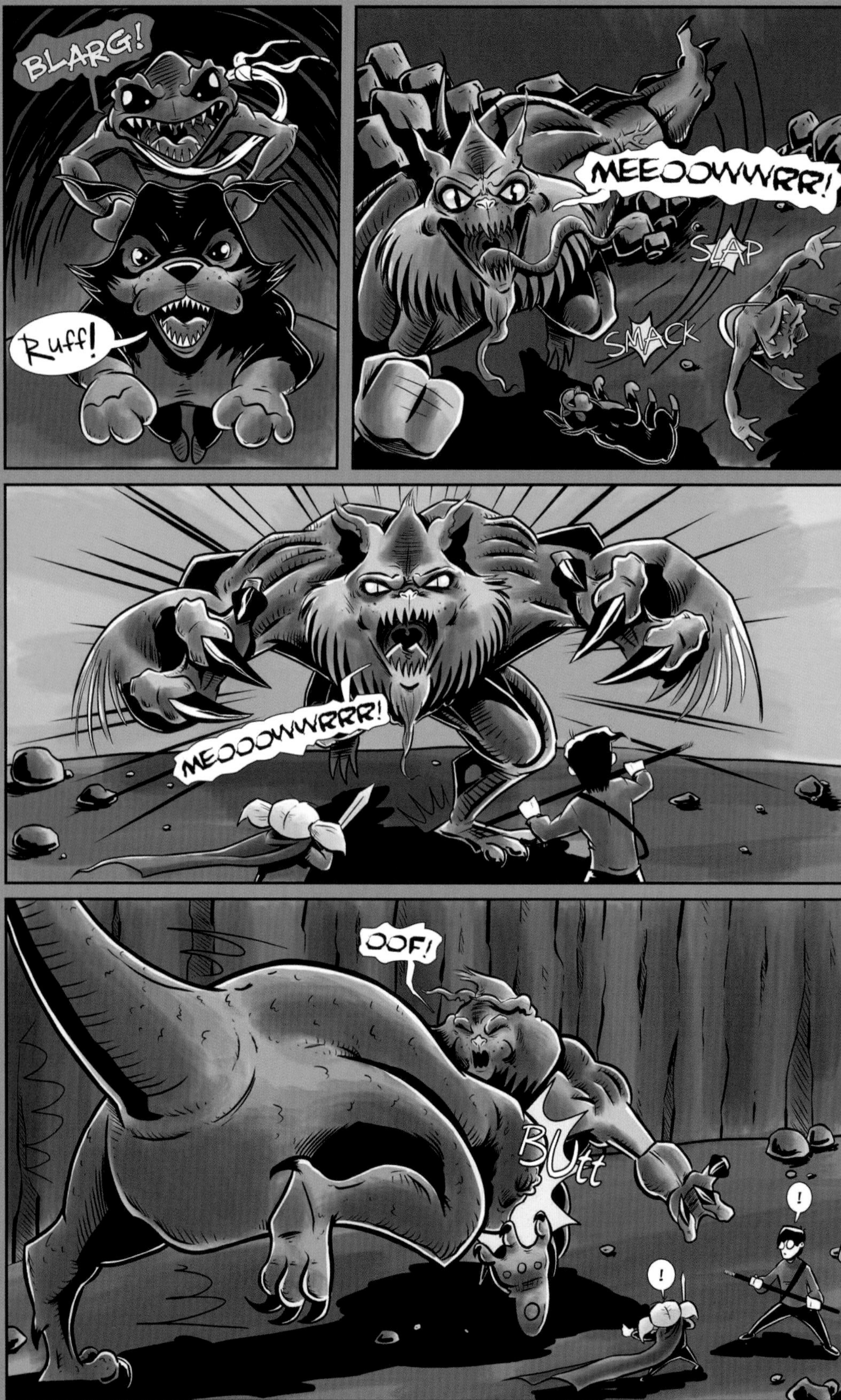
BLARG!
Ruff!
MEEOOWWRR!
SLAP
SMACK
MEOOOWWRRR!
OOF!
BUtt
!
!

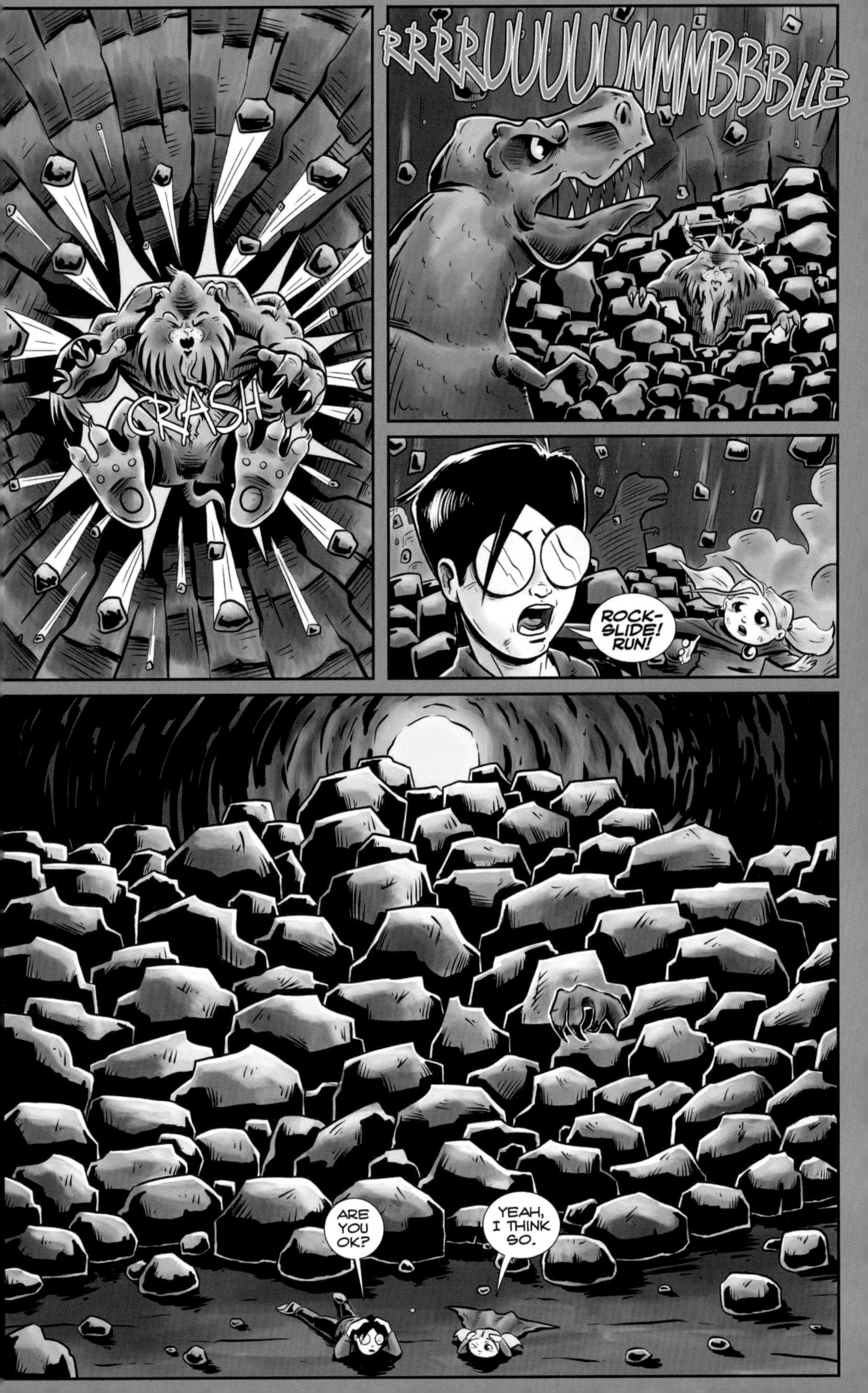
CRASH
RRRRUUUUUMMMBBBLLE
ROCK-SLIDE! RUN!
ARE YOU OK?
YEAH, I THINK SO.

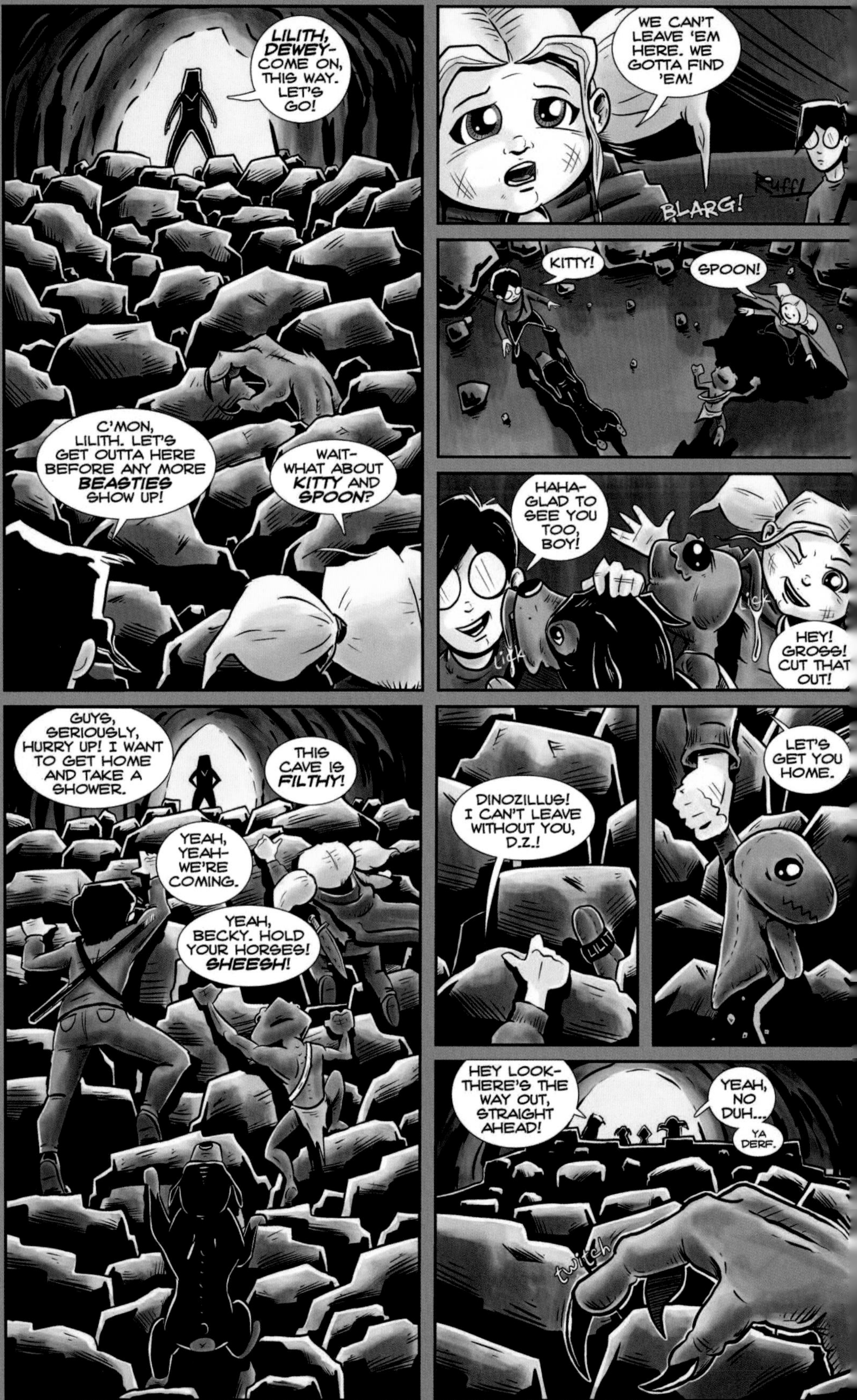

LILITH, DEWEY- COME ON, THIS WAY. LET'S GO!
C'MON, LILITH. LET'S GET OUTTA HERE BEFORE ANY MORE BEASTIES SHOW UP!
WAIT- WHAT ABOUT KITTY AND SPOON?
WE CAN'T LEAVE 'EM HERE. WE GOTTA FIND 'EM!
BLARG!
RUFF!
KITTY!
SPOON!
HAHA- GLAD TO SEE YOU TOO, BOY!
LICK
LICK
HEY! GROSS! CUT THAT OUT!
GUYS, SERIOUSLY, HURRY UP! I WANT TO GET HOME AND TAKE A SHOWER.
THIS CAVE IS FILTHY!
YEAH, YEAH- WE'RE COMING.
YEAH, BECKY. HOLD YOUR HORSES! SHEESH!
DINOZILLUS! I CAN'T LEAVE WITHOUT YOU, D.Z.!
LET'S GET YOU HOME.
HEY LOOK- THERE'S THE WAY OUT, STRAIGHT AHEAD!
YEAH, NO DUH...
YA DERF.
twitch

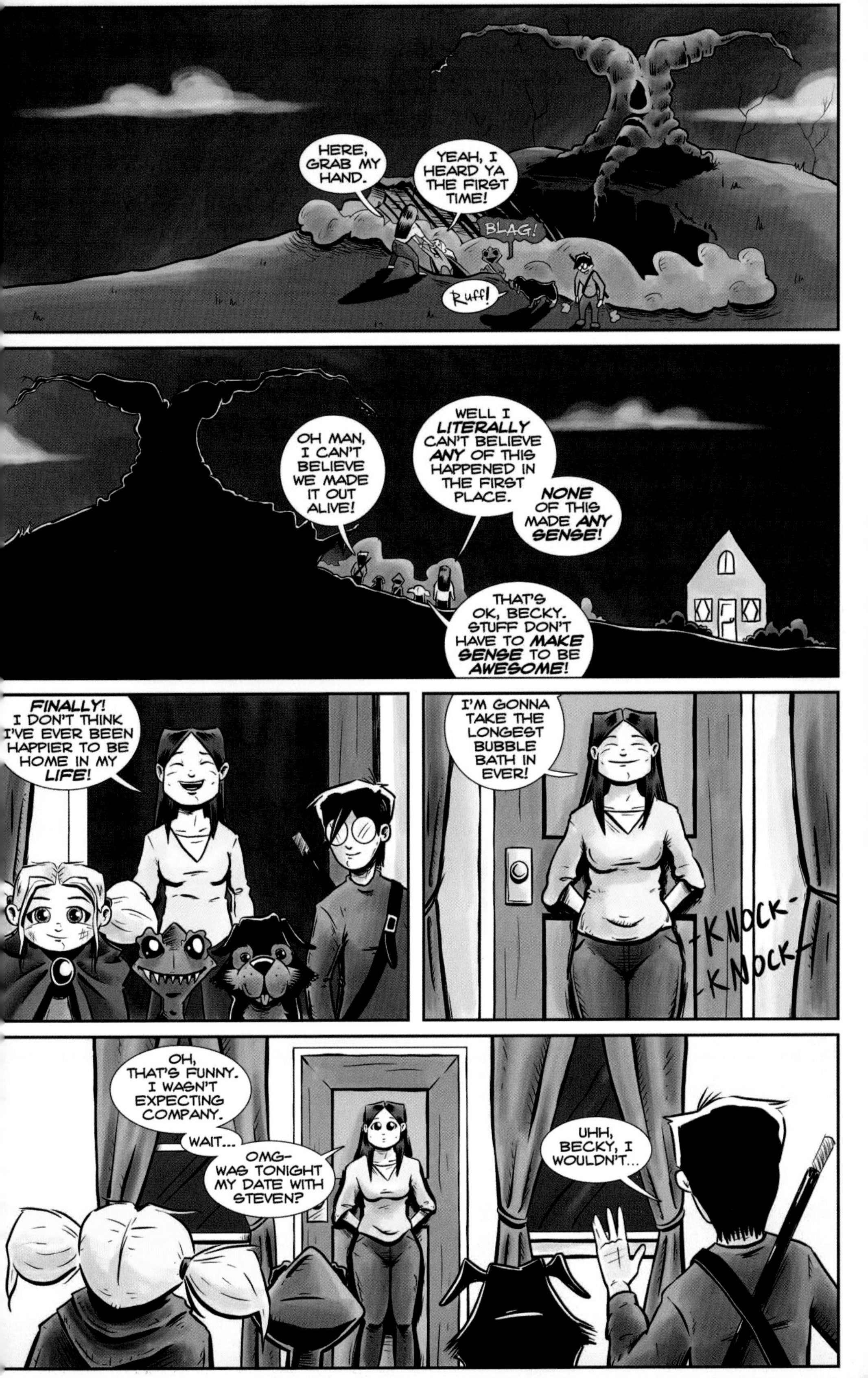
HERE, GRAB MY HAND.
YEAH, I HEARD YA THE FIRST TIME!
BLAG!
RUFF!
OH MAN, I CAN'T BELIEVE WE MADE IT OUT ALIVE!
WELL I LITERALLY CAN'T BELIEVE ANY OF THIS HAPPENED IN THE FIRST PLACE.
NONE OF THIS MADE ANY SENSE!
THAT'S OK, BECKY. STUFF DON'T HAVE TO MAKE SENSE TO BE AWESOME!
FINALLY! I DON'T THINK I'VE EVER BEEN HAPPIER TO BE HOME IN MY LIFE!
I'M GONNA TAKE THE LONGEST BUBBLE BATH IN EVER!
KNOCK- KNOCK
OH, THAT'S FUNNY. I WASN'T EXPECTING COMPANY.
WAIT...
OMG- WAS TONIGHT MY DATE WITH STEVEN?
UHH, BECKY, I WOULDN'T...

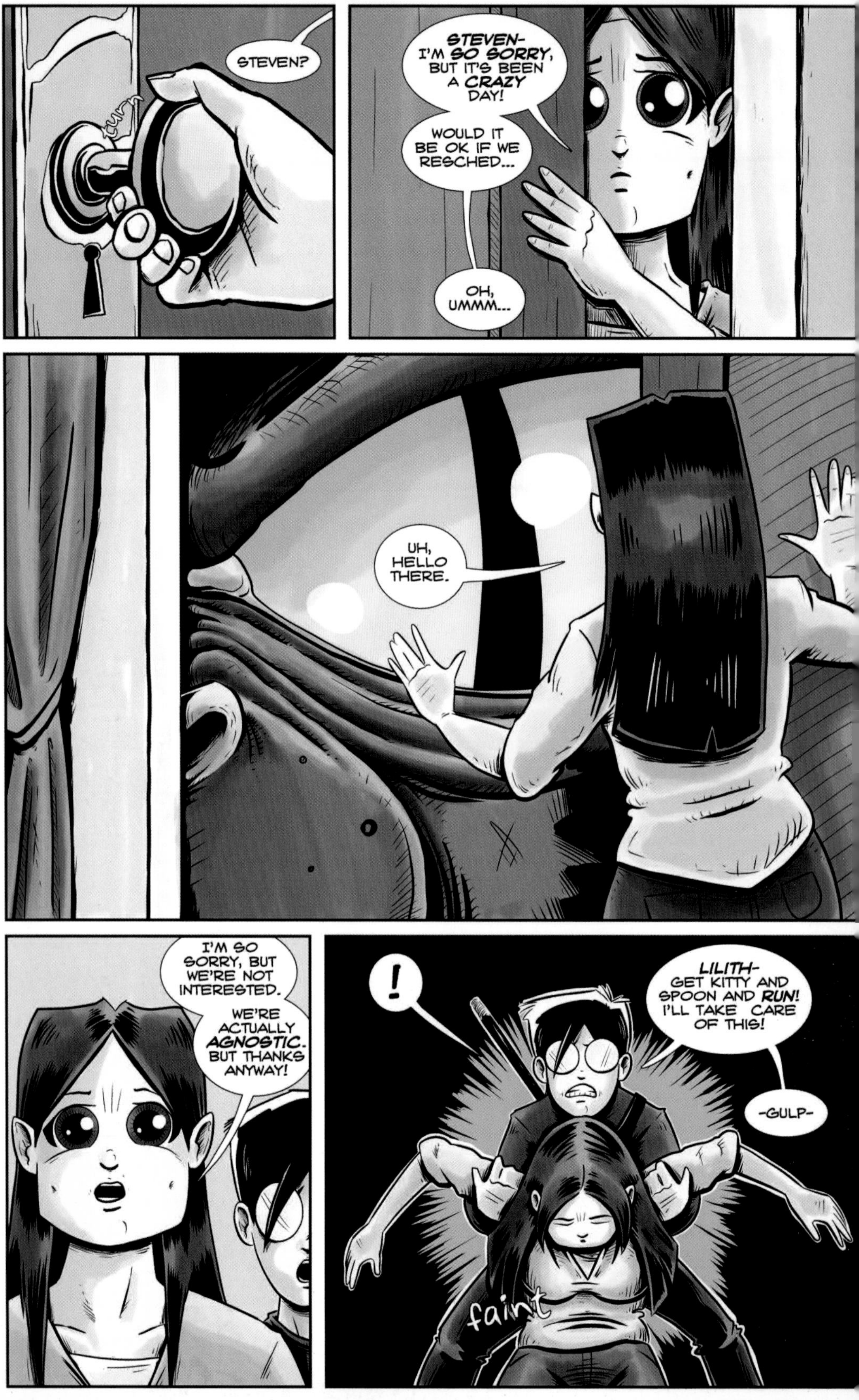
STEVEN?
turn
STEVEN- I'M SO SORRY, BUT IT'S BEEN A CRAZY DAY!
WOULD IT BE OK IF WE RESCHED...
OH, UMMM...
UH, HELLO THERE.
I'M SO SORRY, BUT WE'RE NOT INTERESTED.
WE'RE ACTUALLY AGNOSTIC. BUT THANKS ANYWAY!
!
LILITH- GET KITTY AND SPOON AND RUN! I'LL TAKE CARE OF THIS!
-GULP-
faint

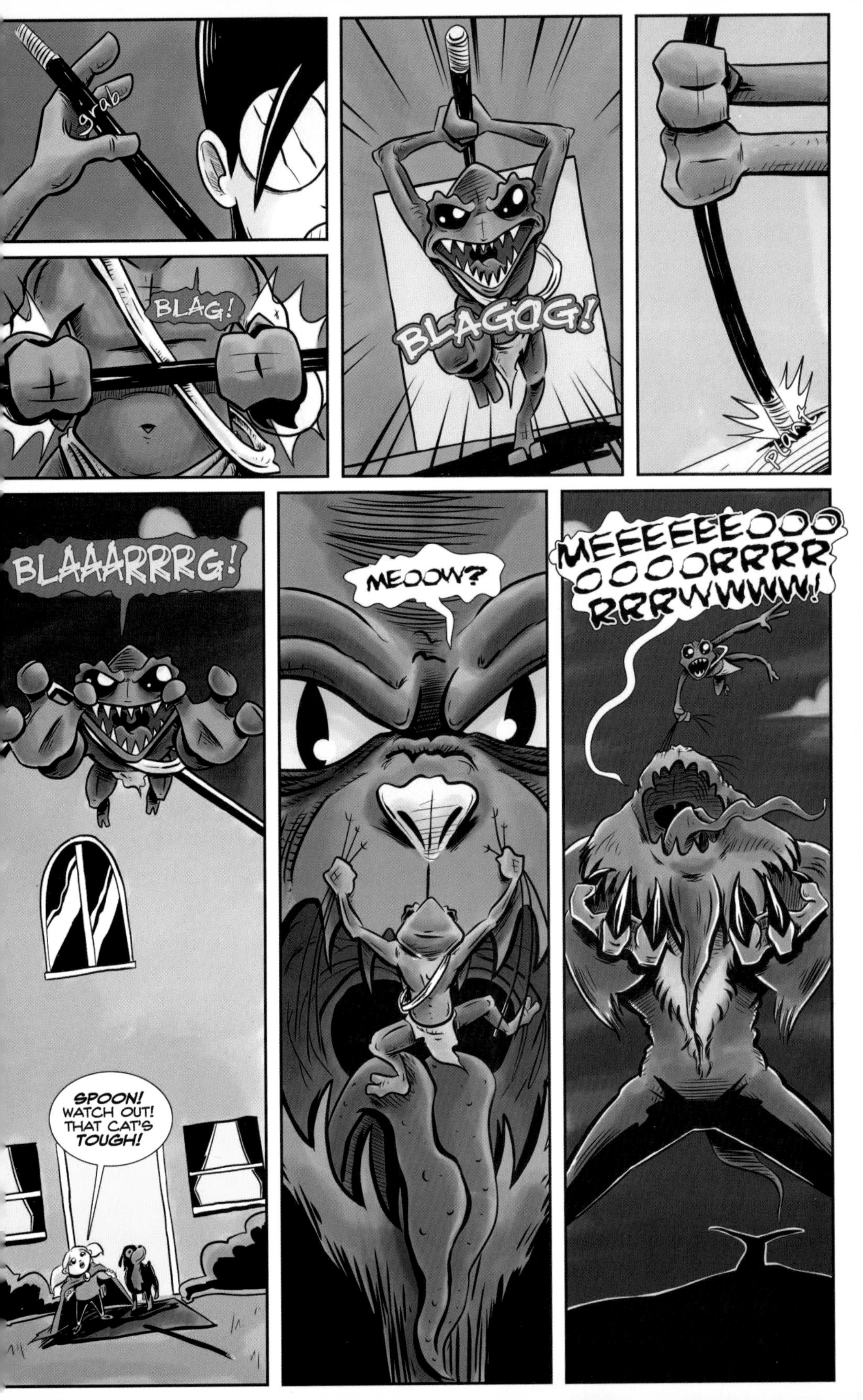

grab
BLAG!
BLAGGG!
plant
BLAAARRRG!
SPOON! WATCH OUT! THAT CAT'S TOUGH!
MEOOW?
MEEEEEEEOOO
OOOORRRR
RRRWWWW!

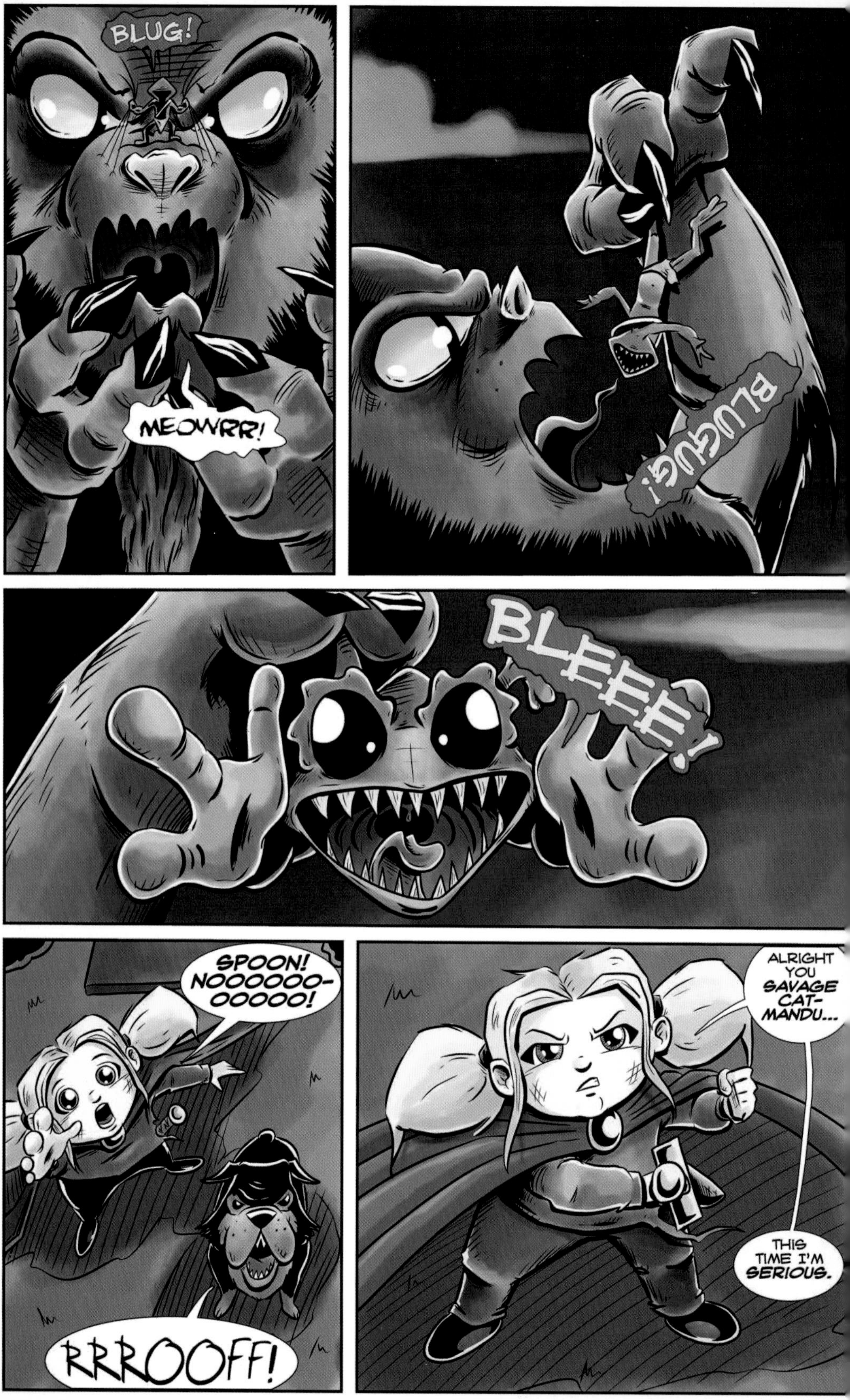
BLUG!
MEOWRR!
BLUGUG!
BLEEE!
SPOON! NOOOOOO-OOOOO!
RRROOFF!
ALRIGHT YOU SAVAGE CAT-MANDU...
THIS TIME I'M SERIOUS.

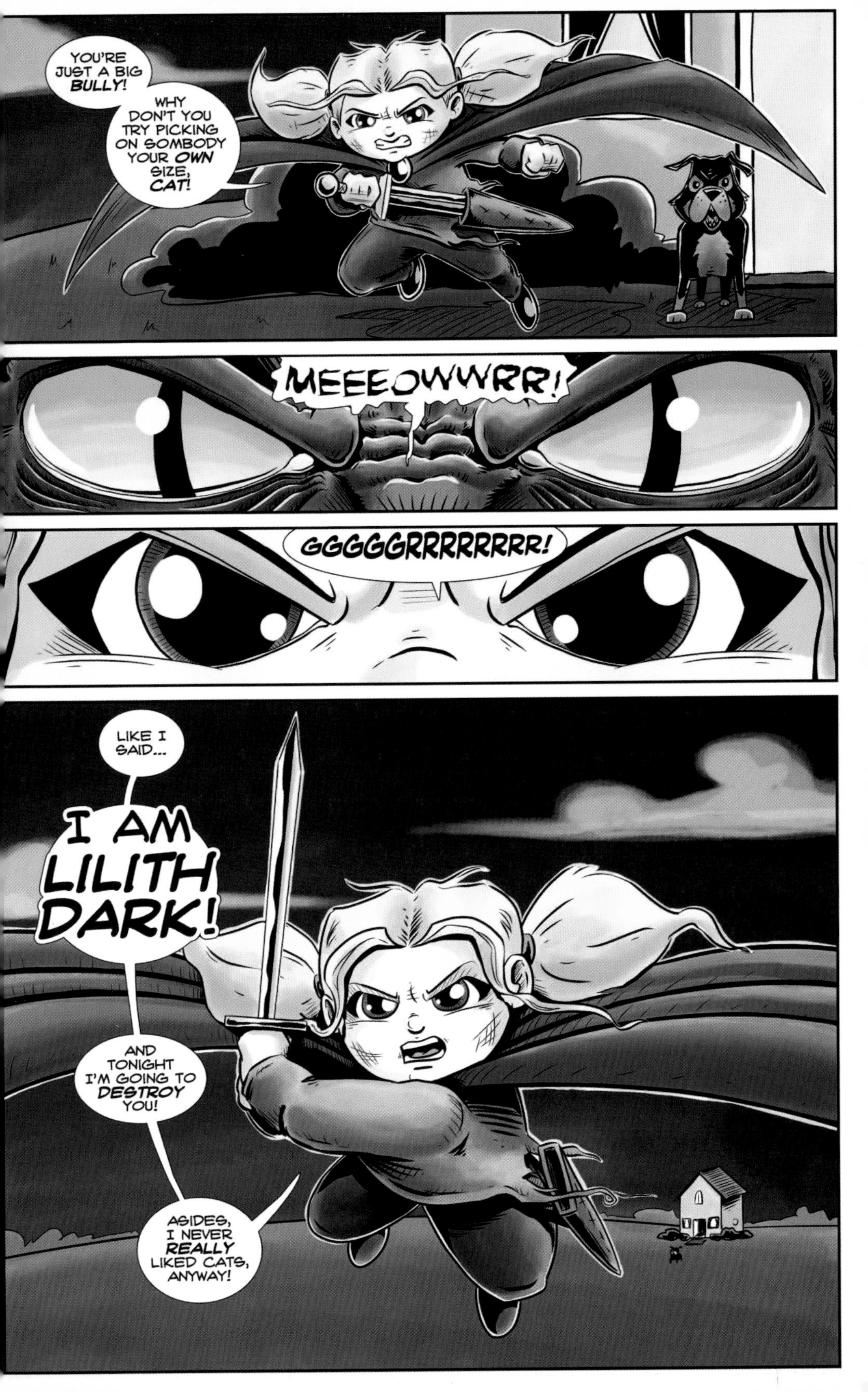
YOU'RE JUST A BIG BULLY!
WHY DON'T YOU TRY PICKING ON SOMBODY YOUR OWN SIZE, CAT!
MEEEOWWRR!
GGGGGRRRRRRRR!
LIKE I SAID...
I AM LILITH DARK!
AND TONIGHT I'M GOING TO DESTROY YOU!
ASIDES, I NEVER REALLY LIKED CATS, ANYWAY!

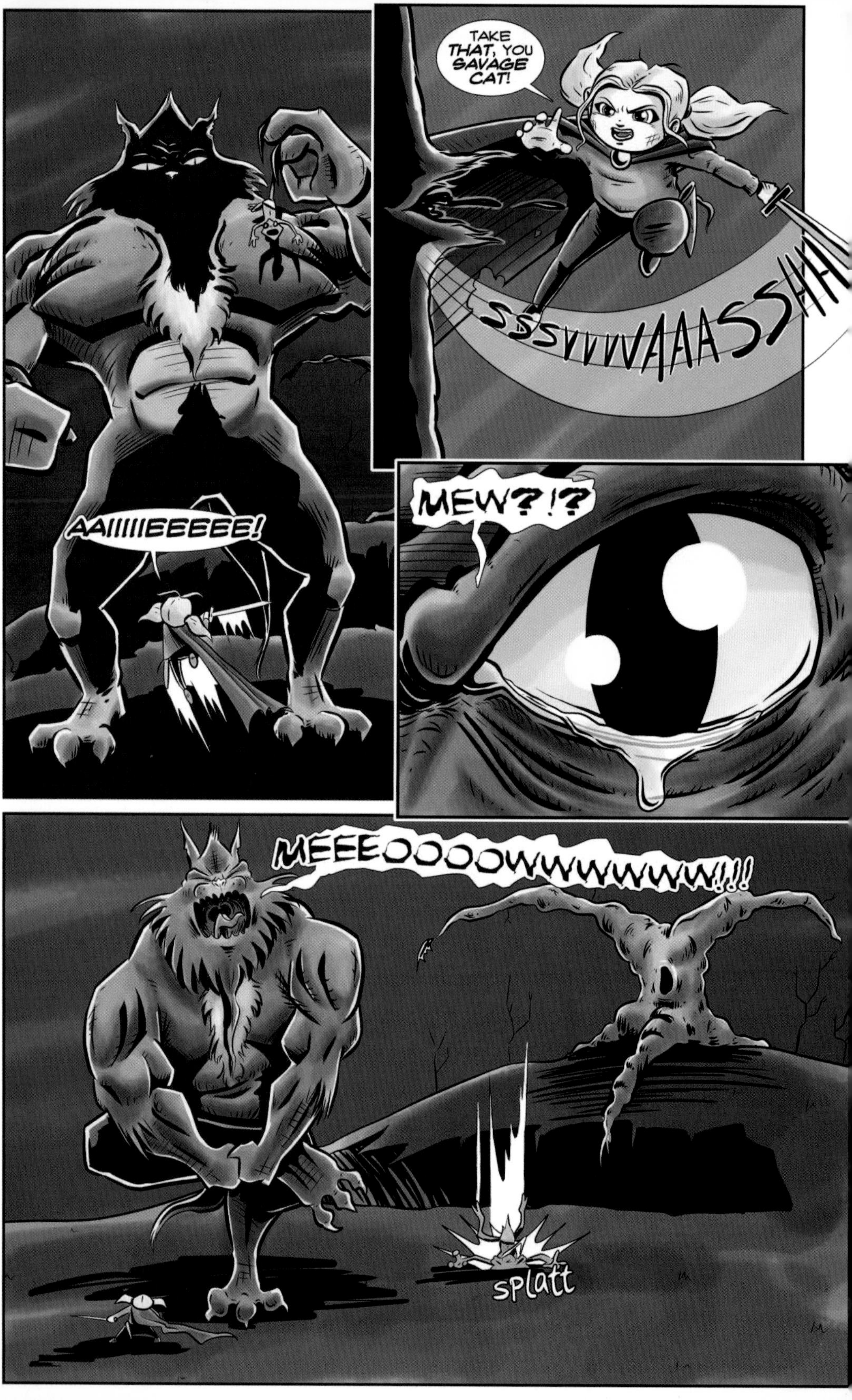
TAKE THAT, YOU SAVAGE CAT!
SSSVVVVVAAASSHH
AAIIIIIIEEEEEE!
MEW?!?
MEEEOOOOWWWWWW!!!
splatt

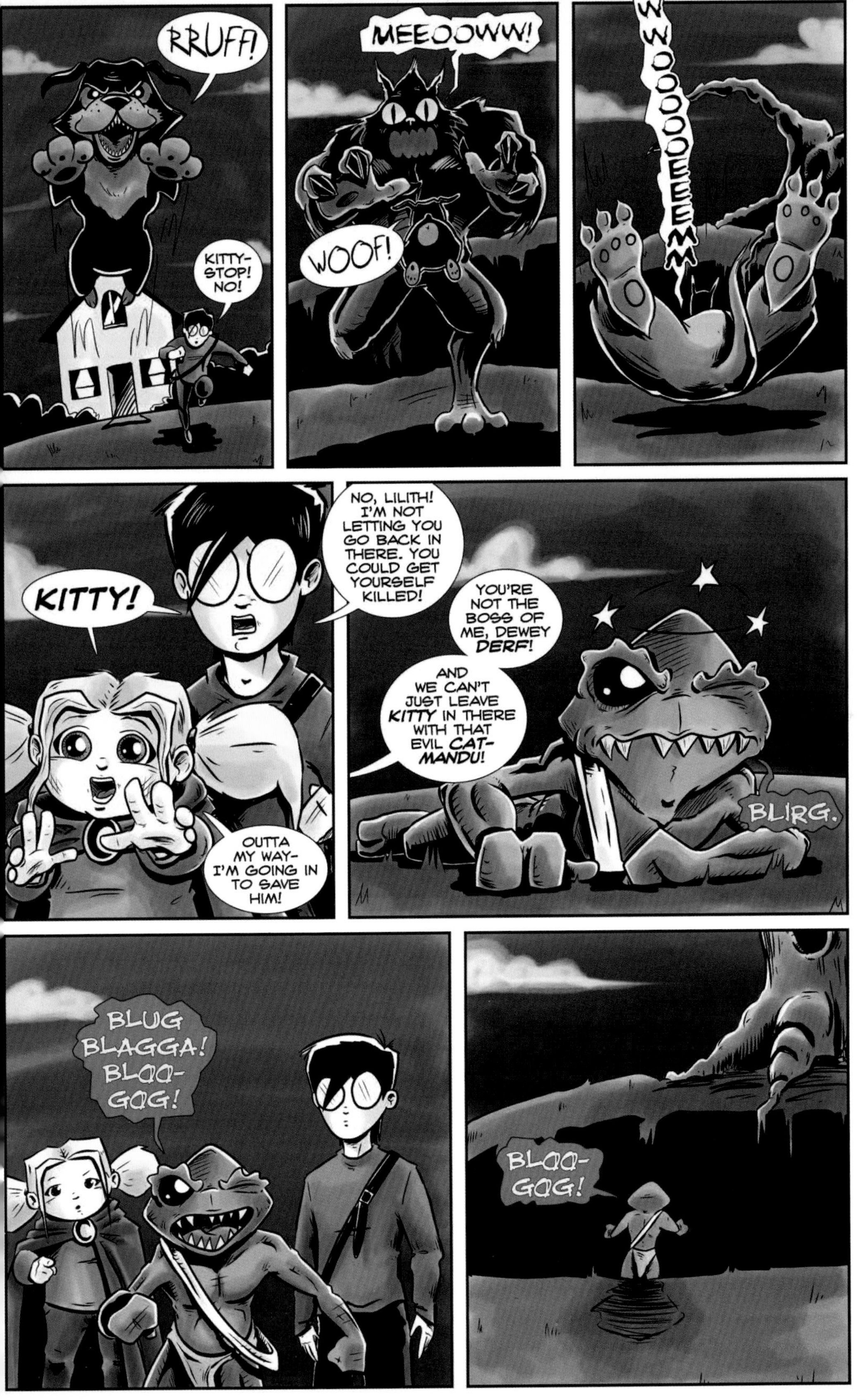
RRUFF!
KITTY-STOP! NO!
MEEOOWW!
WOOF!
WWOOOOOEEEMM
KITTY!
NO, LILITH! I'M NOT LETTING YOU GO BACK IN THERE. YOU COULD GET YOURSELF KILLED!
OUTTA MY WAY-I'M GOING IN TO SAVE HIM!
YOU'RE NOT THE BOSS OF ME, DEWEY DERF!
AND WE CAN'T JUST LEAVE KITTY IN THERE WITH THAT EVIL CAT-MANDU!
BLIRG.
BLUG BLAGGA! BLAA-GAG!
BLAA-GAG!

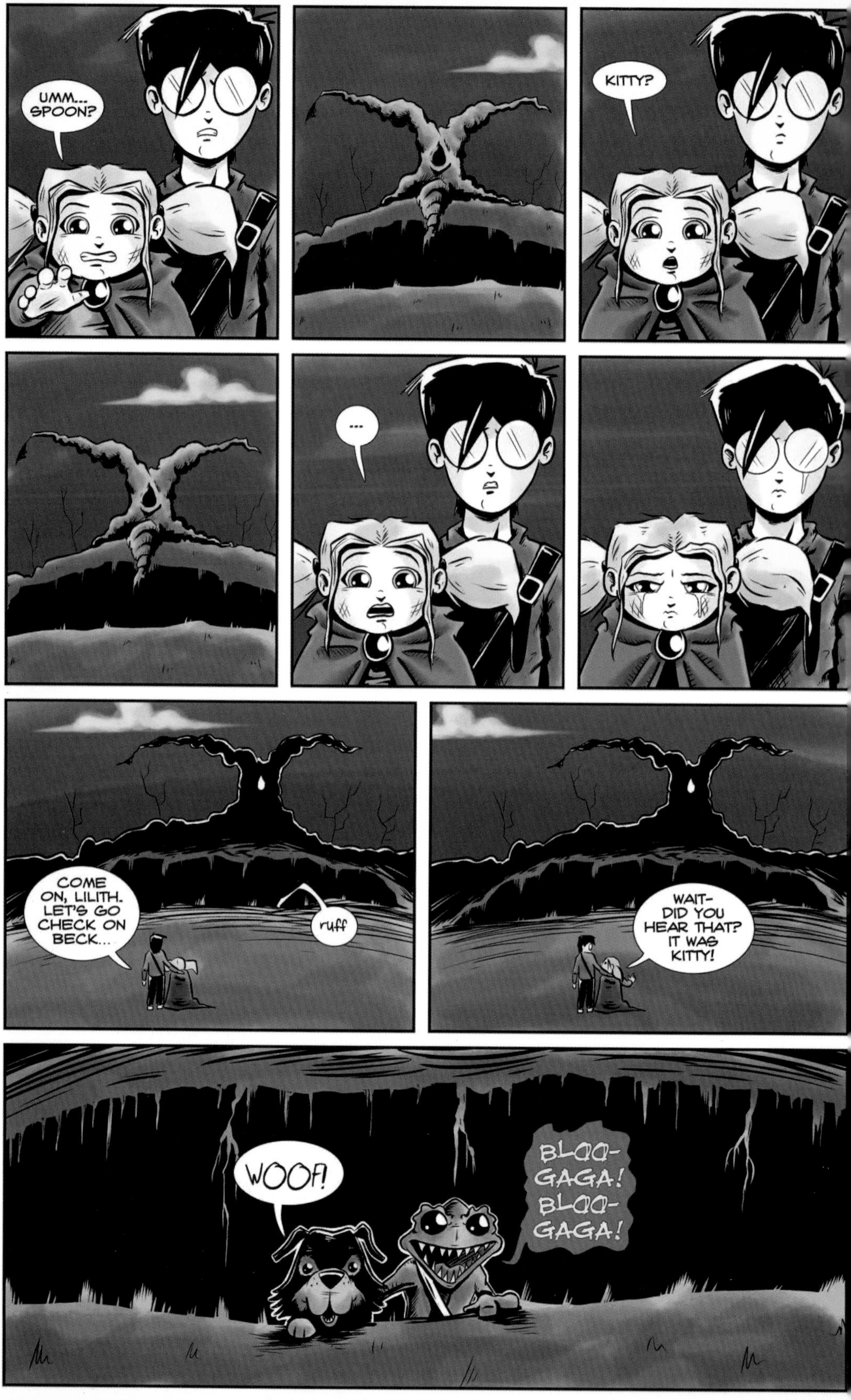
UMM... SPOON?
KITTY?
...
COME ON, LILITH. LET'S GO CHECK ON BECK...
ruff
WAIT- DID YOU HEAR THAT? IT WAS KITTY!
WOOF!
BLOO-GAGA! BLOO-GAGA!

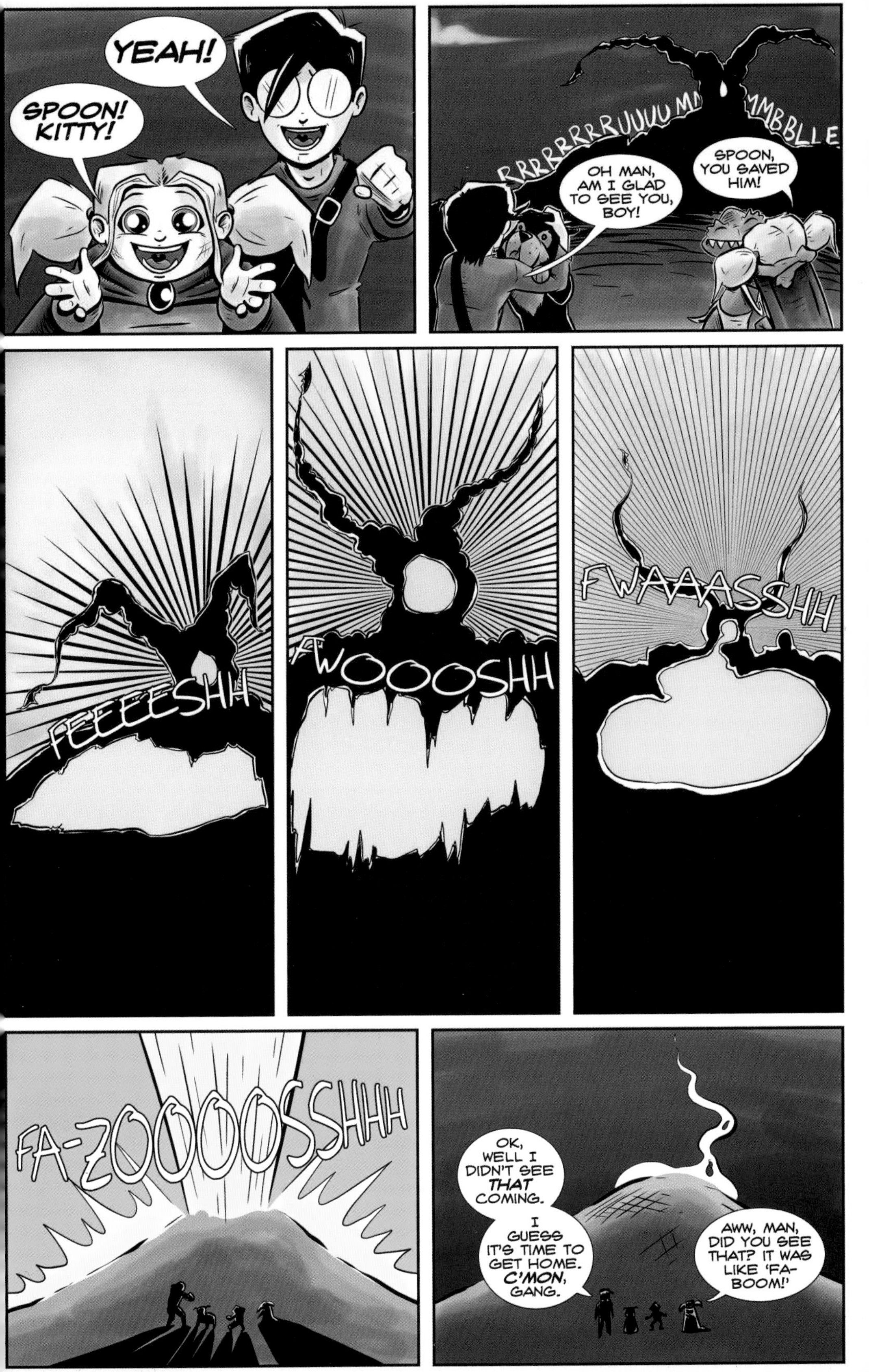
SPOON! KITTY!
YEAH!
RRRRRRRRUUUUMMMMBBLLE
OH MAN, AM I GLAD TO SEE YOU, BOY!
SPOON, YOU SAVED HIM!
FEEEESHH
FWOOOSHH
FWAAAASSHH
FA-ZOOOOOSSHHH
OK, WELL I DIDN'T SEE *THAT* COMING.
I GUESS IT'S TIME TO GET HOME. *C'MON*, GANG.
AWW, MAN, DID YOU SEE THAT? IT WAS LIKE 'FA-BOOM!'

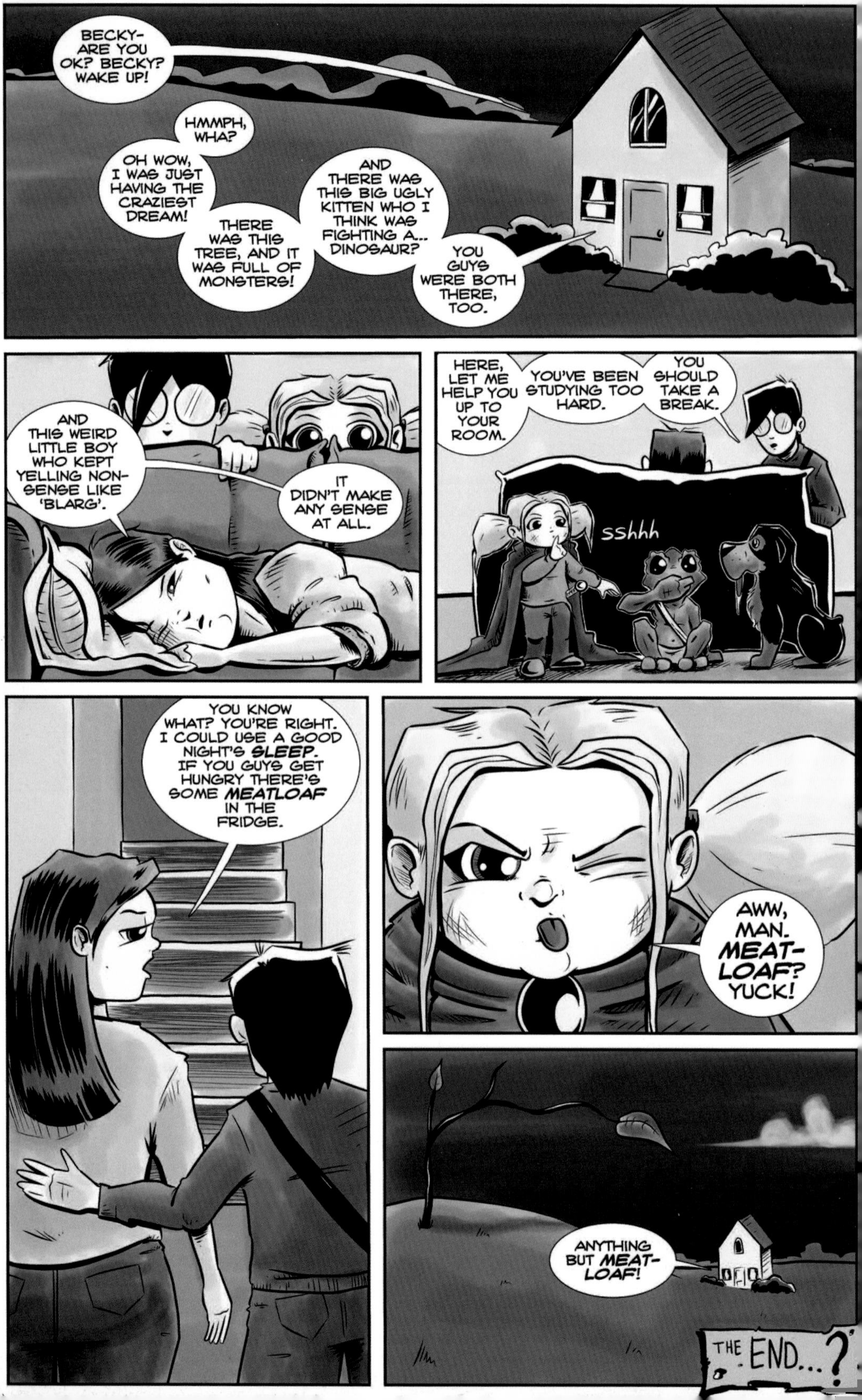
BECKY- ARE YOU OK? BECKY? WAKE UP!
HMMPH, WHA?
OH WOW, I WAS JUST HAVING THE CRAZIEST DREAM!
THERE WAS THIS TREE, AND IT WAS FULL OF MONSTERS!
AND THERE WAS THIS BIG UGLY KITTEN WHO I THINK WAS FIGHTING A... DINOSAUR?
YOU GUYS WERE BOTH THERE, TOO.
AND THIS WEIRD LITTLE BOY WHO KEPT YELLING NON-SENSE LIKE 'BLARG'.
IT DIDN'T MAKE ANY SENSE AT ALL.
HERE, LET ME HELP YOU UP TO YOUR ROOM.
YOU'VE BEEN STUDYING TOO HARD.
YOU SHOULD TAKE A BREAK.
sshhh
YOU KNOW WHAT? YOU'RE RIGHT. I COULD USE A GOOD NIGHT'S SLEEP. IF YOU GUYS GET HUNGRY THERE'S SOME MEATLOAF IN THE FRIDGE.
AWW, MAN. MEAT-LOAF? YUCK!
ANYTHING BUT MEAT-LOAF!
THE END...?

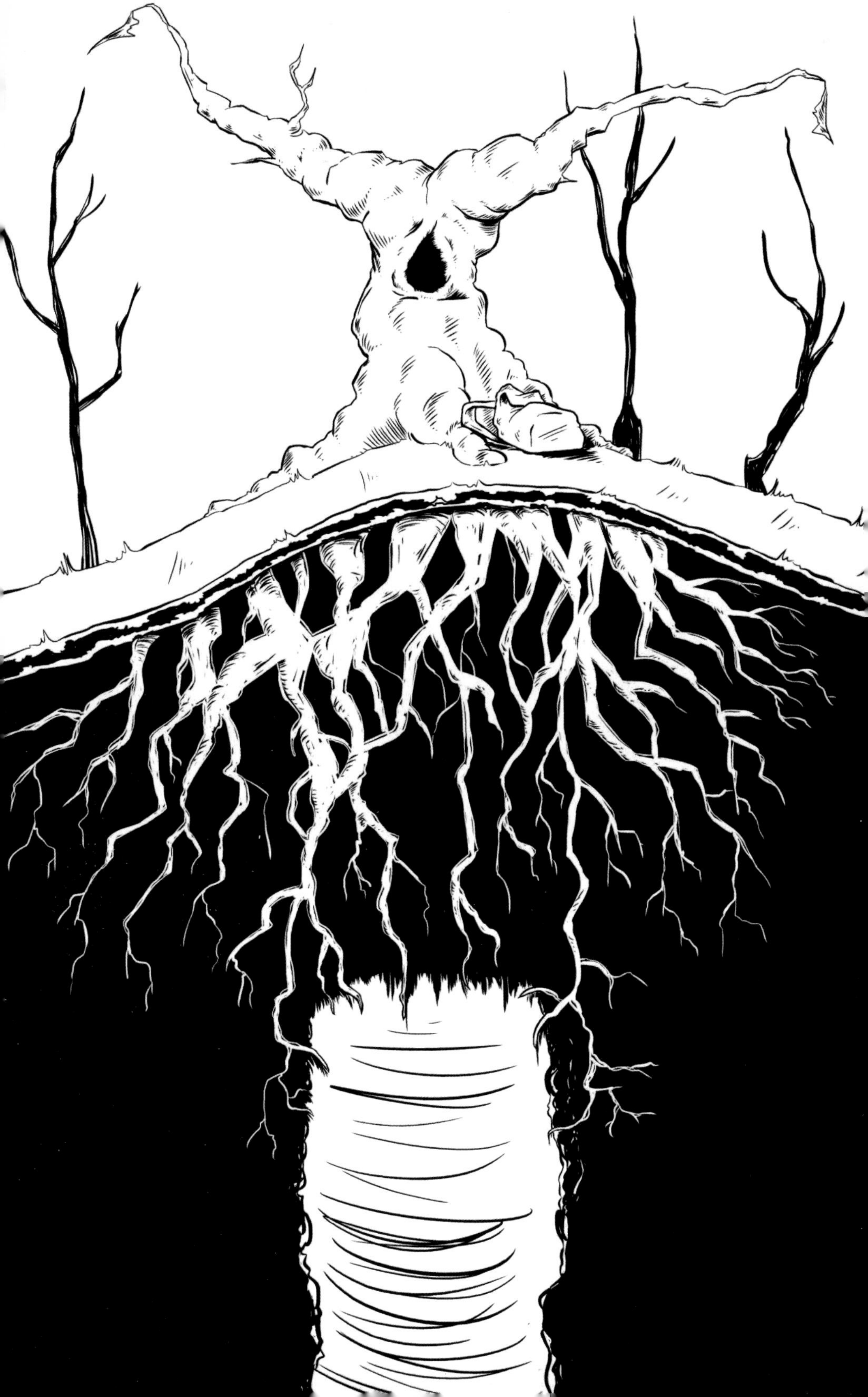

Thank you to the most supportive woman on Earth, Crystal Gayle Dowd. Without you, none of this would have been possible. Love ya, Boo!

Special Thanks To The Following People Who Kickstarted This Book:

Vaile Adams-Fujikawa • Melissa Aho • Abdulaziz Al-Kaboor • Susan Alamo • Cory Altheide • Annika Anderson • Christine Macdonald Anderson • Jeffrey L. Baker • Rob Balzer • Paul Barlow • Jason Barmer • Leah Barr • Sharon Beach • Justin Beeson • Michael Bell • Erik Berglund • Vivian Berkshier • Chris Best • Joel Bezaire • Michael Bird • Christina Bisser • Samantha Blackmon • Holly Blakemore • Kyla Blythe • Adam Boenig • Kira Borders • Jessie Boudrie • Deeter & Samantha Braeden • Martin Brandt Ii • Laurel Bresaz • Amy Gill Britt • Abby & Emma Brown • Tim Browning • Eric Buckley • Tracey Bunch • Danny Burleson • Patrick Cahn • Thaddeus Callahan • Chris Carley • Norman Carpenter • Michael Casamento • Mena Casey • Cesar Cesarotti • Ellia Chaney • Kimberly Chapman • Enrique Chumbes • Nate Cielieska • Rich Clabaugh • Wren Clark • Lindsey Clements • Andrew Clough • John Cmar • Jennifer Cole • J. Cebron Cook • Patricia Copeland • Danny Cordell • Chriss Cornish • Vanessa Cox • William Crisel • Erin Dalton • Robin Dalton • Steve Daly • Nick Davis • Joe Deagnon • Anthony Deaver • Tymothy P Diaz • Rebecca Dobbie • Renae Donohue • Gina Drayer • Charles E. Dyer Iv • James Ebenger • Tom Eckstrand • Jeremy Eda • Bob Eddy • Kate Roberts Edenborg • Beth Endresen • Bryan English • Susan Epler • Taina Evans • Roscoe "Revek" Fay • Michael C. Fedoris • Michael Feldhusen • Ellis Filyaw • Cheryl Fisher • Kahlia Fisher • Rachel Flanagan • Ellen Fleischer • Samantha Forrister • Addison Fox • Paula Frank • Lorinda Freint • Bobby Fruh • Fabio Galluzzo • John D. Garriga • Dan Gibson • Joseph Gifford • Lee Gladen • Nathan Glaesemann • Cathy Goan • Maria Godebska • Wendy Golds • Daniel Gonzales • Bianca Goo • April Goulart • Fallon Goulart • Eugene R. Greenwood • Jennifer Griffin • Trevor Gryffyn • Craig Hackl • Hada-Clan • Ben Halbert • David Haley • Angi C Hansen • Raymond J. Harmon • Thomas Harper • Katy Harrison • Jeremy Helton • Steve Henson • Magi Hernandez • Robert Herrera • Amanda Heslep • Michael Hicks • Anastasia Hinton • Scott Hoben • Chris Hoffmann • Barbara Hoit Griffin • Amber M Holcomb • Tory Holland • Lilith Holmes • Eric Holsinger • Jason Holtschneider • Stephen Honea • Skylar Houston • Krista Hoxie • Vicki Hsu • Ryan Hughes • Shannon Hunt-Scott • Melinda Hunter • Kathryn Huxtable • Lars Ivar Igesund • Tamara Jackson • David Jarvis • Amanda Johnson • Dean Johnson • Mindy Johnson • Kevin Joseph • Greg Jung • Fiona Kacy • Melody Kaufmann (safireblade) • Dylan Keefer • Elisabeth Keene • Lynn Keller • Quinn Kelly • Melissa Kennedy • Amy M. Kindell Behrens • Scott King • Laura Kittleson • Amy Knepper • Einav, David & Lital Knoll • Kathryn Kramer • Michael T. Kramer • Scott Krichau • Karin S. Ku • Debra Kunigonis • Jared Lampson • Christina M. Lanier • Lilith Laurendeau • George Leap • Daniel Leavy • Zoe & Georgia Lefeber • Jason Lempka • Christine Lesher • Sarah Lester • Jessica Lewis • Maria Lewis • Max Lichtman • Yvette Joy Liebesman • Henrik Lindhe • Mia Wookiee Lo • Vince Logreco • Steven Luong • Emma Lysyk • John MacLeod • Kristy-Ann Macpherson • Christina Major • Gary Makries • Joy Mamer • Alan Manganti Lalonde • Dan Manson • Julia Mare • Kurtis Marshall • Karl Martin • Matt 'Doc' Martin • Jenna Mcandrews • Christine Mccann • Jeremiah Mccarty • Morris Mcclelland • Patrick Mccuen • Bhub Mcdavies • Sara Mcdonald • Kathleen Mcgaw • Mike Mcintosh • Stacy Mckeever • Jennifer Mcmillion • Doug Mcnamara • Jason Mcneil • Deanne Medina • Steven Mentzel • Michele Messenger • Erik J. Meyer-Curley • Alexis Rae Miller • Bryan Q. Miller • Ellie & Audrey Miller • Holly, Ryan And Ezra Mills • Randi Misterka • Adam J. Monetta • Cindy Moore • Kathryn Moore • Nick Moore • Joe Mullock • Madeline Munoz- Bustamante • Georgeann Muntin • Elizabeth Myers • Meredith Myers • Kyla Myers • Paul T. Myers • Sue Nakaji • Susan Napier-Myers • Thomas Newman • Leah Newton • Leah Niu • Morte Oakley • Elizabeth Oestreich • Maniyer Olson • Ann Marie Papanagnostou • Diana Paprotny • Sean R Parker • Charles Parsons • Gwen Patton • Timothy Paulson • Sylvia Payne • Markus Perdrizat • Chris Perkerson • Mark Perkins • Joe Perry • Melanie S Perry • Gary Phillips • Remo Pini • Kristen Pitzen • Joel Poirier • Rex Poole • Shelly Poole • Ray Powell • Thom Pratt • Stacey Preston • Annika Quint • Miller Ramos • Rebecca Raven • David Recksiek • Norah Regan • Michael Regina • Jessica Reynolds • Tamsin Haley Rhodes • Lorien Riead • Jennifer Rittmann • Kellie Roach • Dustin Roberts • David Romeyn • Caley Ross • James Rowe • Jande Rowe • Genevieve Ruzich • Charles, Tammie, Olivia & Rowan Ryan • Marc C. Santos • J. Daniel Sawyer • Liz Sayre • Jeanamrie Schlegel-Merrick • Jim Schnepp • William Schubert • Michael Schultz • Jeanette Sefton-Bustamante • Sheelagh Semper • Mia De Seram • Richard Sessions • Aly Severance • Jason Sewell • Amber Sexton • Brianna Sheldon • Mikayla J. Shelton • Arnold Shunneson • Sarah Siekman • Tara Simmons • Brian Smith • Amanda Snodgrass • Daniel Solem • Becky Soto • Kirk Spencer • Jason Sperber • Michael W. Sphar • Susan Spilecki • Lisa Spilman • Chris Spiridigliozzi • Billy Spooner • Tony Springer • Linda Staenberg • Jeremy Stand • Kathleen Standard • Pineapple Steak • Rob Steinberger • Frcory Sticha • Jeremy Stoa • Mark Stokes • Jeff Stoner • Megan Sullivan • Christopher Ta • Edgar Taylor • Beckie Tetrault • Jake Thompson • Brian Toberman • Cindi Todd • Laura Topliffe • Steve Tracy • Rich Vander Klok • Ann Venezia • Wendy Verhulst • Laura Vigander • Tim Viola • Allison Vodicka • Chris Volcheck • Adrian Wailes • Robert Wales • Melissa Walsh • Robert Washburn • Peo Webster • Vernon Welles • David Wells • Micah Weltsch • Tyrone Wested • Sandra Wheeler • Wendy Whipple • W. Byron Wilkins • Emily Williams • Dale Wilson • Jason Wilson • Aaron Wood • Jana Worrall • Xpanding Universe • Scott Yanoska • Cd Ybarra • Elizabeth Young • Alyson Zettlemoyer • Greta Zimmerman • John True • Apples • Brian • Cait • Catdabill • Danial • Dawn • Faust42 • Info • Janice • John • Lork • Ludio92 • Natalie • Rocketpig • Twormus • Wizbang The Mighty